PUTTING THEORY TO WORK:

Implementing Situational Prevention and Problem-oriented Policing

/6100/

Johannes Knutsson

and

Ronald V. Clarke

editors

GUELPH HUMBER LIBRARY
205 Humber College Blvd
Toronto, ON   M9W 5L7

Crime Prevention Studies
Volume 20

Criminal Justice Press
Monsey, NY, USA

Willan Publishing
Cullompton, Devon, UK

2006

ISSN (series):   1065-7029

Cloth
ISBN 10:   1-881798-68-2
ISBN 13: 978-1-881798-68-2

Paper
ISBN 10:   1-881798-69-0
ISBN 13: 978-1-881798-69-9

Printed on acid-free and recycled paper

CRIME PREVENTION STUDIES

Ronald V. Clarke, Series Editor

Crime Prevention Studies is an international book series dedicated to research on situational crime prevention and other initiatives to reduce opportunities for crime. Most volumes center on particular topics chosen by expert guest editors. The editors of each volume, in consultation with the series editor, commission the papers to be published and select peer reviewers.

*   *   *

Volume 1, edited by Ronald V. Clarke, 1993.

Volume 2, edited by Ronald V. Clarke, 1994.

Volume 3, edited by Ronald V. Clarke, 1994 (out of print).

Volume 4, *Crime and Place*, edited by John E. Eck and David Weisburd, 1995.

Volume 5, *The Politics and Practice of Situational Crime Prevention*, edited by Ross Homel, 1996.

Volume 6, *Preventing Mass Transit Crime*, edited by Ronald V. Clarke, 1996.

Volume 7, *Policing for Prevention: Reducing Crime, Public Intoxication and Injury*, edited by Ross Homel, 1997.

Volume 8, *Crime Mapping and Crime Prevention*, edited by David Weisburd and J. Thomas McEwen, 1997.

Volume 9, *Civil Remedies and Crime Prevention*, edited by Lorraine Green Mazerolle and Jan Roehl, 1998.

Volume 10, *Surveillance of Public Space: CCTV, Street Lighting and Crime Prevention*, edited by Kate Painter and Nick Tilley, 1999.

Volume 11, *Illegal Drug Markets: From Research to Prevention Policy*, edited by Mangai Natarajan and Mike Hough, 2000.

continued

Volume 12, *Repeat Victimization*, edited by Graham Farrell and Ken Pease, 2001.

Volume 13, *Analysis for Crime Prevention*, edited by Nick Tilley, 2002.

Volume 14, *Evaluation for Crime Prevention*, edited by Nick Tilley, 2002.

Volume 15, *Problem-oriented Policing: From Innovation to Mainstream*, edited by Johannes Knutsson, 2003.

Volume 16, *Theory for Practice in Situational Crime Prevention*, edited by Martha J. Smith and Derek B. Cornish, 2003.

Volume 17, *Understanding and Preventing Car Theft*, edited by Michael G. Maxfield and Ronald V. Clarke, 2004.

Volume 18, *Designing Out Crime from Products and Systems*, edited by Ronald V. Clarke and Graeme R. Newman, 2005.

Volume 19, *Situational Prevention of Child Sexual Abuse*, edited by Richard Wortley and Richard Smallbone, 2006.

Volume 20, *Putting Theory to Work: Implementing Situational Prevention and Problem-oriented Policing*, edited by Johannes Knutsson and Ronald V. Clarke, 2006.

Volume 21, *Imagination for Crime Prevention: Essays in Honor of Ken Pease*, edited by Graham Farrell, Kate Bowers, Shane Johnson and Mike Townsley, forthcoming 2007.

Contents

(continued)

Contents

Acknowledgments

The papers in this book were presented at a small conference on implementation of crime prevention that took place in May 2005 at Stavern, the Norwegian Justice Sector's Center for Training and Practice. The personnel at the Center made our stay very pleasant and we would like to express our gratitude to the Norwegian National Police Directorate, as well as to the Norwegian Police University College, for funding the conference. Finally, we would like to thank the conference participants for sharing their important insights.

Johannes Knutsson
Norwegian Police
University College

Ronald V. Clarke
Rutgers,
The State University
of New Jersey

Foreword

Crime in the Western world has increased over the past 50 years, and it has become more complicated and more complex. The traditional legal strategy, with the emphasis on punishment as a general and individual deterrent, has proved inadequate as a main strategy alone. More attention has therefore been given to crime prevention measures.

Research on policing methods and strategies brought social science in as a supplement to the legal strategy. Concepts such as community policing and problem-oriented policing rely on social scientific methods as a basis for strategies and measures to prevent and reduce crime. Research also reinforced the recognition that crime cannot be prevented and combated by the police alone. The causes of crime must be dealt with if there is to be any hope of a significant reduction.

Police forces all over the Western world, Norway's included, have been trying to implement new methods and strategies. There has traditionally been a high level of public confidence in the police in the Scandinavian countries, and there is a tradition of close cooperation between the authorities. This makes it easier to invite local authorities, central authorities and other "problem owners" to cooperate in the prevention of crime.

In this book, the authors consider the quality of the work of implementing new strategies and they draw attention to the complexity in regard to competence and responsibility in problem-solving processes that involve several problem owners. They focus on the need for strategic thinking in order to avoid the most common problems that arise in the implementation of new programmes, and they look at experience with practical crime prevention programmes that work – and at what should be done to ensure success in crime prevention.

This is therefore an important book for everyone who shares the responsibility for reducing crime and preserving safety in the community. A group of prominent researchers, all of whom have long experience in this field, give us an insight into possibilities and challenges linked to the implementation of new working methods in crime prevention.

Ingelin Killengreen
National Police
Commissioner, Norway

Introduction

by

Johannes Knutsson
Norwegian Police University College

and

Ronald V. Clarke
Rutgers University

Crime prevention has made rapid progress during the past two decades. This is especially true of situational crime prevention and problem-oriented policing. Each has accumulated a substantial body of evaluated practice and an extensive theoretical and methodological literature to support that practice. In fact, in recent years, the literatures of these two fields have converged, and there has also been some blurring of practice so that, for example, problem-oriented policing projects now make increasing use of techniques and concepts drawn from situational prevention. This is not surprising because, despite their different origins – one in police organizational theory and the other in criminology – the two approaches share some important assumptions about the best way to prevent crime, including the need to focus on immediate causes of highly specific forms of crime and the desirability of adopting an "action-research" methodology (Tilley, 1999). Unfortunately, both crime prevention approaches also share a weakness – the focus of the present volume – which is that they have neglected implementation, i.e., the stage when measures identified during analysis are put into practice.

Crime Prevention Studies, volume 20 (2006), pp. 1–8.

Weaknesses of implementation have been identified by critics (Hope and Murphy, 1983; Grabosky, 1996) and advocates alike (Goldstein, 2003; Clarke, 1998; Scott, 2000). Particularly significant is that Herman Goldstein, the founder of problem-oriented policing, has expressed disappointment with the quality of many projects undertaken in its name. Not only has analysis been weak, but they have also fallen back on traditional policing measures at the response stage and have failed to identify measures that would address the immediate causes of the problem.

These observations serve as the starting point for this volume. All the chapters have been written by academics with a long-standing interest in crime prevention, most of whom have been directly involved in implementing situational or problem-oriented projects. The chapters cover a wide range of topics. Some focus on problems of implementing single crime prevention *projects*, whereas others deal with implementing broader crime prevention *programs* encompassing many different projects. Some are very practical, providing concrete guidance on how to get the most out of crime prevention schemes, while other chapters are almost philosophical in their outlook. In this Introduction, we will not attempt to summarize each chapter since they all carry abstracts and all are clearly written. Instead, we will draw our own conclusions from the chapters and their discussion at the conference held in advance of their publication. While some chapters range more widely, we focus on situational prevention and problem-oriented policing and set out our conclusions under the ten headings below.

1.   Change takes longer than expected

We have already noted that substantial progress in situational prevention and problem-oriented policing has been made. Nevertheless, many contributors expected progress to be faster and some of the chapters have a disillusioned tone. In fact, it takes a long time, perhaps even generations, to effect fundamental change in social policy, and crime policy is no exception. Both the general public and those who work within law enforcement and the criminal justice system believe that the best way to deal with crime is to change offenders, either through treatment or through punishment. These beliefs are strongly held and derive from deeper beliefs about morality and human nature. Consequently, it is very difficult to persuade people that it is more effective to reduce crime opportunities than to change offenders by punishing them or treating them.

2. The theory is robust

However disillusioned some of the contributors might seem to be, none questions the theoretical basis of situational crime prevention and problem-oriented policing and all accept that, (1) immediate situational factors play a strong part in causing crime problems, (2) these factors can generally be changed, and, (3) immediate reductions can result in crime and disorder. Rather, they believe that "implementation failure," not "theory failure," was responsible for the disappointing results of some projects and programs.

3. Implementation is not easy

Advocates of situational crime prevention and problem-oriented policing have often argued that the preventive measures suggested by these approaches, which may entail rather basic improvements in security, are much easier to implement than social prevention measures. That may be true, but at the same time the difficulties of opportunity reduction have been considerably underestimated. Seemingly simple measures can in fact be rather difficult to implement for a variety of technical, managerial and social reasons.

4. The sources of project failure are generally well understood

The many sources of project failure are reviewed in the chapters by Brown and Scott. Brown's discussion is based on his experience of crime prevention and community safety projects in the United Kingdom, while Scott's is based on his knowledge of problem-oriented policing projects in the United States. Consequently they focus on somewhat different factors, but, fortunately, their experience is being distilled for practitioners in a "Problem Solving Guide" on implementation that they are writing together for the Center for Problem-Oriented Policing. Meanwhile, we would identify a short list of requirements for successful implementation as follows: (1) a highly skilled and motivated project manager (see point 7 below), (2) adequate financial resources and staffing, (3) needed support and cooperation from partner agencies, and, (4) measures that are supported by evidence; are aimed at close causes, not distant ones; employ clearly stated mechanisms; are sustainable and do not require supervision; are not too costly or technically complex; and do not take much coordination between organizations. Furthermore, as suggested in Bowers's and Johnson's chapter, experience from crime prevention projects makes it possible to anticipate threats to implementation and to weigh advantages or disadvantages with different courses of action.

5.   Programs seem more vulnerable to failure than projects

The reasons for program failure have been less studied, though three of the chapter authors – Brown, Homel and Hough – draw lessons from the U.K. Crime Reduction Program launched in the late 1990s. This is the largest national crime prevention program to date. It avoided the problem of imposing solutions (see point 6 below) by allowing local projects to choose measures depending on the local situation. Even so, all three authors believe that the program failed to meet its goals because of implementation problems, though each has a different "take" on the specific nature of the problems. Brown views the program from a local perspective, and argues that better project monitoring was needed. Hough blames the political management philosophy that inspired the program, under which central government set the national goals but required local organizations to meet them. An unintended consequence of this approach, according to Hough, is that simplified and populist policies will be advocated, since they reward actors at the central level. To avoid this trap, Hough advocates a more decentralized performance management system, where local authorities set their own goals instead of just determining their own solutions. Finally, Homel argues that the program was supposed to operate in a complex organizational environment, but failed largely because of lack of qualified staff, inadequate leadership and support from central and regional levels, and weak project management at the local level. He reports that the problems encountered are not unique to the U.K. experience, but have emerged in similar programs elsewhere in the world. His remedy is to treat the entire program, with all its different levels, as a single integrated system. It is particularly important to have a well-staffed centre that can provide leadership for the program and that is capable of giving advice and support on crime prevention matters, on budgets, on training, on reporting standards and on a variety of other technical matters.

6.   Programs to implement standard solutions are especially vulnerable

Both problem-oriented policing and situational crime prevention require that tailor-made solutions be identified for specific crime problems. Context is all important, and something that works in one setting will not necessarily work in another, even one that seems similar. This explains why some programs that have sought to introduce opportunity-reducing measures on a wide scale – such as improved street lighting, neighborhood watch and closed-circuit TV surveillance of public places – have usually produced disappointing results, at least when compared with the introduction of the more careful use of these measures in discrete locations. This does not mean that situational or problem-oriented measures can never have broad benefits. One example of such benefits is the European Union's requirement to install immobilizers on all new cars, which seems likely to reduce overall levels of car theft in many EU countries (Brown, 2004). Even in this case, however, the effects of immobilizers will not be uniform. They will probably have a greater effect on joyriding and more opportunistic thefts than on organized, professional thefts of expensive vehicles.

7.   Professional and committed leadership is vital

Homel's chapter argues that strong and committed leadership is vital to the success of crime prevention programs. While not always mentioned in reports (see Knutsson's chapter for an exception), this is equally true for projects. Those who lead successful projects often show considerable energy, as well as tenacity and persistence, well beyond the call of duty. All the contributors to the volume cited examples in discussion of such individuals. In some cases, their efforts were obstructed by colleagues (junior or senior) in their own agencies. More often, they had to beg, threaten and cajole those in other agencies to supply data or make some essential contribution to the project. The Goldstein and Tilley awards in problem-oriented policing (see www.popcenter.org for a repository of submissions) exist partly to recognize the contribution of these individuals.

8.   The need to incentivize implementers has been neglected

In his chapter, Ken Pease focuses on the frequent lack of fit between the intentions of those who promote crime prevention schemes and those who must implement them. In many instances, there is no obvious benefit for the implementer in taking part in a crime preventive scheme. The implementer may also be independent of the intender and hence not susceptible to pressure. Even in organizations with explicit crime prevention goals, there may be little congruence between the preferred activities of the organization and the actions they are expected to undertake for the project. For example, many local community safety and crime prevention agencies in the U.K. have a preference for "social" prevention. In these cases, it is important to find ways of making situational prevention and problem-oriented policing more attractive and rewarding to them.

9. Partnerships can be a trap

Partnerships between different agencies are essential to the success of many crime prevention projects because the solutions often demand coordinated action among a variety of public and private "stakeholders" (see Knutsson's chapter for an example). But partnerships must be very carefully managed or they can doom a project. It is particularly important to avoid forming a partnership before it is clear who can make an effective contribution to the solution. Too often, forming a partnership is the first step in a crime prevention project. This can mean that planning gets bogged down in looking for a role in the solution for every partner, however unrealistic this might be. While this might purchase some temporary goodwill, it is ultimately a source of frustration and delay. Forming a partnership should wait until analysis of the problem has clarified which agencies have the responsibility and the *competence* (see Gloria Laycock's chapter) to implement solutions. Delaying until this point can be difficult, since there is often the expectation that a collaborative venture is needed. It may also be the case that the analysis of the problem requires help from a variety of agencies. However, it is best to seek this help, not in "partnership" meetings, but directly from the agencies concerned. In this way, there need be no presumption that agencies consulted during the project will also have a role in the solution.

10. Ways to communicate "tacit" knowledge must be found

This last conclusion is one of the most important to emerge from the book because it points the way to speeding up the adoption of situational prevention and problem-oriented policing and to helping overcome some of the problems of implementation. All the contributors to this volume are actively engaged in communicating academic knowledge about crime prevention to the practitioners who must put it into practice. Most have provided consultancy advice, but generally they have concentrated on (1) writing pamphlets for practitioners (for example the U.S. COPS Office-sponsored "Problem Solving Guides" and many of the reports in the Home Office Police Research Series), and, (2) helping to develop materials for the Home Office Crime Reduction and the Center for Problem-Oriented

Policing web sites. However, Tilley makes clear in his chapter that, important as these efforts may be, they are not sufficient on their own because the knowledge being communicated is much more complex than was first assumed. For example, preventive measures have to be carefully tailored to the specific context in which they must be implemented. This is a challenging task that takes highly skilled and experienced personnel. Much of the necessary expertise consists of "tacit" knowledge, learned while practicing through personal contact with an accomplished practitioner. Tilley recommends a system of apprenticeship where this type of knowledge can be passed on. It would "involve the simplest possible text guidance backed by personal training and supervised practice, offering limited but growing discretion as the apprentice practitioners come to show that they have sufficient skill and understanding to make their own decisions and depart from strict rules without discussion and approval."

In summary, implementation of problem-oriented policing and situational prevention has been neglected by scholars, who have tended to assume that this stage of the problem-solving process is comparatively straightforward. However, experience has shown that many projects fail for a variety technical, management and "political" reasons. Although there is less experience of implementing crime prevention programs, it is already apparent that these may be even more prone to failure than projects – perhaps because there is so much more to go wrong. On the more positive side, important lessons have also been learned that should guide future practice. Some of the most important of these are that skilled, committed leadership is vital for the success of both projects and programs; that partnerships must be carefully managed if they are to assist, not undermine, implementation; and it must not be assumed that project implementers are fully committed to the opportunity-reduction approach. Finally, it has now been recognized, contrary to early assumptions, that the problem-solving approaches discussed in this book are not straightforward, and that the required knowledge to put them into practice cannot be fully communicated in written texts, even ones that are easy to read and understand. Finding ways to communicate this tacit knowledge will constitute an important challenge to the advocates of situational prevention and problem-oriented policing.

Address correspondence to: Prof. Johannes Knutsson, Norwegian Police University College, Pb 5027 Majorstua, 0301 Oslo, Norway; e-mail: Johannes.Knutsson@phs.no

REFERENCES

Brown, R. (2004). The effectiveness of electronic immobilization: Changing patterns of temporary and permanent vehicle theft. In M. G. Maxfield & R. V. G. Clarke (Eds.), *Understanding and preventing car theft*. Crime Prevention Studies, vol. 17. Monsey, NY: Criminal Justice Press.

Clarke, R. V. G. (1998). Defining police strategies: Problem-solving, problem-oriented policing and community-oriented policing. In T. O'Connor Shelley & A. C. Grant (Eds.), *Problem-oriented policing: Crime-specific problems, critical issues and making POP work*. Washington, DC: Police Executive Research Forum.

Goldstein, H. (2003). On further developing problem-oriented policing: The most critical need, the major impediments and a proposal. In J. Knutsson (Ed.), *Problem-oriented policing: From innovation to mainstream*. Crime Prevention Studies, vol. 15. Monsey, NY: Criminal Justice Press.

Grabosky, P. (1996). Unintended consequences of crime prevention. In R. Homel (Ed.), *Politics and practice of situational crime prevention*. Crime Prevention Studies, vol. 5. Monsey, NY: Criminal Justice Press.

Hope, T., & Murphy, D. (1983). Problems of implementing crime prevention: The experience of a demonstration project. *The Howard Journal, XXII,* 38–50.

Scott, M. S. (2000). *Problem-oriented policing. Reflections on the first 20 years.* Washington, DC: U.S. Department of Justice, Office of Community Oriented Policing Services.

Tilley, N. (1999). The relationship between problem-oriented policing and crime prevention. In C. Sole Brito & T. Allan (Eds.), *Problem-oriented policing: Crime-specific problems, critical issues and making POP work*. Washington, DC: Police Executive Research Forum.

Implementing Crime Prevention: Lessons Learned from Problem-oriented Policing Projects

by

Michael S. Scott
University of Wisconsin Law School
Center for Problem-Oriented Policing

Abstract: *Problem-oriented policing initiatives are one important form of crime prevention, and they offer opportunities for learning about implementation success and failure. Problem-oriented policing initiatives can succeed or fail for a variety of reasons, among them: inaccurate identification of the problem, inaccurate analysis of the problem, inadequate implementation, or application of an incorrect theory. This paper draws upon both the research literature and reports on problem-oriented policing initiatives to identify those factors that best explain why action plans do or do not get implemented. It identifies and provides examples of five clusters of factors that help explain implementation success or failure: (1) characteristics, skills, and actions of project managers; (2) resources (3) support and cooperation external to the police agency; (4) evidence; and (5) complexity of implementation.*

INTRODUCTION

The literature on community and problem-oriented policing is replete with analyses and explanations for many aspects of failed efforts to adopt these approaches. Much of the literature is focused at the organizational level: that is, exploring why the approach did not take hold as a systemic, organizational framework for the operations and administration of the police agency or as a guiding philosophy for governmental and nongovernmental responses to crime and disorder (Skogan, Hartnett et al., 2000; Alarid, 1999; Sparrow, 1988; Laycock and Farrell, 2003; Greene, 1998; Rosenbaum, 1994; Grinder, 2000). Less well studied is failure at the problem level: that is, exploring why a crime or disorder reduction initiative undertaken to address one particular problem did not achieve its objectives.

Using the basic framework of a problem-solving model, there are four basic reasons why any particular problem reduction initiative might fail (or, conversely, succeed):

1. The problem was inaccurately *identified*: the underlying problem was something other than what it first appeared, the problem was not as acute as initially believed, or the police agency or the community was not as concerned about the problem as first thought.

2. The problem was insufficiently or inadequately *analyzed*: either the real contributing or causative factors were not discovered, or insufficient or inadequate evidence was mounted to persuade others to take interest in the problem.

3. The responses developed from the problem analysis were improperly or insufficiently *implemented*, or not implemented at all.

4. The problem was properly identified and analyzed, and responses were implemented, but the responses did not have the desired effect on the problem.

This paper concerns itself principally with the third of these four reasons: successful or failed implementation of responses.

At first blush, *implementation* seems the simplest and most straightforward of the four basic problem-solving steps. Invoking the simple admonition adopted by the Nike Corporation as its slogan, one might think that implementation requires merely that one "just do it." In reality, implementation is often infinitely more complex than it first appears, demanding much greater attention and care than is commonly imagined (Larson, 1980).

The implementation phase of problem-oriented policing initiatives may well be the most crucial yet least well-understood phase. Indeed, the early literature on problem-oriented policing paid scant attention to this phase, owing largely to the absence of a sufficiently robust body of case studies from which an improved understanding of implementation might be gleaned. Goldstein's (1990) seminal work on the concept devoted entire chapters to identifying problems (chapter 6), analyzing problems (chapter 7), and developing and choosing from among alternative responses (chapter 8), but only alluded to some of the challenges associated with implementing responses, and then only in the context of choosing from among a range of response options (1990:143–45). Even later studies of problem-oriented policing initiatives – which carefully studied such questions as how problems were identified, how they were analyzed, what sorts of responses were developed, and what results were achieved – paid less attention to the factors that explained whether, why, and how well the responses developed were implemented (Capowich and Roehl, 1994; Scott, 2000).

Partly out of a desire to make the problem-solving process appear less daunting, many proponents and practitioners of problem-oriented policing promoted the use of simplified problem-solving processes, the most common being the SARA (Scanning, Analysis, Response, Assessment) model (Eck and Spelman, 1987). One unfortunate consequence of this simplified model is that it conflates into one stage – the Response stage – several rather distinct processes.

Goldstein's original conceptualization of a problem-solving model for problem-oriented policing saw this "Response" stage as comprising at least three distinct processes: (1) conducting a broad, uninhibited search for response alternatives; (2) choosing from among those alternatives; and (3) implementing the chosen alternatives (Goldstein, 1990).[1] Each of these processes requires careful attention to minimize the risk of failure. With regard to the first of these processes – conducting a broad search for responses – conventional thinking creates the risk that police will be blind to innovative responses that have greater potential to be effective than conventional police responses. Decision makers can prematurely settle upon a response strategy and become fixated on one strategy to the exclusion of potentially more viable alternatives. With regard to the second of these processes – choosing from among alternatives – failing to fully account for the advantages and disadvantages of each potential response (e.g., likelihood of effectiveness, community reaction, financial costs, available resources, legality, practicality) can lead police to try to implement responses that are doomed to fail or backfire. So too with regard to the third of these processes – implementing chosen responses – is careful attention required to minimize the risk of failure.

Although implementation failures are every bit as instructive as successes, they are, of course, harder for researchers to uncover for the simple reason that they are less likely to be documented by police agencies.

A variety of factors explaining why problem-oriented initiatives appear to succeed or fail appear in the research literature and in police reports on problem-oriented policing projects. The factors are of five general types:

1. characteristics, skills, and actions of project managers,

2. resources,

3. support and cooperation external to the police agency,

4. evidence, and

5. complexity of implementation.

Further explanation and examples of these factors follow.

1. Characteristics, Skills, and Actions of Project Managers

The degree to which POP initiatives succeed or fail depends greatly on the characteristics, skills, and actions of key individuals, most especially those individuals who have assumed the responsibility for managing the initiatives. Several personal characteristics and skills stand out in the literature as especially significant, among them: leadership, personal engagement by the police chief executive, continuity of assignment, ownership of the initiative, effective communication to others of the project objectives and directives, and technical and managerial competence.

Leadership At or Near the Level of the Principal Project Agents

It is perhaps a truism that strong leadership is necessary to successful implementation of problem-oriented policing initiatives, or that weak leadership is a key factor in failed implementation: however, the strength or weakness of leadership is at least partially defined by the success or failure of the task one is leading. It nonetheless bears saying that in so many POP initiatives project leadership stands out among the factors cited for successful implementation of responses (Skogan et al., 2000).

POP initiatives are undertaken at various levels of aggregation and at various levels within a police bureaucratic hierarchy (Scott, 2000; Goldstein

1990). Some initiatives are undertaken at the beat level, some at the jurisdictional level, some at cross-jurisdictional levels, and some at various intermediate levels. Thus we find project leadership and management being exercised by individuals at varying ranks and position within and outside the police organization, from line-level officers or civilian staff, to mid-level supervisors and managers, to senior executives.

Few police agencies seem to have well-established systems for ensuring that the action plans developed in POP initiatives are carried out. Consequently, to the extent that they are carried out, it seems often to be due to the diligence, persistence, and perseverance of one or a few individuals. These individuals schedule and lead meetings, perform the tasks they have agreed to and hold others accountable for doing the same, and generally do whatever is necessary to keep the project a priority concern. It is often the case that these individuals exercise a degree of leadership not commonly expected of their rank and position. They press ahead unless made to stop.

Personal Support and Involvement of High-Ranking Police Executives

Particularly when the POP initiative requires a significant commitment of resources, a change in policy or legislation, or the exercise of significant political influence, the police chief executive's personal engagement in and commitment to implementing a response plan can be critical.

This was exemplified when the police chief in Fremont, California spearheaded his agency's initiative to change its response to burglar alarms. In the face of strong opposition by the alarm industry, the police chief pressed the case for a policy change by carefully presenting his agency's internal analysis of its response to burglar alarms to audiences of alarm owners, elected officials, and the public at large (Aguirre, 2005).

Similarly, the police chief in Racine, Wisconsin used his influence and contacts within the political and business community to advance a POP initiative to reduce drug- and gang-related crime by sparking community redevelopment. The police chief worked with other influential community leaders to set up a nonprofit foundation through which private donations could be received and spent on community redevelopment and crime control efforts. The foundation purchased blighted houses, renovated them, permitted police to use them as community police stations for awhile (in order to help stabilize the neighborhood), and then sold them as owner-occupied homes. A combination of community development and targeted law enforcement were deemed to have significantly reduced reported crime and fear (Racine Police Department, 1999). This initiative was recognized as a finalist in the Herman Goldstein Award for Excellence in Problem-Oriented Policing in large measure due to the distinctively-involved role of the police chief.

The police chief executive can similarly stifle the implementation of a response plan. In one instance, a detective working to improve investigations of child sexual abuse requested that his police chief solicit the local district attorney's support to purchase an expensive piece of equipment for medical examinations of child victims. Although the police chief dutifully placed a call and left a message for the district attorney, when the chief was notified during a meeting that the district attorney was returning his call, the chief replied that the district attorney should be told that the matter wasn't important. The detective then became discouraged and the initiative effectively ended. Ironically, the meeting in which the police chief did not want to be interrupted concerned implementing a community policing plan in the agency.[2]

Even where a police chief executive does not intentionally squelch a POP initiative, his or her lack of engagement at critical junctures in the project can mean that the project achieves less than it might otherwise. Police chief executives typically operate in a tumultuous political and professional environment in which organizational priorities change relatively rapidly and somewhat unpredictably. Accordingly, some POP initiatives that begin as high priorities for the chief executive can drop down the priority list as the project progresses and as new issues supersede the problem at hand. An initiative by the Savannah, Georgia Police Department (now the Savannah-Chatham Metropolitan Police Department) to address burglary of single-family houses yielded interesting and useful insights in the problem analysis and a comprehensive set of practical recommendations for action. However, even though the project confirmed that the problem was persistent and the community's overall response to it inadequate, other priorities – counterterrorism (in the wake of the terrorist attacks on New York City and Washington, D.C. and an anthrax scare), violent crime (owing to a spike in its incidence), and merger of the city and county police departments – came to dominate the chief executive's attention after the project began. Few of the response recommendations developed in the burglary project were implemented and, for the most part, the project was abandoned. The time and attention of key burglary project staff were consumed attending to these competing priorities of the chief executive (Scott, 2004).

At least part of the implementation failures in the St. Louis Consent-to-Search initiative (an initiative designed to remove guns from the hands of young people known to be involved in youth gangs) was attributed to a fundamental philosophical change at the level of the police chief executive. Wrote the project researchers:

> After the first chief left, the St. Louis Police Department had no organizational commitment to either problem solving or community policing. The prevailing departmental philosophy . . . was that consent searches were ineffective and too soft on offenders. Departmental leadership placed a high priority on taking offenders rather than guns off the streets. (Decker and Rosenfeld, 2004:15)

Continuity of Project Leadership and Management

Many POP initiatives take months, even years, to bring to fruition. When key project leaders and managers stop working on the project (due to transfers, promotions, retirements, new project assignments, and the like), it is often difficult to maintain interest in and commitment to the project (Bullock, Farrell et al., 2002). This is typically the case when POP initiatives are perceived within the agency to be matters of personal, rather than organizational, interest and priority. Absent a formalized system in which project management is officially transferred to a successor, the departure of the project's key leaders often spells the end of the initiative.

In order to take on the task of trying to reduce domestic-violence homicides in Newport News, Virginia, a police detective requested and was granted a transfer to a special task force set up for that purpose. The effort required extensive problem analysis and the careful development, implementation, and monitoring of a new domestic violence protocol and program. The police detective assumed the central coordinating role among a host of other agencies that were brought together to address the problem (Newport News Police Department, 1998).

The continuity of a police captain's assignment as project manager for an initiative to address drug dealing in private apartment complexes in Newark, New Jersey – through a change in the top leadership of the police agency – was deemed essential to the project's success (Zanin, Shane et al., 2004).

Ownership of the Initiative

Most people are more committed to their own ideas than to others'. In the context of implementing POP initiatives this means that it is desirable

that the people needed to implement responses feel some sense of ownership of the action plan (Bullock, Farrell et al., 2002, citing Read and
Tilley, 2000). A sense of ownership can be cultivated in key individuals
by providing them with opportunities to meaningfully influence the direction of the project such that they feel they are not merely implementing
somebody else's plan, but implementing their own plan. Conversely, a lack
of input by key individuals at meaningful stages of the project can lead to
their lack of commitment to implementation (Long et al., 2002).

Much of the problem-oriented policing literature stresses the importance of maintaining a strong link between the analysis and response
development phases, and the response implementation phase. Ideally, the
same individuals remain actively involved in the project throughout, from
initial problem identification to analysis to response development to response implementation to assessment. Ownership of an action plan can
either be assumed or assigned (or neither) in a police organization. Ideally,
the individual or individuals who spearheaded the problem analysis would
likewise have the capacity and desire to put their resultant plan into action.
The emergence of professional grant writers working for police agencies
increases the risk that the plan of action, which often must be specified
in the funding application, will be developed without the input or commitment of those who will be tasked with putting the plan into action. Where
it is not possible for the lead problem analysts to implement the plan, the
next best possibility is for the action plan to be officially assigned to one
or more individuals who will be held accountable for carrying it out. When
responsibility for implementing an action plan is neither assumed nor
assigned, the plan typically lies dormant.

The lead researchers of the earliest POP initiative examining the
problem of drinking drivers concluded that the failure to fully implement
the recommendations for action arising out of the inquiry was largely
attributable to the fact that no one individual within the police agency
had or was given responsibility for doing so (Goldstein and Susmilch,
1982:108–09). By contrast, the recommendations for action that emerged
out of the same researchers' analysis of a second problem – repeat sex
offenders – were promptly and effectively implemented owing largely to
the fact that a police lieutenant was tasked with doing so (Goldstein and
Susmilch, 1982:109). Similarly, the researchers who worked and reported
on the Boston Gun Project's Operation Ceasefire attributed some of the
project's success to the clear accountability mechanisms established
through an interagency task force (Kennedy, Braga and Piehl, 2001).

A sense of ownership of a response plan is unlikely to be engendered merely by assigning it to someone nor by extrinsic motivations such as financial reward. For example, where police officers or others agree to carry out certain assignments principally because there is overtime compensation to be earned from doing so, it is often the case that the commitment to carrying out the plan as originally designed is weakened. Wrote one project manager:

> Police supervisors, who were brought in from other districts to work overtime, were not implementing the program in a consistent manner. . . . It became apparent that the lack of ownership for the problem by other district supervisors was jeopardizing the attempt to deal with the problem. As a result, the original designed response was being implemented inconsistently, causing confusion and frustration. (Halton Regional Police, 2002)

Creating a specialized assignment to address a problem appears to increase the likelihood that action plans will be implemented. Specialized assignments might be in the form of special task forces, specialized units, secondments, and other similar arrangements. The specialization of the assignment might be either to the particular problem or to some sort of problem-solving unit within which the individuals assigned can choose problems to address and concentrate their work on them. From among the POP initiatives regarded as most successful one more commonly finds them occurring within the context of specialized rather than generalized assignments.

Typically, specialized assignments provide not only the time and other resources necessary to the task, but also greater accountability because responsibility for addressing particular problems is more firmly established. Additionally, specialized assignments offer other intangible benefits to the individuals assuming those assignments: prestige, freedom from ordinary duties, greater autonomy over working conditions, and so forth. To the extent the individuals value these benefits, they have incentives to ensure that action plans are implemented; that the project appears to be moving forward and producing results. Of course, specialized assignments have a built-in dilemma: if those so assigned are too successful and the problem is eliminated or dramatically abated, there may no longer be a justification for perpetuating the specialized assignment. It is a tendency of bureaucracies (and by extension, the subdivisions thereof) that the individuals holding desirable positions in them will do whatever is necessary to perpetuate the existence of the bureaucratic entity. Consequently, individuals holding specialized assignments often seek an optimal rather than maximum degree of success: just successful enough to convince decision makers that the specialized assignment is *effective*, and just unsuccessful enough to convince decision makers that continuation of the specialized assignment is *necessary*.

Where a specialized assignment is intended as a sort of pilot initiative to develop a response strategy that is then to be rolled out more widely to general assignment officers, a new set of challenges arise. The factors that make specialized work effective – commitment to the plan, esprit de corps, flexible time and other resources, and so forth – are often difficult to replicate outside the specialized context.

Externally-funded research projects are similarly a mixed blessing in terms of translating the research into action. The external funding provides resources and expertise that might otherwise be unavailable to the project. It can also serve as an incentive to project participants who want to make a favorable impression to external funders (and not to be embarrassed in published reports). But the external aspects of the initiative can undermine the police agency's sense of ownership of the project. A subtle attitude can develop among police agency participants that the point of the whole exercise is to satisfy the researchers' and funding agency's needs rather than to solve the problem at hand. This appeared to be the case in the initiatives addressing drunk driving in Madison, Wisconsin (Goldstein and Susmilch, 1982) and burglary of single-family houses in Savannah, Georgia (Scott, 2004). Where this attitude develops, there is a tendency to view the project as complete once the problem analysis is complete.

Even where ownership of an initiative is once firmly established, it can degrade over time because of other factors discussed elsewhere in this paper such as staff turnover, complacency, loss of resources, loss of control over the initiative, and so forth.

Effective Communication of Policy Objectives and Directives to those Responsible for Implementation

Where it is beyond the capacity of the project leaders to themselves implement responses, it becomes crucial that they be able to persuasively and effectively communicate to others tasked with implementation what needs to be done and why (Long, Wells et al., 2002, citing Van Horn and Van Meter, 1977; Bullock and Tilley, 2003; Clarke and Eck, 2003). Wrote Larson (1980:5): "As a general rule of thumb, the greater the number of actors and agencies involved in a program, the less likely it is to succeed."

Problem-solving is, for the most part, not sufficiently well institution-alized in most police agency's operations for it to be self-evident that the tasks needed to implement a POP initiative response plan must be dutifully performed. Notwithstanding that police agencies are perceived to be highly disciplined quasi-military organizations in which orders are faithfully obeyed, police officers, like most workers, comply with directives better when they understand and agree with the objectives and see value in their contributions toward them. Accordingly, getting others to carry out essential tasks often requires a careful effort to get them to "buy in" to the initiative. This is more readily accomplished if those tasked with implementing the responses have at least some input into the design of those responses.

As difficult as it often is for police officers to obtain "buy-in" within their own agency, it is often even more difficult to convince people outside the police department to carry out specific tasks faithfully and properly. The success of an anti-bullying initiative led by a police officer in South Euclid, Ohio was heavily dependent on the capacity of the officer and his project colleagues to persuade school administrators and teachers, students, and parents to address bullying differently than they had in the past. The officer's analysis of the problem led him to conclude that teachers, administrators, parents, and students had a far greater capacity to control bullying than did the police, but only if they learned to adopt a new understanding about and attitudes toward bullying, and then translated that new awareness into new behavioral responses to the problem. The officer and his project colleagues deliberately involved school administra-tors and teachers, parents, and students in the process of interpreting their analysis findings and proposing new responses. Extensive training and education of all key groups was instrumental in conveying what could and should be done to control bullying. Program evaluation surveys confirmed that the training and education components of the initiative were a critical factor in the successful implementation of new responses (South Euclid Police Department, 2001).

The St. Louis initiative to confiscate guns from young persons through consent searches suffered from difficulties in convincing regular patrol officers and supervisors of the value of this approach, which was developed by a specialized unit. Many officers who were not part of the unit that designed the initiative never came to believe in the value of the particular response. Little training was provided outside of the specialized unit (Decker and Rosenfeld, 2004).

Professional Capabilities of Key Individuals

Even where strong leadership is present, successful implementation requires that the individuals responsible for carrying out essential implementation tasks must have the requisite technical knowledge, skills, and abilities (Larson, 1980; Bullock and Tilley, 2003; Ekblom, 2002; Clarke and Eck, 2003). These requisite proficiencies extend both to project management and supervision, as well as to service delivery or the acquisition, installation, and operation of things.

The St. Louis gun control initiative cited above also suffered because an outside clergy group that was supposed to make follow-up visits to the homes where guns were confiscated failed to make these visits when referred by police (Decker and Rosenfeld, 2004).

2. Resources

Whether POP initiative action plans get properly implemented also depends heavily on the sufficiency and availability of the resources necessary for implementation (Grabosky, 1996). Such resources typically include, at a minimum, finances, authority, and staffing. It is seldom sufficient that the resources exist; they must also be sufficiently accessible to project decision makers and flexible in their adaptation to particular needs.

Sufficiency of Legal and Organizational Authority

It is often the case that the responses developed in POP initiatives are sufficiently innovative that they present a significant challenge to the status quo. Accordingly, POP initiative managers must acquire and use new forms and grants of authority in order to properly implement new responses. This authority might come in the form of a change in the law – a new regulation, ordinance, by-law, statute, or judicial interpretation – or in the form of a change in administrative or organizational policy or practice.

In problem-oriented policing, key decision making should occur at an organizational level closest to where the problem is experienced, consistent with the need for meaningful oversight and review. This has typically meant that authority has generally been pushed down in the traditional police hierarchy, whereby police officials are encouraged to use this newly granted authority to push forward the POP initiatives in which they are personally engaged. Naturally, such a shift in orientation can give rise to new tensions, both within the police organization and in its relations with external organizations. Police officials pressing for the implementation of new responses might well be challenged by others who perceive that the officials pressing for action lack the requisite authority to do so.

How these tensions get resolved varies from agency to agency and project to project. Much turns on the skill with which the project manager exercises his or her authority, whether the exercise of that authority is backed up by a formal grant of authority, and the extent to which higher-ranking police officials defend their subordinates when they exercise that authority and are challenged by others for doing so.

Some line-level police officers, whether by virtue of their personalities or their training and experience in leadership roles outside of policing, are tremendously effective at making authoritative requests of others to do certain things. For example, a police officer working on a problem involving noise complaints emanating from a railroad switching yard, when met with resistance from lower-level railroad employees, promptly placed a telephone call to the chief executive officer of the railroad corporation in another state, requesting his cooperation and appealing to the corporate executive's desire to avoid bad publicity to the corporation for disturbing local citizens. The corporate executive was receptive to the officer's recommendations and ordered that steps be taken to reduce the noise. The police officer, taking steps that even some police chief executives might be reluctant to take, relied upon assurances from his department that this was the sort of initiative he was expected to take, as well as on his experience as an officer of higher rank in his military service.[3]

Availability and Flexibility of Sufficient Resources

Some responses to problems do not require the commitment of new resources; perhaps all that is required is a shift of existing resources or revision of a policy. But most projects involve at least some responses that do require additional resources: staffing, money, equipment, and so forth. This often presents significant challenges to police agencies, particularly during times when resources are tight. The regular operating and capital budgets of most police agencies are set well before most problem-oriented initiatives are crystallized and few police budgets have pools of funds set aside for unanticipated needs. Accordingly, many POP initiatives, to the extent they require the commitment of significant new resources, are heavily dependent on other funding sources: grants, special police funds such as drug asset forfeiture funds, or corporate or community donations.

Even where external resources are available, the strictures of those re-sources – delays between application for and receipt of resources, timelines for expending the resources, reporting requirements, use restrictions, and so forth – can make them less useful for the purpose of addressing an evolving public safety problem than they might first appear.

To the extent that a POP initiative in Charlotte-Mecklenburg, North Carolina succeeded in addressing the problem of thefts of appliances from construction sites, it did so in large measure because two police officers were assigned to work on the project on a full-time basis for about two years (Clarke and Goldstein, 2003). Given the labor-intensive nature of their analysis of and responses to the problem, and given the competing priorities for police attention, it is highly unlikely that this initiative would have yielded the results it did without this substantial staffing commitment.

An initiative undertaken in the Fenlands area of England to reduce repeat burglaries was intended to follow an earlier burglary reduction model in which all houses once burglarized would receive a heightened level of protection from police and others. However, in the final analysis, far fewer houses received this heightened protection, a fact attributed by project evaluators to the inadequacy of resources necessary for the scope of the task (Jones, 2003:82).

3. Support and Cooperation External to the Police Agency

There are some responses that police can implement solely on their own authority, but more commonly, police need support and cooperation from outside their agency to implement new responses to public safety problems. Obviously, it is easier for police to get things done in the absence of strong opposition to the plan of action, but even in the absence of strong opposition, getting things done still calls for cultivating external support and cooperation.[4]

Grass-Roots Community Support

Response plans that enjoy grass-roots community support tend to be more likely to be implemented than those without it because such community support can be converted into political influence which can mobilize re-sources and action. Police have influence themselves, to be sure, but their influence alone is not always sufficient to persuade reluctant government officials. St. Louis police expedited the demolition of derelict buildings that were serving as crime magnets by getting citizens to write letters to the government agency responsible for demolishing buildings. In the same project, police mobilized a large group of citizens to testify at a liquor licensing hearing, persuading the licensing authority to revoke the license of a troublesome tavern (Risk, 1992).

Grass-roots community support can also be essential to forestall opposition to police action. Indianapolis police were able to sustain an intensive effort to stop vehicles, search for guns, and investigate suspicious drivers and occupants in a predominantly minority community owing in large part to preparatory work done by the police to gain community understanding of and support for the initiative (McGarrell, Chermak et al., 2002).

Supportive Media Coverage

Where media coverage of a police effort to address a problem presents the police perspective in a favorable light, this can provide a substantial boost to the implementation of responses. It can do so in several ways: by engendering public understanding of and support for the course of action recommended by police (and thereby giving elected officials incentives to ensure that the problem is addressed), by shaming and holding to account certain parties deemed to be responsible for contributing to the problem or parties deemed not to be cooperating in the effort to remediate the problem, by keeping the problem in the consciousness of key officials (including police officials) until it is properly addressed, by providing a reasonably objective assessment of the case being made by police for new responses to the problem, and by encouraging police officials through the intrinsic satisfaction of positive publicity and recognition.

Media coverage, however, is not universally supportive of a police plan to address a particular problem, and can in fact thwart it. A plan by Manchester, UK police to conduct an enforcement crackdown on certain gang members was put on hold because lawyers representing some gang members on trial at the time prevailed in their argument that the media coverage of a police crackdown on gangs would unfairly prejudice the jury in the instant trial (Bullock and Tilley, 2003:122). When Lauderhill, Florida police filed a nuisance abatement action against the owner of a commercial property as a means of controlling an open-air drug market operating on the property, local newspaper coverage was hostile to the police action, adopting the editorial view that only drug dealers and buyers should be held responsible for the drug market, not the property owner, and further questioning the police motives. Although the adverse media coverage did not ultimately hinder the legal action, it did weaken public support for it (Lauderhill Police Department, 1996).

Existence of Organizations with the Capacity and Mandate to Implement Responses

Where there already exist organizations outside the police agency with the clear mandate and capacity to implement responses, the probability that the responses will actually be implemented appears to be higher. Conversely, where the response would require creating a new organization or unit to implement the response, or where it is unclear which organization or unit has the mandate and capacity to implement the response, successful implementation is less likely (Long, Wells et al., 2002; Bullock, Farrell et al., 2002).

The Newark (New Jersey) Police Department's analysis of problems associated with drug dealing in privately-owned apartment complexes led them to conclude that reengineering a major arterial roadway was likely to be the most effective response to a particular problem. Traffic reengineering on such a scale as this is clearly beyond the authority and capacity of the police agency alone. That it nonetheless was contemplated and approved owed largely to the fact that the city's Traffic Engineering Department became deeply engaged with the Newark police on this project. Traffic engineers had the authority and the technical competence to undertake such a large project. The Traffic Engineering Department had already secured the authority and funding from the state for this reengineering project. Traffic engineers were therefore positioned to work closely with the police because doing so only required relatively minor modifications to their existing plans rather than a major reprioritization of traffic projects. The actions deemed necessary to control the drug problem in the short term while awaiting completion of the long-term roadway redesign and construction were within the capacity of the police (drug enforcement), city fire, code, and health inspectors (code enforcement against problem properties), and traffic engineers (temporary roadway redesign) to effect at a reasonable cost (Zanin, Shane et al., 2004).

This same factor can apply to units within the police agency. The Oakland, California Police Department implemented a sophisticated set of responses to address a problem pertaining to a budget motel. It negotiated with the motel's on-site manager to improve management practices, assisted with some clean-up of the motel property, negotiated changes in management practices with corporate executives, conducted undercover surveillance and enforcement operations at the motel, and ultimately filed a nuisance abatement lawsuit against the motel's parent corporation. All of these actions called for careful attention to detail, legal and procedural expertise, and persistent monitoring of the problem. That the responses were executed so well was largely attributed to the fact that the police agency had in existence a special unit – known as the Beat Health Unit – that over the course of many years had developed procedures, systems, and expertise to address just these sorts of problems. Particularly given the high financial stakes in this problem and the formidable corporate resources aligned against the police, it is highly unlikely these responses could have been implemented, let alone have proven so successful, without the mandate and capacity that the Beat Health Unit could bring to bear on the problem (Oakland Police Department, 2003).

Fortuitous Timing

Some POP initiatives benefit from fortuitous timing. A critical incident (such as a heinous crime) or budget pressures might generate public interest in and attention to a problem that might not otherwise occur merely through a more painstaking presentation of evidence and arguments (Goldstein and Susmilch, 1982). Police ought to exploit such opportunities responsibly, taking care to complete a careful analysis of the problem so that they are able to justify their new responses to the problem if called upon to do so in a more deliberate and reasoned fashion. The recommendations made to improve the overall response to repeat sex offenders emerging from a study of that problem in Madison, Wisconsin took on urgent importance when a repeat sex offender murdered a young girl just as the study's recommendations were coming out (Goldstein and Susmilch, 1982). The California Highway Patrol's efforts to reduce injuries and fatalities in farm-vehicle crashes met with less resistance in the wake of a horrific crash that killed 13 farm workers. Legislation applying mandatory seat belt laws to farm vehicles, enhancing farm-vehicle inspections, and providing funding for educating farm employers and workers was enacted speedily (California Highway Patrol, 2002).

The Newark Police Department's plan for controlling drug dealing in private apartment complexes through major roadway redesign benefited from the fortuitous timing of the project: the city had already received state funding and approval for reengineering of that particular roadway, albeit not for the purpose of controlling drug markets. The project was able to take advantage of the plans already on the drawing board intended merely to address traffic congestion concerns and modify them slightly to also address drug market problems (Zanin, Shane et al., 2004).

Congruence of Perspectives and Objectives

Problem-oriented policing generally urges police to engage other organizations in the effort to address problems. While such engagement often yields a synergetic effect, it can also have an inhibiting effect. Where the perspectives, objectives, performance indicators, or cultures of the various collaborating organizations are too divergent and are not effectively reconciled, implementation plans can suffer (Bullock, Farrell et al., 2002; Bullock and Tilley, 2003; Grabosky, 1996; Clarke and Eck, 2003; Laycock and Tilley, 1995). For example, if police personnel are motivated to undertake activities with which they are familiar and for which they believe they will be rewarded – such as law enforcement – and the particular project calls for them to undertake different sorts of activities – such as providing social services – police might be less than enthusiastic or diligent in providing the social services.

Ordinarily, responses are more likely to be implemented if the individuals and organizations tasked with implementation recognize and legitimate the activity as one that they feel competent to carry out and which fits their conception of what they or their organization ought to be doing. For example, police are more likely to conduct criminal law enforcement activities because such activities fit squarely within the scope of police competence and self-image. They are likely to be more reluctant to engage in other sorts of tasks such as providing social services. So too with other agencies. The Boston Gun Project, which was coordinated by an interagency task force, appears to have apportioned the various tasks that were part of its overall response plan in accordance with the respective competencies and self-images of the participating agencies. The police engaged in enforcement crackdowns, the clergy and gang outreach workers offered assistance to gang members, probation officers supervised their clients, prosecutors prosecuted crimes, and so forth. Responses were faithfully implemented perhaps in part because no agency or individual was asked to stretch its conventional sense of its own function. To be sure, the various participants, with their conventionally divergent perspectives on the problem, endorsed one another's work in a unified fashion, but the work itself was performed by the individuals and organizations most comfortable with the respective tasks. Moreover, the various elements of the response plan were developed mindful of the practicality of what participating agencies could do to address the problem. So, for example, economic development was not made part of the response plan in large measure because none of the participating organizations had the capacity to do that work (Kennedy, Braga and Piehl, 2001).

Divergent perspectives and objectives can often be reconciled, of course, but doing so typically requires a conscious and concerted effort and is best done at the outset of the project before hard feelings and recalcitrance develop. Sometimes it is just a matter of having key individuals spend time with one another to learn and appreciate one another's professional perspectives. Other times it requires some third party – sometimes an individual with supervisory authority over all involved organizations – to intervene and help establish some common perspectives and objectives. Such appeared to be the case when the Joliet, Illinois Police Department first tried to work collaboratively with its city Neighborhood Services division to enforce rental property management laws against neglectful property owners. The city manager eventually stepped in to reconcile differences, which led to the two agencies developing and implementing a new process for enforcing rental property management laws, a process which proved to help both agencies achieve results they both desired (Joliet Police Department, 2000).

A related pitfall is what has been termed "mission drift" (Bullock and Tilley, 2003) whereby the initial project objectives morph into either more ambitious or different objectives altogether. This can occur as a result of an insufficient understanding of the causes of the problem or lack of clarity and agreement about which aspects of a larger problem to concentrate upon. Large, ill-defined problems such as "juvenile delinquency," "violent crime," "gangs," "repeat offenders," or "drugs" are especially susceptible to this phenomenon. Spelman (1990) noted that projects and programs to target high-rate repeat offenders often turn into efforts to target especially dangerous offenders who may or may not also offend at high rates. The original implementation plan becomes diluted or diffuse as the various actors responsible for implementation go off in divergent directions. While multiple objectives might be worthwhile, confusing them can render the response ineffective for either.

Although much of this discussion assumes that all those engaged in a problem-oriented initiative share common outcome objectives, this is not always the case. Sometimes it becomes apparent after the start of the project that there are conflicts among the various interests of those involved in the project; that what police hope to achieve in the initiative does not square with what others hope to achieve. Such was the case when Lauderhill, Florida police sought to work with the merchants and owner of a commercial property comprising several shops to eradicate an open-air drug market. Although all parties initially claimed to want to eradicate drug dealing, when police concluded that certain business practices – failing to maintain the property, selling drug paraphernalia, operating pay telephones, and so forth – were significant contributing factors to the problem, several merchants actively resisted police efforts to implement prevention measures. The merchants believed that police should control the drug market exclusively through criminal arrests and that the merchants should be free to pursue their business interests without regard to any effects on drug trafficking (Lauderhill Police Department, 1996).

4. Evidence

Adequacy of Hard Data Support and Effective Communication of the Evidence to Key Decision Makers

Hard evidence that a particular response is justifiable and is or is not known to be effective, and effective communication of that evidence to decision makers, is a powerful factor influencing whether or not that response is ultimately implemented. This is often a significant challenge. Much of what police and others do to control public safety problems has not been rigorously and thoroughly evaluated. The body of evidence from accumulated practice and evaluation research is rather slim indeed. Moreover, it is often the case that police are advocating that new, relatively untested responses be tried in the hope and belief that trying these new responses will, if nothing else, be preferable to continuing with conventional responses that have not proven as effective as hoped. In these circumstances, police must cross two thresholds: one to establish that the old methods ought to be abandoned and a second to establish that the new methods should be tried. For some decision makers, this is more uncertainty than they care to embrace.

When the Salt Lake City, Utah Police Department set out to change its agency's response to burglary alarms, it met with tremendous resistance from the alarm industry because the proposed change would have far-reaching financial ramifications for many alarm companies. The police proposed that police officers would only be dispatched to investigate burglary alarms if the police received some verification that the alarm was not false, that suspicious activity was indeed afoot. Because the alarm companies would no longer be able to count on the police making the initial investigation of the alarm, it would be incumbent upon them to investigate prior to summoning the police. It quickly became apparent to the alarm industry that if the Salt Lake City Police Department were to prevail in its effort to shift responsibility for initial response to burglary alarms in that city, the idea might catch hold in other cities across the country and might trigger a paradigmatic shift in the burglary alarm business model. Consequently, the alarm industry mounted a vigorous opposition to the police proposal. Because the Salt Lake City police chose to secure the authority for this new response via a change in city law, this meant that the police and the alarm industry would be engaged in a public debate over the merits of the proposal. To overcome substantial political pressure generated by the alarm industry, the police would have to marshal substantial hard evidence in support of their proposal. The police prevailed in a close vote of the local city council and several council members who voted for the police proposal cited the persuasive evidence presented by the police as justification for their vote (Salt Lake City Police Department, 2001).

Compelling evidence was equally, if not more, critical when a city ordinance regulating the operations of convenience stores, which was proposed by the Gainesville, Florida Police Department and enacted by its city council, was challenged in the courts by the convenience store industry. Whereas elected officials can be influenced by political pressure as well as hard evidence, the courts tend to be persuaded only by hard evidence and compelling interpretations of the law. Wrote Goldstein (1990:81) in his account of the Gainesville experience:

> The minimum staffing requirement was challenged in the courts
> but upheld as an appropriate exercise of local government authority
> to increase public safety, in large measure because of the persuasive
> data the police had carefully collected and analyzed.

The response plan developed by a task force established to reduce vehicle crashes and injuries along a highway corridor in California included a number of responses that would require significant resources to implement, including funding overtime for enforcement, redesigning and rebuilding roadways, installing emergency communications equipment along roadways, and producing public education materials. The rigorous and detailed analysis of the problem conducted by the task force was almost certainly essential to justify such public expenditures (California Highway Patrol, 2001).

5. Complexity of Implementation

Ease of Implementation

The relative ease with which a response *can* be implemented is obviously a significant factor in explaining whether and to what degree it *is* implemented: simple responses are more likely to get implemented, complex ones less likely (Clarke and Eck, 2003). Hope and Murphy (1983) cite one project in which a seemingly straightforward response – to use toughened glass for school windows to reduce vandalism – was never implemented because it created fire safety hazards and the alternatives simply required more effort than officials were willing to make. Responses that require a one-time effort tend to be simpler than those that require ongoing effort. The degree of complexity is in turn influenced by such factors as the number of individuals or entities that must approve or act upon a response proposal and the form of authority required.

Absence of Delays

Delays in implementation, for whatever reason, can stall the momentum of the project and create doubt about the viability of the plan (Larson, 1980; Bullock, Farrell et al., 2002). To the extent that project managers can keep the project moving forward, the likelihood that the action plan developed will actually be implemented appears to increase.

There is another aspect of delay that can profoundly influence whether a particular response strategy is implemented: where key decision makers feel pressured to demonstrate crime reduction results quickly, those response measures that are likely to take a long time to implement are unlikely to be adopted, however promising they might be. This is one of the unintended consequences of police management accountability schemes that set short timelines for achieving measurable results: police problem-solvers' response options are narrowed and those responses that can be implemented quickly and without need for securing external authority, support, or resources are preferred (see Moore, 2003).

CONCLUSION

When one reflects on the litany of factors and conditions that seem essential for any POP project action plan to actually be put into effect, and the concomitant factors and conditions that can preclude implementation, it is a wonder that police get anything accomplished at all. And yet they do. Among governmental bureaucracies, police seem especially capable of getting things done. Indeed, oftentimes that is precisely why some problems are left to, or assumed by, the police to address. Policing is at its core an action-oriented occupation. It tends toward impatience with deliberate analysis in favor of immediate and dramatic action. The overriding sense one gets from reviewing POP initiatives – both the successfully and the unsuccessfully implemented – is that when police really want something accomplished, it usually gets accomplished. Police POP project managers are remarkably adept at navigating the shoals of implementation failure. The determining factor, therefore, is police desire. And, as with most human endeavors, desire is driven by individual or organizational self-interest, however determined. Problem-oriented policing is a promising means of enlightening that self-interest through rigorous analysis and careful weighing of alternatives, but the underlying desire to get problems solved through a new course of action would appear to be extrinsic to the concept itself. Accordingly, researchers and practitioners alike who are interested in advancing problem-oriented policing would do well to better understand why the best laid plans go oft awry.

Address correspondence to: Michael S. Scott, Center for Problem-Oriented Policing, 120 S. Allen St., Madison, WI 53726; e-mail: mscott@wisc.edu

NOTES

1. Others have conceptualized program implementation as comprising such distinct phases as interpretation (translating the response into written guidelines and regulations), organization (assigning responsibility for tasks), and application (carrying out the tasks): see Larson, 1980.

2. This example is known to the author from personal experience and involvement in the initiative.
3. This example is known to the author from personal experience and involvement in the initiative.
4. For further reading on how police can overcome opposition to their implementation plans, see Buerger (1998), Scott (2005), and Scott and Goldstein (2005).

REFERENCES

Aguirre, B. (2005, January 20). To serve, protect – with proof: Fremont police, looking to cut costs, will soon stop responding to burglar alarms without knowing if a crime has been committed. *Inside Bay Area*.

Alarid, L. F. (1999). Law enforcement departments as learning organizations: Argyris's theory as a framework for implementing community-oriented policing. *Police Quarterly*, 2(3), 321–337.

Buerger, M. (1998). The politics of third-party policing. In L. G. Mazerolle & J. Roehl (Eds.), *Civil remedies and crime prevention*. Crime Prevention Studies, vol. 9 (pp. 89–116). Monsey, NY: Criminal Justice Press.

Bullock, K., & Tilley, N. (2003). From strategy to action: the development and implementation of problem-oriented projects. In K. Bullock & N. Tilley (Eds.), *Crime reduction and problem-oriented policing* (pp. 89–125). Cullompton, UK: Willan Publishing.

Bullock, K., Farrell, G., & Tilley, N. (2002). Funding and implementing crime reduction initiatives. RDS Online Report 10/02. London: Home Office. Retrieved May 25, 2005, from Center for Problem-Oriented Policing Web site: http://www.homeoffice.gov.uk/rds/pdfs2/rdsolr1002.pdf

California Highway Patrol (2002). SAFE: a safety and farm vehicle education program. Submission to the Herman Goldstein Award for Excellence in Problem-Oriented Policing. Retrieved May 25, 2005, from Center for Problem-Oriented Policing Web site: http://www.popcenter.org/Library/Goldstein/2002/02-07(W).pdf

California Highway Patrol (2001). Corridor safety program: a collaborative approach to traffic safety. Submission to the Herman Goldstein Award for Excellence in Problem-Oriented Policing. Retrieved May 25, 2005, from Center for Problem-Oriented Policing Web site: http://www.popcenter.org/Library/Goldstein/2001/01-09(W).pdf

Capowich, G., & Roehl, J. (1994). Problem-oriented policing: actions and effectiveness in San Diego. In D. Rosenbaum (Ed.), *The challenge of community policing: Testing the promises* (pp. 127–146). Thousand Oaks, CA.: Sage Publications.

Clarke, R., & Eck, J. (2003). *Becoming a problem-solving crime analyst*. London: Jill Dando Institute of Crime Science.

Clarke, R., & Goldstein, H. (2003). *Reducing theft at construction sites: Lessons from a problem-oriented project*. Washington, DC: U.S. Department of Justice, Office of Community Oriented Policing Services. Retrieved May 25, 2005, from Center for Problem-Oriented Policing Web site: http://www.cops.usdoj.gov/mime/open.pdf?Item=804

Decker, S., & Rosenfeld, R. (2004). *Reducing gun violence: The St. Louis consent-to-search program*. Research report. Washington, DC: U.S. Department of Justice, National Institute of Justice.

Eck, J., & Spelman, W. (1987). *Problem-solving: Problem-oriented policing in Newport News*. Washington, DC: Police Executive Research Forum.

Ekblom, P. (2002). From the source to the mainstream is uphill: The challenge of transferring knowledge of crime prevention through replication, innovation and anticipation. In N. Tilley (Ed.), *Analysis for crime prevention*. Crime Prevention Studies, vol. 13 (pp. 131–204). Monsey, NY: Criminal Justice Press.

Goldstein, H. (1990). *Problem-oriented policing*. Philadelphia: Temple University Press.

Goldstein, H., & Susmilch, C. (1982). *Experimenting with the problem-oriented approach to improving police service: A report and some reflections on two case studies*. Vol. 4 of the project on development of a problem-oriented approach to improving police service. Madison, WI: University of Wisconsin Law School. Retrieved May 25, 2005, from Center for Problem-Oriented Policing Web site: http://www.popcenter.org/Library/researcherprojects/DevelopmentofPOPVolIV.pdf

Grabosky, P. (1996). Unintended consequences of crime prevention. In R. Homel (Ed.), *The politics and practice of situational crime prevention*. Crime Prevention Studies, vol. 5 (pp. 25–56). Monsey, NY: Criminal Justice Press.

Greene, J. (1998). Evaluating planned change strategies in modern law enforcement: Implementing community-based policing. In J. P. Brodeur (Ed.), *How to recognize good policing: Problems and issues* (pp. 141–160). Thousand Oaks, CA: Sage Publications and Police Executive Research Forum.

Grinder, D. (2000). Implementing problem-oriented policing: a view from the front lines. In C. Solé Brito & E. Gratto (Eds.), *Problem-oriented policing: Crime-specific problems, critical issues and making POP work*, vol. 3 (pp. 141–156). Washington, DC: Police Executive Research Forum.

Halton Regional Police Service. (2002). Let's dance: A community's collaborative response to an all ages nightclub. Submission to the Herman Goldstein Award for Excellence in Problem-Oriented Policing. Retrieved May 25, 2005, from Center for Problem-Oriented Policing Web site: http://www.popcenter.org/Library/Goldstein/2002/02-14(F).pdf

Hope, T., & Murphy, J. (1983). Problems of implementing crime prevention: The experience of a crime reduction project. *The Howard Journal, XXII*, 38–50.

Joliet Police Department (2000). Licensing rental property in Joliet: repairing neighborhoods with partnerships. Submission to the Herman Goldstein Award for Excellence in Problem-Oriented Policing. Retrieved May 25, 2005, from Center for Problem-Oriented Policing Web site: http://www.popcenter.org/Library/Goldstein/2000/00-12(F).pdf. (Also published in: U.S. Department of Justice, National Institute of Justice (2001). *Excellence in problem-oriented policing: the 2000 Herman Goldstein award winner* (pp. 22–30). Washington, DC: U.S. Department of Justice, National Institute of Justice.)

Jones, B. (2003). Doing problem-solving across borders in low-crime areas: The Fens experience. In K. Bullock & N. Tilley (Eds.), *Crime reduction and problem-oriented policing* (pp. 69–88). Cullompton, UK: Willan Publishing.

Kennedy, D., Braga, A., & Piehl, A. (2001). Developing and implementing Operation Ceasefire. In *Reducing gun violence: The Boston gun project's Operation Ceasefire.* Research report. Washington, DC: U.S. Department of Justice, National Institute of Justice.

Larson, J. (1980). *Why government programs fail: Improving policy implementation.* New York: Praeger Publishers.

Lauderhill Police Department (1996). Mission: Mission Lake Plaza. Combating an open-air drug market in a shopping complex. Submission to the Herman Goldstein Award for Excellence in Problem-Oriented Policing. Retrieved May 25, 2005, from Center for Problem-Oriented Policing Web site: http://www.popcenter.org/Library/Goldstein/1996/96-25(F).pdf

Laycock, G., & Farrell, G. (2003). Repeat victimization: Lessons for implementing problem-oriented policing. In J. Knutsson (Ed.), *Problem-oriented policing: From innovation to mainstream.* Crime Prevention Studies, vol. 15 (pp. 213–238). Monsey, NY: Criminal Justice Press.

Laycock, G., & Tilley, N. (1995). Implementing crime prevention. In M. Tonry & D. Farrington (Eds.), *Building a safer society: Strategic approaches to crime prevention* (pp. 535–584). Chicago: University of Chicago Press.

Long, J., Wells, W., & De Leon-Granados, W. (2002). Implementation issues in a community and police partnership in law enforcement space: Lessons from a case study of a community policing approach to domestic violence. *Police Practice and Research, 3*(3), 231–246.

McGarrell, E., Chermak, S., & Weiss, A. *Reducing gun violence: Evaluation of the Indianapolis Police Department's Directed Patrol Project.* Research report. Washington, DC: U.S. Department of Justice, National Institute of Justice.

Moore, M. (2003). Sizing up Compstat: An important administrative innovation in policing. *Criminology, 2*(3), 469–494.

Newport News Police Department (1998). PRIDE: Police response to incidents of domestic emergencies. Submission for the Herman Goldstein Award for Excellence in Problem-Oriented Policing. Retrieved May 25, 2005, from Center for Problem-Oriented Policing Web site: http://www.popcenter.org/Library/Goldstein/1998/98-50(F).pdf

Racine Police Department (1999). The power of partnerships: revitalizing neighborhoods through community policing houses. Submission for the Herman Goldstein Award for Excellence in Problem-Oriented Policing. Retrieved May 25, 2005, from Center for Problem-Oriented Policing Web site: http://www.popcenter.org/Library/Goldstein/1999/99-50(F).pdf

Read, T., & Tilley, N. (2000). *Not rocket science? Problem-solving and crime reduction. Crime Reduction Research Series.* Paper No. 6. London: Home Office Policing and Reducing Crime Unit.

Risk, S. (1992). Untitled memorandum documenting a community policing initiative. St. Louis Metropolitan Police Department. On file with the author of the present chapter.

Rosenbaum, D. (1994). *The challenge of community policing: Testing the promises.* Thousand Oaks, CA: Sage Publications.

Salt Lake City Police Department (2001). The false alarm solution: verified response. Submission to the Herman Goldstein Award for Excellence in Problem-Oriented Policing. Retrieved May 25, 2005, from Center for Problem-Oriented Policing Web site: http://www.popcenter.org/Library/Goldstein/2000/00-55 (F).pdf

Scott, M. (2004). Burglary of single-family houses: A final report to the U.S. Department of Justice Office of Community Oriented Policing Services on a project undertaken in Savannah, Georgia to test the utility of the problem-oriented guides for police. Retrieved May 4, 2006 from Center for Problem-Oriented Policing web site: http://www.popcenter.org/Library/researcher projects/BurglarySingleHouses.pdf

Scott, M. (2005). Shifting and sharing police responsibility to address public safety problems. In N. Tilley (Ed.), *Handbook of crime prevention and community safety.* Cullompton, UK: Willan Publishing.

Scott, M. (2000). *Problem-oriented policing: Reflections on the first 20 years.* Washington, DC: U.S. Department of Justice, Office of Community Oriented Policing Services.

Scott, M., & Goldstein, H. (2005). *Shifting and sharing responsibility for public safety problems.* Problem-oriented guides for police. Response guide series #3. Washington, DC: U.S. Department of Justice, Office of Community Oriented Policing Services.

Skogan, W., Hartnett, S., DuBois, J., Comey, J., Kaiser, M., & Lovig, J. (2000). *Problem solving in practice: Implementing community policing in Chicago.* Washington, DC: U.S. Department of Justice, National Institute of Justice.

South Euclid Police Department (2001). The South Euclid school bullying project. Submission for the Herman Goldstein Award for Excellence in Problem-Oriented Policing. Retrieved May 25, 2005, from Center for Problem-Oriented Policing Web site: http://www.popcenter.org/Library/Goldstein/2001/01-65(F).pdf

Sparrow, M. (1988). Implementing community policing. *Perspectives on Policing,* No. 9. Cambridge, MA and Washington, DC: Harvard University and U.S. Department of Justice, National Institute of Justice.

Spelman, W. (1990). *Repeat offender programs for law enforcement.* Washington, DC: Police Executive Research Forum.

Van Horn, C., & Van Meter, D. (1977). The implementation of intergovernmental policy. In S. Nagel (Ed.), *Policy Studies Review Annual, 1,* 97–120. Beverly Hills, CA: Sage.

Zanin, N., Shane, J., & Clarke, R. V. (2004). Reducing drug dealing in private apartment complexes: A final report to the U.S. Department of Justice Office of Community Oriented Policing Services on a project undertaken in Newark, NJ to test the utility of the problem-oriented guides for police. Retrieved May 4, 2006 from Center for Problem-Oriented Policing web site: http://www.pop center.org/Library/researcherprojects/DrugsApartment.pdf

The Role of Project
Management in Implementing
Community Safety Initiatives

by

Rick Brown
Evidence Led Solutions Limited

Abstract: *One of the common features of recent evaluations of community safety and crime reduction initiatives has been the observation that project management has often been weak and ineffectual. The implications of this are that improving project management skills of the staff involved in such initiatives and implementing effective management processes would increase the likelihood of success. This chapter explores the various weaknesses found in project managing community safety initiatives and presents a model of the "dynamic project lifecycle." This model helps to identify how projects evolve and helps to identify ways in which common problems can be resolved.*

INTRODUCTION

Over the past 20 years, project management has increasingly become a key skill associated with delivering community safety initiatives in the U.K. From the development of the "Five Towns Initiative" in the mid-1980's through to the current "Safer and Stronger Communities Fund," government-funded community safety programmes have been typified by a plethora of local projects funded over relatively short timescales (usually 9 to

12 months). These local projects have had varying degrees of success, due partly to the quality of the project management. This chapter examines the nature of implementation problems identified by previous evaluators before moving on to discuss the characteristics of projects and their management that can be problematic.

Evidence of Project Management Weaknesses

Project management has been identified by a number of previous researchers as a key ingredient in successful community safety initiatives. This has commonly been articulated as an absence of project management coinciding with an absence of implementation success. Schemes that fail to achieve often exhibit defective project management processes. This has most recently been identified in relation to the Crime Reduction Programme. The Crime Reduction Programme was a £500 million programme designed to tackle a range of crime problems through a series of locally implemented projects. Launched in 1998, the Crime Reduction Programme eventually funded over 1,350 projects across England and Wales. In evaluating the process of implementing the Crime Reduction Programme, Homel et al. (2004) noted that there was, *"A general lack of project management competency among those responsible for project implementation, especially in relation to financial management"* (Homel et al., 2005, p. 50; emphasis added). This sentiment was echoed by Hearnden et al. (2004), who found a skills gap between the requirements to manage projects funded under the Reducing Burglary Initiative and the abilities of staff employed in those roles.

There have been a number of areas in which community safety / crime reduction-related project management has been particularly weak. One issue has been the governance, or oversight of projects. In discussing the implementation of the Safer Cities Programme, Sutton (1996) identified three types of project board – passive, dominant and consultative. Passive project boards were described as those that showed limited interest in the implementation of projects. These would be characterised by little discussion of the problems experienced by projects, with meetings becoming no more than a "rubber-stamping" exercise to provide legitimacy for the project. Dominant project boards described the opposite extreme, in which the board wished to take an active role in the day-to-day decision making on projects. However, the fact that these boards met on an irregular basis meant that the implementation timetable would often slip and creativity would be stifled. This approach was also characterised by a degree of subversive behaviour by project managers, who would seek to circumvent the project board in order to deliver the planned interventions. The third type of project management board identified by Sutton provided a balance between these two extremes. Consultative project boards generated a true dialogue about project delivery and provided assistance in overcoming barriers, without stifling day-to-day decision making.

Hedderman and Williams (2001) highlighted the importance of having steering groups hold the project manager to account by reviewing progress on the project at key stages and querying a lack of progress. These authors also highlighted the importance of protecting project manager's time, so that s/he were not drawn into additional non-project work that could dilute the effort devoted to the project. Indeed, one of the problems associated with implementation of burglary reduction projects examined by Hedderman and Williams was the delays that resulted from insufficient time spent managing projects.

Conversely, there have been observed successes when sufficient resources have been devoted to project management. An evaluation of arson reduction projects by Brown et al. (2005) attributed the high degree of implementation success in part to the fact that the funding programme (the Arson Control Forum's New Projects Initiative) had encouraged the employment of project managers. This provided a dedicated resource to deliver local interventions. It was, however, noted that there was a need to balance the employment of project managers with sufficient "working capital" to implement interventions. In some cases, the failure to allow for this "working capital" meant that a significant amount of the project manager's time was spent fundraising from local partners.

It should be noted that employing project managers has been shown to be a time-consuming business. Brown et al. (2005) found that in some cases it took more than six months to employ project managers, which was clearly problematic when the project was short term. Millie et al. (2004) provide examples of recruitment processes that took eight months or more. This was felt to be particularly problematic when local authority employment procedures were used, which required jobs to be advertised internally, before being opened to external applicants.

In some circumstances, posts simply cannot be filled through recruitment processes. Short-term posts are often unattractive to applicants because of the uncertainties of tenure they create for employees. Assuming that a project manager can be employed, there is no guarantee s/he can be retained. Homel et al. (2004) reported that community safety / crime reduction projects funded under the Crime Reduction Programme were often characterised by high levels of staff turnover. Hedderman and Williams (2001) noted that in at least a third of the 21 burglary reduction projects they evaluated the project manager had changed since the original bid document had been written – in one case there had been three project managers.

Even with a project manager employed for the duration of a project, this is by no means a guarantee of implementation success. Here, a number of problems can emerge in the project management process, including the length of time it takes to implement, the cost of implementation exceeding that originally planned, and problems with the quality of the project that is implemented.

Project or Programme Management?

While there is evidence to show how the weaknesses associated with project management affect the delivery of community safety initiatives, good *programme* management can also be an essential ingredient in successful implementation. A programme will usually consist of a series of projects, joined together to achieve a common strategic aim. Like projects, a programme will be focused on delivery with an expectation of achieving an impact on a specified problem. However, the focus of concern will be more focused on how projects as a whole are delivering, rather than on the minutiae of individual local interventions. Good programme management will ensure that funding is delivered in an appropriate and timely manner and will aim to resolve blockages at the strategic level that may threaten successful implementation. There is scope for further research in this area as poor programme management can have a serious impact on the ability to address problems at a macro level. The present chapter, however, focuses on the project level and simply acknowledges that good *programme* management can facilitate good *project* management.

People or Processes?

Before moving on to examine ways in which project management can be improved, it is worth spending a moment to ask whether improving such processes can make better projects. In evaluating community safety initiatives, it often seems as though the key ingredient is the quality of the people employed on such projects. Regardless of how simple or difficult an intervention may appear, some project managers have the ability to implement effectively, while others do not. In evaluating a series of burglary reduction projects, Hedderman and Williams (2001, p. 2) stated that, "*We have also found that in all projects (multi-agency or not), the personal qualities and abilities of the project manager seems to be **the** factor which determines whether implementation is successful*" (italics added).

This highlights the fact that good project management processes are no substitute for good people – the two must go together. The following pages focus solely on that which can be learned and applied in project management and assumes that the personal qualities that make for a good project manager are a given.

Who Needs to be Concerned with Project Management?

While much of the discussion presented here is targeted towards project managers, it is important to ensure that all those involved in projects are aware of the requirements and processes associated with effective project management. This includes project staff, stakeholders, members of a project board and funders. An agreed understanding of these issues will help to avoid conflicts resulting from a misunderstanding of roles.

The Role of Paperwork

Effective project management should not be viewed as a bureaucratic process. Indeed, many good project managers will follow project processes as a matter of instinct, rather than as a form-filling process. Indeed, it is important to view project management as a mindset, or way of working, rather than as a form-filling exercise. While there will inevitably be a degree of paperwork, this will usually be for the purposes of accountability or as a means of protection for the project manager. This should act as a warning against imposing project management through the introduction of additional paperwork. Such attempts are likely to end in failure, with project staff finding ways to avoid form filling while at the same time failing to apply the principles of good project management. In short, the thinking processes are more important than the form-filling processes.

Why Implement through Projects?

Given the many problems associated with managing projects, one might ask why this form of implementation has been so prevalent. At least part of the answer lies in the fact that, from a funder's perspective, the character-istics of projects make them relatively easy to administer. Projects tend to have a defined beginning, middle and end, which means a funding agency will know when their funds start to be spent and can keep track of progress in spending their money through regular reporting processes. Projects also tend to involve working structures that are distinct from mainstream delivery. This may include specific personnel devoted to a project, separate governance structures (through project boards) and separate budgets. This enables a funding agency to identify more readily what they get for their money than if funding were subsumed into mainstream ways of working. In mainstream working, where the resources of a funding agency may be combined with the resources of other organisations, it becomes more difficult to identify the additional benefit gained from the funding organis-ation's involvement. It can also be more difficult for a funding organisation to withdraw support, as the recipient organisation will no doubt claim that the continued funding is essential for the delivery of the initiative.

While there are clear benefits in organising community safety initia-tives into projects from a funder's perspective, they can also cause difficult-ies at the point when they come to an end. Projects are often established as "pilot" or "pathfinder" initiatives in which innovative approaches, or new ways of working, are tested on a small scale before being "rolled-out" on a larger scale. This can be problematic for a number of reasons. First, it assumes that the context of implementation for the pilot (for example in terms of the environment in which intervention was undertaken) will be similar when rolled out more widely. If a project is rolled out in a different context, there is no reason to assume that a similar level of impact as observed in the original project will be achieved (Pawson and Tilley, 1997).

A second problem relates to the very structures that make projects attractive from the funder's perspective. Projects come in a kind of "wrap-per" that separates them from mainstream work. As described above, this can include separate staffing, budgets and ways of working. However, this "wrapper" can be difficult to remove at the point at which projects are mainstreamed. For example, working structures established for a project may be incompatible with mainstream working practices, and may result in initiatives not working quite as they had done under a project framework. This can mean that projects sometimes have to be "shoe-horned" into existing structures.

A third problem relates to the basis upon which decisions are made to mainstream projects. Evaluations of projects usually extend beyond the life of the project in order to allow a period of reflection and in order to gather sufficient data upon which to conduct a robust analysis of impact. This, however, causes a problem at the point at which decisions must be made about whether to continue to fund a project, mainstream the activity or close it down. These decisions will usually need to be made some weeks or months prior to the end of a project in order to allow for future planning and in order to avoid losing staff who may otherwise find new jobs. This means that future funding decisions are often made in the absence of evaluation findings or on partial results. This can lead to embarrassing situations in which funding organisations have to justify their decisions to continue to fund projects that are later shown to be ineffective.

UNDERSTANDING THE DYNAMIC PROJECT LIFECYCLE

Given the fact that project working is so prevalent in community safety work and that managing such projects has clearly proven problematic, it is worth exploring in more detail the various facets of projects that can make them so difficult to control. One model for understanding projects is the dynamic project lifecycle, developed by Young (1998). Figure 1 illustrates a modified form of the dynamic project lifecycle that reflects the structure of many community safety-related projects.

The dynamic project lifecycle consists of four key phases and, in theory, all projects more or less go through each of these phases. The first phase involves "Conception and Definition." This represents the "thinking" stage in which the problem to be addressed by the project is identified, further analysis is undertaken to understand the problem and suitable interventions are selected. The second phase, "Planning and Scheduling," involves more detailed planning, such as identifying the activity required to deliver a project, timetabling the activity, costing the work and planning for risks. This stage results in a project plan that provides the "road-map" for how the project will be delivered. The third phase, "Executing the Project Work," involves delivery of the planned interventions. At this stage project monitoring becomes important for identifying emerging problems and rectifying them in order to avoid implementation failure. The final phase, "Handover and Closure," marks the end of a project, with the delivery of an exit strategy and the production of a final evaluation.

As would seem clear from its name, the dynamic project lifecycle has a series of in-built change mechanisms. This recognises the fact that projects

Figure 1: Illustration of the Dynamic Project Lifecycle[1]

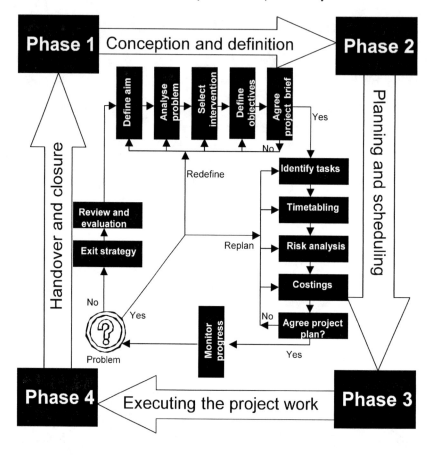

seldom run smoothly and often change considerably between the initial idea and the completion of implementation. The dynamic project lifecycle identifies a number of points at which changes can occur. For example, following the completion of the "Conception and Definition" phase there is an opportunity to share a "project brief" with colleagues and stakeholders, and this may provide a basis for changing the focus of the project.[2] Similarly, on completion of the initial "Planning and Scheduling" phase, there is again an opportunity for consultation that may result in changes to the project plan. At the stage of "Executing the Project Work," projects will typically follow a loop in which monitoring identifies minor problems (typically associated with timescales and resource allocation) that are rectified through re-planning. However, more fundamental problems may require greater attention through a re-definition process that involves returning to the drawing-board and may result in the selection of alternative interventions felt to be more suited to the new understanding of the problem.

The following pages examine each of the four phases of the dynamic project lifecycle in turn and discuss the project management problems that can emerge at each stage.

Conception and Definition

Conception and definition is the initial planning stage in which problems are identified and understood, and interventions are selected. While, on the face of it, this would appear a straightforward process, experience has shown that a myriad of problems can emerge at this early stage.

Identifying the Problem

When identifying the problem in the first instance, it is important to ascertain whether the problem is *real*. Problems may be identified initially through opinions and knowledge of individuals associated with an area, but these perceptions should be tested against the available data (Curtin et al., 2001). This is because the perception of the nature and extent of a problem can differ markedly from its actual occurrence. The political nature of the environment within which community safety projects operate can also affect the targeting of problems. There are often vested interests in encouraging projects to be undertaken which may not be solely due to the extent of a local problem. Such interests can include elected politicians (both at national and local government levels) who are keen to be seen promoting their constituents' interests, or community safety professionals who are keen to be seen working in partnership to tackle a problem, where the partnership working is seen as the primary outcome.

It is also important to recognise that there will be diminishing marginal returns in replicating a project that has been shown to be effective. Pilot projects may target the areas or groups with the most severe problem. However, once the most severe problems have been tackled, only lower-level problems are left to tackle and can result in projects being undertaken to tackle problems that really do not deserve attention. This most frequently would appear to occur within the auspices of a local organisation, such as a police force. A project that has been shown to be effective within a particular area may subsequently be rolled out on a force-wide basis, regardless of whether the problem exists in the same way in other parts of the force area.

Even where the problem is real and has been "proven" with available data, projects can be targeted in the wrong place. Tilley et al. (1999) document a visit to a burglary project in which members of the local Crime and Disorder Reduction Partnership (CDRP) described in detail the nature of a local burglary problem in a particular police beat area. Subsequent analysis of the police crime data revealed that no such burglary problem existed in the beat in question. It later transpired that, when undertaking the crime analysis, the analyst had entered the wrong beat code. The area that actually had a burglary problem was a neighbouring beat – yet a team of community safety professionals was able to articulate in some detail the nature of a burglary problem in an area that in fact had no burglary problem at all. This highlights two lessons – the importance of testing one's assumptions about a problem and the importance of challenging crime analysis that conflicts with one's perceptions.

Defining the Aim

The preceding discussion on identifying a problem highlights the importance of ensuring that a project is problem-oriented. Ideally a project aim should specify the problem that is to be tackled. While this sounds obvious, all too often projects fail to specify an aim, or specify it in terms of the activity that is to be undertaken. Examples of this might be to undertake a project to target prolific offenders, or to undertake a project to build youth shelters in local parks. The problem with these process-oriented approaches to specifying aims is that they can be achieved without having any impact on the problem they set out to address. For example, a project aimed at targeting prolific offenders with enforcement activity and intensive support may be successful in the sense that it has identified the right people and engaged with them in programmes of enforcement and support, but may result in no change in their individual levels of offending. In such circumstances, the project has successfully delivered its intervention, but has failed to impact on the problem. From a community safety perspective, such projects should be viewed as failures as they result in the community being no safer than before.

Specifying a clear, problem-oriented aim can also help to avoid "mission creep" in which a project that originally set out to address one problem, subsequently has other issues added to it. Identifying the project aim can help to highlight that additional suggestions for project activity may fall outside the remit of the project and would therefore detract from addressing the original problem. A clear project aim should therefore help to maintain a focus. It will also help with any subsequent evaluation, as the first consideration should be whether the project has indeed achieved the aim of the project.

At this point it is worth mentioning targets. Like much of the public sector in the U.K., community safety activity is beset with target setting. As a result, there is often a desire among community safety professionals to place targets on their project aims. Examples of such targets might be *"to reduce the extent of vehicle crime in the area by 15%,"* or *"to reduce the rate of violence against the person to the national average."* There are, however, a number of dangers in this practice. First, there is the question over how targets are set. These are often based on a professional judgement about what can be achieved, or are given by funding organisations. They are seldom based on a careful analysis of how much of a reduction can be achieved by planned interventions. This can create problems if the target is not met. For example, it can demoralise staff involved in delivering a project and may fail to take into account other positive outcomes that can result from projects, but which are more difficult to measure – such as improved community cohesion, or greater local awareness of activity.

Perhaps the most problematic aspect of targets is that they generally fail to take into account the counterfactual. Yet this is extremely important in community safety projects. The fact that a project meets its outcome target is not necessarily a success if one expected to achieve a greater reduction (based on what has been achieved elsewhere). Furthermore, a failure to achieve the project outcome is not necessarily a negative result if one would actually have expected to achieve a worse result. To illustrate this point, a recent evaluation of the Arson Control Forum's New Projects Initiative by Brown et al. (2005) estimated that the combined effect of 19 arson reduction projects was an 8% increase in deliberate primary fires. However, this was a much better performance than a series of comparison areas, which witnessed an increase in deliberate primary fires of 27%. On this basis, the programme was shown to be very cost-effective, yet if a simple arson reduction target had been used, the programme would have appeared to have failed.

Analysing the Nature of the Problem

Once a problem has been identified and agreed as the focus of a project, further analysis should be undertaken to gain a detailed understanding of the problem, prior to selecting interventions that fit what is known about the problem. However, there is a whole host of issues that can arise with such analysis. These have been well documented by others (see Clarke and Eck, 2003) and this section briefly examines the most common.

One of the key problems relates to the completeness of the data being analysed. Indeed, the quality of the analysis will only be as good as the data being examined. Common issues here relate to the reporting and recording of police crime data, which can skew the understanding of the problem. However, such issues can be even more problematic when other sources of data are used. For example, an audit of drugs misuse in one area identified that no discarded syringes had been found on the streets for the last two years. However, further analysis revealed that there had been two "needle-stick" incidents in which council street cleaning staff has been pricked by a discarded syringe. It transpired that the lack of data on discarded needles was due to the fact that street cleaners were unwilling to fill in forms. This highlights the fact that social processes always mediate data available for analysis.

A second problem is related to the ability to get the analysis done in the first place. With ever increasing demands on data analysts, it can be difficult to secure an analyst's time to conduct ad-hoc analysis for a specific project. This can delay the planning stage of the project. Even once it is undertaken, such analysis can lack the imagination to examine the problem from different perspectives, with analysis restricted to bland frequency counts of the database fields.

Thirdly, it is important not to forget about the "softer" forms of analysis that can inform a project, such as observation of a target area and discussions with those who live and work in the area. In short, the more care and attention paid to analysing the nature of a problem, the better equipped one will be to implement effective interventions.

Selecting Interventions

In ideal circumstances, detailed analysis should result in the selection of interventions that are best suited to addressing that problem. In selecting interventions, there are a number of important issues to consider. Probably the most important issue associated with developing interventions is understanding the "mechanism of change" – that is, how will the intervention bring about the desired change? For example, the mechanism involved in target-hardening schemes can be described as "increasing effort," while the mechanism behind improved street lighting might be "increased risk of detection" (see Laycock and Tilley, 2002). In general these mechanisms are relatively straightforward for situationally-based approaches and become more difficult to specify when individual behavioural change is involved. For example, an evaluation of summer SPLASH schemes (involving diversionary activities with young people) identified eight potential mechanisms by which engaging with young people could bring about reductions in area crime and disorder rates (Loxley et al., 2002). Mechanisms of change have been found to work best when they are simple to specify and provide a realistic explanation about how the intervention may work. If an intervention fails either of these tests, it often fails to bring about the desired change.

The ease with which an intervention can be implemented can also be an important consideration. Indeed, implementation is often best achieved when a project involves simple interventions that are easy to implement. Conversely, complex interventions that require a great deal of decision making, or involve the sequenced activity of a range of different agencies, can be the most difficult to implement. Partnership working can in many instances aid the process of implementation by bringing together disparate skills, knowledge and resources, but this can also be a source of frustration if a partner agency fails to deliver.

Projects seldom consist of single interventions. Tilley et al. (1999) noted the importance of understanding how interventions interacted with each other. They identified three kinds of interaction, described as interactive (in which an interventions benefited from another intervention being present), contradictory (in which an intervention was impeded by the presence of other interventions), and combined interventions (in which interventions coexist with no positive and negative influences on each other). In most cases, projects consist of combined interventions, with relatively few examples of contradictory and interactive approaches.

Defining Objectives

There is often confusion in terminology between an aim and objective, and this results in the terms being used interchangeably. However, one way to clarify this difference is to view objectives as an operationalization of the aim, which describe how the aim is to be achieved. This can be achieved by formalising interventions in terms of objectives, with one objective being used to describe each of the project interventions. For example, a project aim may be *"to reduce thefts from vehicles in an area"* while two objectives may be *"to provide an additional 100 hours of high visibility patrol in hot spot areas"* and *"to notify all vehicle owners who leave items on display in their vehicles."* This approach means that, while project aims are about "outcomes" (what will be achieved), project objectives are about "outputs" (what will be delivered on the ground). This important distinction helps to clarify the logic of a project, with a clear explanation of how the aims will be achieved. It also helps to highlight interventions that may not be addressing the problem. If one cannot explain how the objective will help to achieve the aim, the objectives have either been inappropriately specified, or the intervention it describes will fail to address the problem.

Agreeing on a Project Brief

The project brief is the document that provides the information collected during the conception and definition phase. This is usually a relatively short document that offers an opportunity to agree on the direction of a project with stakeholders prior to undertaking more detailed project planning. The arrows that feedback into each of the conception and definition boxes in Figure 1 demonstrate the first of the dynamic aspects of the dynamic project lifecycle. For example, it offers an opportunity to change, or refine a project aim. An initial project brief may aim to reduce anti-social behaviour, but this may later be refined to address a particular subset of this behaviour, such as graffiti, or nuisance neighbours. Alternatively, the analysis of the problem may be challenged, or the selected interventions may be felt to be unsuitable for the target area / group. Each of these issues offer an opportunity to return to the drawing board and to make changes to the project before undertaking more detailed work. In this way, the project brief can act as a checking mechanism to avoid unnecessary work in future and to shape a more effective project.

In most community safety projects, something akin to a project brief will be produced. Indeed, funding applications often follow a similar format,[3] with this kind of information being used to judge the suitability for future funding. However, experience has shown that this is often the sum total of planning that is undertaken prior to the implementation of a project. From the perspective of the dynamic project lifecycle, this excludes the important processes of planning and scheduling. Skipping this stage and moving straight to the execution of the project can have severe consequences in terms of managing timescales, costs and risks.

Planning and Scheduling

Phase two of a project should involve more detailed planning and scheduling, resulting in a project plan. Within this project plan there are a number of key issues that are often overlooked by community safety project managers and these are addressed below.

Identifying Tasks and Timetabling

Ask anyone how long a particular job will take and they will probably be able to give you a rough estimate. Ask them how they came up with that estimate and they will probably be unable to give a clear reason. This is how most of us tend to work – estimating roughly how long work will take to complete and working towards that timescale. Often it won't matter if things take longer than anticipated as time can be made up at a later date. However, part of the "wrapper" of any project is the timescale over which it has to be completed. No project has an infinite amount of time and delivery by a specified time can mark the success or failure of a project. One way to address this constraint on time is to start with the end date and work backwards, fitting the planned tasks into place as one goes. This approach has the uncanny knack of always managing to fit the implementation of a project into the available time. This is because one has a tendency to be over-optimistic about how quickly tasks can be completed in a desire to make the project look like it can be achieved on time. As a result, projects often take longer to complete than anticipated.

Under-estimation of how long tasks will take to complete is a common problem associated with implementation failure in community safety work. Common issues that have been identified in previous evaluations include the time it takes to secure funding from external organisations, to recruit staff, to undertake public consultation, to tender for work to be undertaken by outside contractors and to actually implement some interventions. The evaluation of the Reducing Burglary Initiative showed how interventions that appeared simple on paper could be deceptively complex and time consuming when it came to the implementation stage. A prime example of this was the process of restricting access to alleyways that ran to the rear of terraced properties by placing gates on the alleys' access points (Johnson and Loxley, 2001). These were found to take much longer to install than anticipated due to the time it took to gain agreement from all property owners affected by the changes. This was, at the time, a pre-requisite to obtaining a closure order from a magistrates' court, which was necessary on alleyways that formed a public right of way. Such applications for closure orders also received objections from the Ramblers Association, which was opposed in principle to the notion of closing public rights of way – even when located in densely urban and deprived neighbourhoods.

There are, however, processes that can be used by project managers to provide a little more certainty in planning how long interventions will take to complete. This starts with the identification of all the possible tasks associated with the implementation of a project. As a general rule, the smaller the task, the greater the degree of accuracy that will be exhibited in the timetable. Once these tasks have been identified, they can be se-quenced into a logical order. A timetable can then be drawn up on the basis of estimates of how long each of the individual tasks will take to complete.

Risk Analysis

Risk analysis in community safety projects would seldom appear to be undertaken in an explicit way. Potential risks may be taken into account as part of the tacit knowledge of project managers, but these risks are seldom documented and addressed in a systematic way. In nine times out of ten, this lack of risk analysis and risk planning will have no detrimental impact on a project, simply because potential risks do not arise. However, the failure to plan for potential risks can in some circumstances have a significant impact on implementation. In one project worked on by the author, a detailed risk analysis was developed as part of the evaluation process, which was conveyed to the project team. This risk analysis actually identified over 60 potential risks. One important risk was the likelihood that the team of ten staff seconded to the project would have left before the end of the two-year project to take up posts elsewhere. This is a common problem with short-term funded project work, which results in capable staff finding new, more secure jobs well before the end of their existing short-term contracts. When this risk was highlighted to the project manager, the response indicated that he felt this was unlikely to happen with such a team of dedicated professionals. Six months prior to the end of the project, only two of the original team of ten were left working on the project, with the remainder leaving to take up posts elsewhere. This severely hampered the ability of the project to deliver its objectives.

In undertaking risk analysis, it is important to identify the potential risks in the first instance and then to assess both the likelihood of the risk occurring and the potential impact that each risk will have on a project. A decision can then be made regarding which risks need to be addressed prior to implementation and which can be addressed as and when they occur.

Costings

Costing projects and budget management is a key aspect of the community safety project manager's role. This tends to be an area that is now relatively well addressed, with most organisations having clear procedures for budgeting and auditing. However, there remain problems in terms of producing "spending-profiles" (the equivalent of cash flow forecasts) that can be matched against the stage of delivery of a project. Ideally a project manager will want to know whether a project is on track in terms of how much has been spent to reach a certain point in the project. However, these two factors often exist in isolation, with budget profiles produced by finance departments being incompatible with other monitoring used by the project manager.

A second problem can relate to projects that run for more than one financial year. With uncertainty of budgets from one year to the next, many CDRPs are unwilling to take the risk of funding projects over two years for fear of being unable to continue to support such commitments. This naturally limits the kind of projects that can be undertaken. It also raises the risk of project under-spends in any one financial year. Projects that must be completed by March each year can cause problems if implementation takes longer to complete that anticipated. This results in having surplus funds exactly at the point when one doesn't want it (at the end of a financial year) and the uncertainty of how to pay for the remainder of the implementation in the following financial year. In general, as CDRPs have become more used to this way of working these kinds of problems have diminished.

Agreeing on the Project Plan

As with the project brief, once the project plan has been produced, there is an opportunity to share this with colleagues and stakeholders and to agree on the direction of the project. This provides an opportunity to challenge whether timescales and costings are realistic and whether the full range of tasks associated with the project has been identified. In Figure 1, this is represented by the arrows that feedback into each of the boxes connected with the planning and scheduling phase. This process of consultation should ultimately result in a more robust project plan, which in turn, should result in better implementation.

The dynamic project lifecycle pays careful attention to project planning, as evidenced by the fact that two of the four phases focus on this aspect of project management. This is in recognition of the importance that planning plays in ensuring effective delivery. However, planning should not be used as an excuse for failing to get on with the implementation phase. Sooner or later, the plan will need to be put into practice and it is at this stage that unforeseen problems invariably arise.

Executing the Project Work

The "executing of the project work" phase of the dynamic project lifecycle is in many ways the most straightforward aspect of the model. This generally involves implementing interventions, monitoring them to ensure they are delivered correctly and addressing problems as they arise.

Monitoring Progress

Monitoring progress in implementing interventions is a key part of the project management process. However, all too often community safety project managers view monitoring as something you do to appease funding organisation, which usually impose their own monitoring forms. This form of monitoring is different to that which is useful for ensuring the project remains on track and can consist of monitoring information, which, while serving a purpose for the funding body, is of little or no use for day-to-day project monitoring. The danger is that this becomes the only form of monitoring undertaken, thereby leaving the project vulnerable to unidentified problems.

The focus of attention in monitoring community safety projects will depend on the type of interventions involved. Here we need to distinguish between interventions that produce a fast, recurring output and interventions that take a long time to deliver the outputs. An example of the former would be a target-hardening scheme in which a project aims to target-harden 50 households per month. In this kind of project, the monitoring should focus on the outputs associated with the intervention. If the project delivers only 25 target-hardened households per month, then this highlights the likelihood that the project will fail to deliver the planned level of intervention. This would subsequently require one to examine the *process* of intervention (how referrals are received, the time it takes to improve security of each household etc.) to determine where the problems lie. Although the process of intervention will be the subject of attention, the identification of the problem in the first instance would be through the output monitoring.

An example of an intervention that might take a long time to deliver an output is the installation of "alley-gates," as described earlier. Evaluation of such projects has shown that it is not unusual for such interventions to take a year or more to implement (Johnson and Loxley, 2001). If monitoring is focused solely on the output (the installation of the gates) one would be unaware of any problems emerging during the project, thereby increasing the risk of implementation failure. Where this kind of project is concerned, the focus of monitoring attention should, in the first instance, be on the process of implementation.

Addressing Problems

All projects experience problems and a key role of a project manager is to identify and address these problems before they impede implementation progress. Hearnden et al. (2004) identified three key ways in which projects funded under the Reducing Burglary Initiative developed over time in response to emerging problems. These resulted from:

- A change in the capacities and priorities of participating organisations

- A project's initial approach being ill-suited to the evolving problem context

- A project appearing ineffective in reducing crime.

This notion of responding to emerging problems introduces the main dynamic element of the project lifecycle, in which the nature of the original project changes in response to current circumstances. Most problems will be small scale in nature and require relatively minor adjustments. Examples of such problems include particular aspects of an intervention being over budget, or taking longer than anticipated. These problems will usually be resolved through minor "tweaking" of the project plan to put it back on track, as represented by the re-planning route in Figure 1.

In a small proportion of projects, the problems will be more fundamental, with minor re-planning being unable to rectify weaknesses. In these circumstances, the project may require more serious attention. This can happen, for example, when an intervention that was initially felt to be suitable for a particular community, later turns out to be inappropriate or ineffective. This should not be surprising, given the fact that the very process of implementation is itself a form of analysis, with a greater understanding of the target area / group generally unfolding as the project develops. In these circumstances, a process of re-definition may be required, with a change to the problem analysis and selected interventions required. Decisions to enter a re-definition process can, however, be hard to make. It requires a project manager to accept that mistakes were made at the planning stage and that the project simply isn't working. It can also require these mistakes to be admitted in a semi-public forum, especially if agreement to changes needs to be obtained from a CDRP, or funding organisation. In an environment in which successful projects reflect well on a project team, there can be good reasons for not being willing to admit failure. This can result in a project that is implementing defective interventions simply limping on to the finishing line and therefore failing to achieve the original aim, rather than accept the need to make significant changes.

Handover and Closure

The final stage of the dynamic project lifecycle is the process of closing down the project. As noted earlier, projects should have an end – indeed this is one of their defining characteristics that marks them out as different from mainstream work. Here, there are two main considerations for the project manager – exit strategies and the process of review and evaluation.

Exit Strategies

An exit strategy simply sets out how the project will be closed down. Although put into progress at the end of a project, it would ideally be developed during the planning stages. This is, however, relatively unusual, with little thought generally given to this issue until the point at which project closure becomes imperative. This most commonly occurs when project funding comes to an end and intervention needs to cease. This would particularly appear to be the case in projects involving some form of community development, or youth work. In these kinds of projects, the end of funding for staff posts or sessional work marks the end of intervention in that community. Yet the problems that originally inspired the community development work will often persist, resulting in another community development project at a later point in time. This can create a stop-start approach to intervention, which leaves members of local communities sceptical about how long and how effective any new project will be in an area. Ending projects in an abrupt way can also leave unfulfilled demand for the service being provided. For example, one project that undertook a widespread target-hardening project over a two-year period as part of a large regeneration programme, built up considerable interest in the service and by the time funding ceased for the project, there were still many households that wanted the target-hardening, but were unable to receive it.

In general, there are three main exit strategies. These involve either a) continuation funding that creates a serial project approach in which one project leads on to another, b) mainstreaming of the project in which the service will still be provided, but as part of routine delivery by an organisation, or c) closure of the project, in which intervention is ceased.

Regardless of the approach that is eventually taken to exit strategies, it is important to communicate this to those associated with the project at the earliest opportunity. This is important for project staff, intervention recipients and stakeholder organisations involved in the project. All may have to make adjustments as a result of exit strategies.

Review and Evaluation

Once a project has concluded, there will be a need to review and evaluate progress. This is important as a mark of completion of the project and as a record for future project implementation. However, the extent of evaluation that is undertaken will vary from project to project. Short-term projects, those involving limited resources and "tried-tested" interventions, will probably not require rigorous formal evaluations of the kind conducted by independent evaluators. To do so would constitute a waste of valuable resources that could otherwise have been spent on project implementation. For these kinds of projects, a process evaluation - in which progress in project delivery is documented, along with details of problems and how they were overcome – will probably be sufficient.

For larger-scale projects, or projects involving innovative approaches, there is often benefit in conducting a more detailed evaluation of both process and impact, although it is important to recognise that such evaluations are unlikely to report until some time after the project implementation has been completed.

Regardless of the form that evaluation takes, the findings should be used to assist with future projects. Whether similar projects are undertaken with different communities, or different projects undertaken with the same communities, there is likely to have been valuable learning that will assist with future implementation. This is represented in Figure 1 by the arrow from review and evaluation back into project aims.

Relationship with Other Frameworks

The dynamic project lifecycle has similarities with other frameworks used in community safety and crime reduction work, such as the SARA (Scanning, Analysis, Response and Assessment) model (Eck and Spelman, 1987) and the "5 Is" (Intelligence, Intervention, Implementation, Involvement and Impact) (Ekblom, 2002). All three are *problem-oriented*. They provide a means of understanding the nature of a particular problem and of finding a way to resolve the problem. This brings us to the second similarity – all three are *action-oriented*. They are not only about understanding the problem, but focus on ways in which action can be taken to address the particular problems concerned. A third similarity is that all three provide a similar *intervention lifecycle*. Each starts with an articulation of a problem, followed by a detailed understanding of the nature of the problem, based on sound analysis. Each then provides a means of addressing the problem and each measures the extent to which the problem has been eliminated. A fourth similarity is that all three tools are designed to be used by community safety practitioners as a framework for tackling local problems. Each is a means of ordering a way of working.

Advantages of the Dynamic Project Lifecycle

While there are clearly similarities among the three approaches, there are a number of advantages to using the Dynamic Project Lifecycle. The first advantage relates to the clarity with which the dynamism of projects is articulated. While SARA is taught as an iterative process, it still tends to be perceived and, indeed, operationalized by practitioners, as a linear process. This involves steady, forward, progress through the four stages, moving from Scanning, to Analysis to Response and finally Assessment.

By contrast, the Dynamic Project Lifecycle treats as a virtue the process of making changes through the life of a project. This is particularly important at the "Response" / "Executing the project work" phase in which changes will be made on a continual basis.

A second advantage of the Dynamic Project Lifecycle is that accountability is built into each stage of the project, creating a series of checks and balances. At the end of each of the four phases there is an opportunity to share information with stakeholders to help ensure the project remains on track. For example, the project brief, project plan, project monitoring and project evaluation each offer an opportunity for consultation with stakeholders and, where necessary, allow for challenges to be made.

Another advantage of this approach is that it pays particular attention to the planning process prior to implementation. Indeed, this is the focus of two of the four lifecycle phases. The emphasis on planning should result in more effective implementation as potential problems are addressed in advance. By contrast, the notion of planning is implied, rather than clearly spelled out in both the SARA and 5Is models.

The Dynamic Project Lifecycle also highlights the importance of continuous monitoring throughout the implementation phase and shows how problems identified through monitoring can be addressed by replanning, or redesigning a project. Neither SARA nor the 5Is place such an emphasis on monitoring, although they do regard monitoring as necessary during the Response / Implementation phases.

Although it is no project manager's favourite subject, paperwork is a necessary part of any project, although as noted earlier, the paperwork should not be the key driver of the project. The Dynamic Project Lifecycle treats paperwork as an integral part of the process and highlights three key documents – the brief, the plan and the evaluation. This paperwork process is not so clearly defined in SARA or the 5Is, although there is an expectation that each of the stages will have been documented in some way.

The Dynamic Project Lifecycle also has applications beyond community safety work. This means that the skills and knowledge built up in one area can be transferred to other environments in which projects are undertaken. This can be a useful feature in an environment of rapid staff turnover, as would seem to typify community safety and crime reduction work. For example, the project management skills and processes employed on a community safety initiative can be transferred to another part of an organisation's work (such as procurement, IT, change management etc.) By contrast, the principles behind SARA and 5Is, while not impossible, are certainly more difficult to transfer to other environments.

Disadvantages of the Dynamic Project Lifecycle

While there are advantages to using the Dynamic Project Lifecycle, there are aspects of the model that make its application problematic. The first issue is that, by definition, it focuses specifically on project working. As such, it is not so applicable to other forms of working, such as "mainstream" activity. By contrast, both SARA and 5Is can be applied within the context of projects and mainstream work and the stages embodied in each model are applicable to both ways of working.

Another concern is that the focus on planning in the Dynamic Project Lifecycle can be a time-consuming activity. Community safety practitioners often complain about not having the time to plan their work, and it is therefore likely that it is this activity that will be squeezed in the rush to get the job done. The obvious challenge to this is that careful planning will save time in the long run by being able to avoid potential implementation problems. However, this requires an up-front investment in time to plan and it is this investment that practitioners are often unwilling, or unable to make.

The Dynamic Project Lifecycle is a structured approach that requires a number of key processes to be undertaken. Given the time involved in this (as noted above), the model is probably unsuitable for small-scale projects in which the planning could take longer than the implementation. This suggests that the model is best suited to larger-scale projects where the risks of implementation problems means there would be benefit in conducting rigorous project management.

The final disadvantage is a cosmetic one. The Dynamic Project Lifecycle can be daunting at first sight and has been described by some as looking like a "wiring-diagram." Unlike SARA it does not have a memorable acronym, and unlike the 5Is it does not have a common word association (i.e., all five phases beginning with the letter "I"). This factor alone may be enough to prevent wide-scale adoption of the Dynamic Project Lifecycle.

Towards a Synthesis of Models

Given the relative advantages and disadvantages of the Dynamic Project Lifecycle, it would be unwise to advocate the replacement of one of the existing models with this new approach. However, there may be benefit in combining aspects of the Dynamic Project Lifecycle into, for example, the SARA process. This is particularly relevant at the Response phase of the cycle. Indeed, the response could be broken down to include the planning processes embodied in the Planning and Scheduling phase and the dynamic problem-solving aspect of the Executing the Project Work phase. It could also ensure that an exit strategy (as outlined in the Handover and Closure phase) is built into the Response stage.

The relevance of the Dynamic Project Lifecycle to SARA and the 5Is will vary on a case-by-case basis. This is dependent on whether the work is a project or mainstream working and on the size of the task involved.

CONCLUSIONS

Project management of community safety and crime reduction initiatives has been identified as a major weakness by many previous researchers and has been related to the failure of projects to implement. Common problems emerging from weak project management include poor articulation of the problem, weak interventions, delays in implementation and cost overruns. These issues point towards the need for stronger project management.

The dynamic project lifecycle provides a tool for understanding how projects develop over time and for identifying how such projects can be managed more effectively. For example, it helps to identify the particular stage reached by a project and for identifying when changes are required, either in terms of re-planning or re-designing. It also helps to identify the range of issues that should be addressed by the project manager during the course of planning and implementing community safety initiatives.

While this chapter has concentrated on examining how project management can be enhanced, it is important to recognise that this is only one small factor in ensuring implementation success. Other key ingredients – such as the qualities of the staff (their enthusiasm, as well as their ability to lead, communicate and innovate), support from senior management and access to appropriate resources – are all important factors in ensuring that projects are managed effectively.

Address correspondence to: Rick Brown, Evidence Led Solutions Limited, 48 High Street, Swinderby, Lincoln, England, LN6 9LW; e-mail: rick.brown@evidenceledsolutions.com

NOTES

1. Modified from Young (1998).
2. This is represented by the feedback arrows into each of the boxes in the phase.
3. It should be noted that project briefs will usually also include an indication of timescales and costings. Indeed, these are necessary to determine the kind of interventions that may be appropriate given these constraints. However, they are addressed under the planning and scheduling phase of the dynamic project lifecycle as it is at this stage that a much firmer understanding will be obtained of how long interventions will take to implement and how much they will cost.

REFERENCES

Brown, R., Hopkins, M., Cannings, A., & Raybould, S. (2005). *Evaluation of the Arson Control Forum's New Projects Initiative: Final Report: Technical Annex.* London: Office of the Deputy Prime Minister.

Clarke, R. V., & Eck, J. (2003). *Become a problem solving crime analyst in 55 small steps.* London: Jill Dando Institute of Crime Science, University College London.

Curtin, L., Tilley, N., Owen, M., & Pease, K. (2001). *Developing crime reduction plans: Some examples from the Reducing Burglary Initiative.* Crime Reduction Research Series Paper 7. London: Home Office.

Eck, J., & Spelman, W. (1987). *Problem solving: Problem oriented policing in Newport News.* Washington DC: Police Executive Research Forum.

Ekblom, P. (2002). *Towards a European knowledge database.* Paper presented to the European Crime Prevention Network Conference 2002. Volume 1: Presentations and Conclusions (pp. 62–97). Glostrup: Danish Crime Prevention Council.

Hearnden, I., Millie, A., Hamilton-Smith, N., & Willis, J. (2004). Action and reaction: Delivering local burglary reduction projects In N. Hamilton Smith (Ed.), *The Reducing Burglary Initiative: Design, development and delivery.* Home Office Research Study 287. London: Home Office.

Hedderman, C., & Williams, C. (2001). *Making partnerships work: Emerging findings from the Reducing Burglary Initiative.* Policing and Reducing Crime Unit Briefing Note 1/01. London: Home Office.

Homel, P., Nutley, S., Webb, B., & Tilley, N. (2004). *Investing to deliver: Reviewing the implementation of the UK Crime Reduction Programme.* Home Office Research Study 281. London: Home Office.

Johnson, S., & Loxley, C. (2001). *Installing alley-gates: Practical lessons from burglary reduction projects.* Policing and Reducing Crime Unit Briefing Note 2/01. London: Home Office.

Laycock, G., & Tilley, N. (2002). *Working out what to do: Evidence-based crime reduction.* Crime Reduction Research Series Paper 11. London: Home Office.

Loxley, C., Curtin, L., & Brown, R. (2002). *Summer Splash Schemes 2000: Findings from six case studies.* Crime Reduction Research Series Paper 12. London: Home Office.

Millie, A., Hearnden, I., & Hamilton-Smith, N. (2004). From paper to action: Setting up local burglary reduction projects. In N. Hamilton Smith (Ed.), *The Reducing Burglary Initiative: Design, development and delivery.* Home Office Research Study 287. London: Home Office.

Pawson, R., & Tilley, N. (1997). *Realistic evaluation.* London: Sage.

Sutton, M. (1996). *Implementing crime prevention schemes in a multi-agency setting: Aspects of process in the Safer Cities Programme.* Home Office Research Study 160. London: Home Office.

Tilley, N., Pease, K., Hough, M., & Brown, R. (1999). *Burglary prevention: Early lessons from the Crime Reduction Programme.* Crime Reduction Research Series Paper 1. London: Home Office.

Young, T. (1998). *The handbook of project management: A practical guide to effective policies and procedures.* London: Kogan Page.

Implementing Crime Reduction Measures: Conflicts and Tensions

by

Gloria Laycock

Jill Dando Institute of Crime Science
University College London

Abstract: *It has been recognised for some time that implementation is not as easy as was once assumed. This chapter looks at some of the conflicts and tensions associated with implementation and suggests that they form major obstacles to achieving effective action. An appreciation of these difficulties can assist with their resolution, which on occasion might result in the need to apply leverage against individuals, companies or even governments to change the contingencies under which they operate and persuade them that crime prevention is a high priority and ultimately in their interest. The problem of "carding" – i.e., the placing of advertisements for prostitution in telephone kiosks – is discussed as a means of illustrating the complex issues that can arise in the course of attempting to implement a crime prevention scheme.*

INTRODUCTION

That crime reduction involves individuals and agencies working in partnership is probably one of the most overworked notions of the past decade. It transpires, however, that there are a lot of problems with the approach (see for example, Hough, this volume), including the fact that as a concept it is too vague to be meaningful. It does, nevertheless, have the air of motherhood and apple pie about it. Who could argue but that we all should work together in common (good) cause? But of course reality is never so simple. Implementation failure has long been acknowledged as a significant threat to the delivery of crime reduction initiatives (Rosenbaum et al., 1986), and it often happens because someone within a partnership didn't do something that they needed to do. The partnership in this sense failed. In this chapter some of the possible reasons for this are explored. In practice, of course, there are conflicting and vested interests at all levels of operation from the individual to the international, and it is these conflicting priorities that get in the way of efficient implementation and change. And, significantly, the whole scenario is played out against an historical backdrop of assumptions and expectations about the way in which crime is or might better be reduced.

This chapter begins with a brief discussion of that backdrop and its relevance to implementation. It goes on to define and discuss the notions of responsibility and competency, which are seen as crucial to the proper development of effective implementation. There then follows a discussion of the roles and responsibilities of individuals, the private sector, police and their statutory (in England and Wales) local government partners in crime reduction. The roles of regional and central governments are also noted and a few points are made about their responsibilities and competencies in this field.

The next section describes an attempt in the U.K. by a major international company to implement a crime reduction policy directed at the public telephone kiosks for which they were responsible, and which were being used by prostitutes[1] to advertise their services (known as "carding"). This case study illustrates the tensions and difficulties faced by the company and how they are being dealt with. It is an unfinished tale and raises questions about the role of research in the development process of projects of this kind. At present it is a case study in partial implementation failure, but it illustrates many of the problems that can be encountered in trying to engage large companies in generating crime prevention action when they are not suffering from victimisation themselves.

The chapter concludes with a brief discussion of some of the issues arising from the case study and a checklist for the local practitioner that is intended to assist the process of achieving successful implementation of projects at that local level.

The Crime Control Backdrop

It is tempting to observe that throughout the 20th Century the official focus of responsibility for the control of crime was the criminal justice system (CJS) and all the associated paraphernalia of police, courts, sentencing policy and prisons. Tempting because of the vast sums spent on them and because whenever crime rates went up (or even sometimes when they didn't) the cry was for more police patrols and stiffer sentences. This seemed particularly to be the case at the time of political elections. In practice however, people and organisations protect themselves from crime insofar as they are able. In the main they lock their doors and windows, look out for their children and other family members, and take sensible precautions to ensure that they are not victimised. Similarly the major institutions – banks, shops, industries – wherever relevant, install safes and burglar alarms and employ the private security industry on a grand scale to protect themselves from crime. They do not, in other words, rely solely on the CJS. When the chips are down – when any of us might be the victims of crime – preventive measures including situational approaches are taken.

Despite this observation on what people do, research using the British Crime Survey (BCS) shows that after taking the influence of other factors into account, the strongest predictor of perceiving an increase in the national crime rate was believing that the CJS was not effective at reducing crime (Nicholas and Walker, 2004). It is possible to reverse the direction of causality here and say that the strongest predictor of thinking the system is ineffective is believing that crime is rising (or indeed that the two statements are independently driven by some other factor). But this does not alter the observation that there is some conflict between what people appear to believe – i.e., that the operation of the CJS is central to crime reduction – and what they do, in taking appropriate measures to protect themselves. This belief that the CJS is intimately linked to controlling crime is of more than academic interest. As is discussed below, it can be used as an excuse for inaction on the part of key players and thus contribute to implementation failure and to increasing crime rates.

RESPONSIBILITY AND COMPETENCY IN CRIME CONTROL

Engstad and Evans (1980) first introduced these two notions to the crime prevention scene, arguing that they needed to be differentiated if crime prevention were to flourish. According to Engstad and Evans, responsibility for crime prevention may rest with individuals in that they are, for example, expected to lock their cars when leaving them. But Engstad and Evans note that it is not the individual who has the competency to put a good lock on the car in the first place – that rests with the manufacturer. In this case there needs to be a partnership, albeit a virtual one, between the individual car owner and the car designers. The individual has the responsibility to use the lock provided by the competent manufacturer. These ideas have been expanded in relation to car crime by Laycock (2004), although the principles apply not only to car crime but to many elements of crime reduction insofar as they affect the design of goods, services, management practices and housing styles and layout. There is even evidence that poorly crafted legislation or regulation can lead to increases in crime (Morgan and Clarke, 2003; Webb and Marshall, 2004).

In relation to goods, for example, Clarke (1999) has developed the acronym CRAVED to characterise those goods most at risk of criminal attention. They are Concealable, Removable, Available, Valuable, Enjoyable and Disposable. Any item of property fitting that acronym is likely to be at risk of theft. The most highly craved item in these terms is cash, but goods that are attractive to young people, particularly those that are marketed as fashion items or have hi-tech characteristics, are also at risk. In the U.K., and more broadly across Europe, the mobile phone is a frequent target of theft having the characteristics outlined by Clarke (Harrington and Mayhew, 2001).

In thinking through the relevance of these concepts to implementation a few points can be made. First, it seems important to be clear on who the likely victim of the crime might be. For example, if the individual with both responsibility and competency is also the potential victim of the crime in question, then action will be more likely to follow. Banks do not have to be pressed to hold their highly craved cash in safes or otherwise protected locations. Similarly when mobile phone manufacturers were themselves victims of phone cloning (Clarke et al., 2001) they took rapid action to redesign the phones so that cloning became impossible.

It is when those with the competency to design the goods and etc. differently are not themselves the victims of the crimes associated with those goods, that problems arise. Clarke and Eck (2003) talk about finding the "owner" of a problem, by which they mean the agency or individual with the competency to change the opportunity structure that might make offending less likely. In this chapter I regard the "owners" of the crime problems as the victims – they are the people with the personal interest in addressing the opportunities that have arisen and they are *not* always the agencies with the competency to do so. We might think of those who are competent in this sense as "owning" the solution. Nevertheless Clarke and Eck helpfully suggest four reasons why those competent to address the problem may have ignored it. The first is that they may be *unable* to prevent the crime due to ignorance of the problem, a lack of resources or institutionalised procedures that make it difficult to change the situation. Secondly some institutions might be *unwilling* to prevent the crime. They may dwell on the individual responsibility of offenders and argue that they should control themselves or be controlled by the threat of the CJS. This is one of the reasons why the "baggage" associated with crime control is so important and needs to be challenged. The idea that the CJS alone can successfully control crime is simply wrong, and those manufacturers arguing that it should be used to address the crime problems caused by their poorly designed goods are being rather disingenuous. They do not apply that argument when they are the victims themselves – then they tend to take situationally-oriented action.

The third reason suggested by Clarke and Eck is that the institutions may *gain* more by ignoring the problem than by responding to it. There are almost invariably costs to prevention and these may be perceived to outweigh the benefits. The final reason suggested is that some institutions may actually *profit* from the offending against their goods. The example given by Clarke and Eck in this case is of the second-hand goods shop owner who does little to verify the legitimacy of the goods being offered to him for purchase. A more appropriate example in the context of this chapter, and the definitions being used, would be the mobile phone manufacturers who can additionally benefit from the theft of their phones in that they can sell insurance against theft, making a profit on that, and can benefit when the victim of crime buys another phone. There were, for example, reports in the 1980s that in redesigning the style of car radios so that they were much less vulnerable to theft, Vauxhall motors lost money on the sale of replacement radios.

Table 1 below sets out a few examples of types of offending or targets of theft, and it notes those who might be held responsible for taking protective action and those with the competency to do so. (It should also be noted that the CJS might be seen as responsible throughout the table for prevention through deterrence.) In the table, those expected to take responsibility for crime prevention are also those who are the victims or

Table 1: Responsibility and Competency for Crime Prevention by Crime Type: Some Examples

Crime type	Responsibility	Competency
Theft of cars	Car owner to lock car and park in a secure place or garage it	Car manufacturer to provide good lock, parking lots to be secure or house designers to provide appropriate garaging space
Theft from cars	Car owner not to leave goods in car or lock away out of sight	Manufacturers to provide secure places, out of sight, inside cars
Domestic burglary	Home owners to use locks, alarms and etc.	House builders to build to "secure by design" standards; house owners to retrofit security devices (this is particularly problematic when the house is owned by a private landlord)
Violence in public houses	"Responsible drinking" by individuals	Publicans to operate responsible policies in drink marketing, door staff, design of public house etc.
Theft of mobile phones	Users not to use phone in high risk locations (e.g., leaving transport nodes); not to leave phones on café tables or otherwise on view	Mobile phone manufacturers to design phone so that it will not work if stolen

potential victims of the offence (where the CJS is held responsible, it is in representing the State as victim), but they are not necessarily the ones with the competency to deal with it. In such cases some pressure may need to be applied in the form of leverage to ensure that the necessary action is actually taken.

Goldstein (1997) has discussed the ways in which such pressure might be brought to bear in persuading those with the competency to take action to actually do so. He suggests a hierarchy of ways, ranging from education, or simply providing information (on the assumption that the agency would be perfectly prepared to address the problem if they knew about it), to civil action in the courts. Before applying Goldstein's hierarchy, an agent of some description has to be identified to apply any necessary pressure. In many cases, in the U.K., that would be the crime and disorder partnerships[2] at the local level, and might be the police or a government agency at regional or national level. In addition there has to be clarity about who is responsible for what, and where the competency lies for effective action. It might also be helpful if there were some consideration of the relationship between competency, responsibility and victim vulnerability. It is a contention in this chapter that many of the implementation problems observed result from a lack of such clarity. Some ideas on responsibility, competency and victimisation are outlined in the next section

WHO IS RESPONSIBLE FOR WHAT?

Being "irresponsible" is quite a comfortable position. It is one of the many advantages of youth! As we become older responsibilities of all sorts increase, including greater responsibility for our own safety or security. Garland (1996) describes "responsibilisation," as he calls it, as an adaptive process within high-crime societies, which is characterised by prevention and partnership. He discusses responsibilisation as it applies to the individual and contrasts it with the "sovereign state strategy" of crime control. The latter has the characteristics of enhanced and oppressive state control and expressive punishment and operates through the CJS. It is the prevalence of this view which gets in the way of the development of alternative and particularly more preventively-oriented approaches, although Garland tends to see their development as parallel and independent.

I discussed the various responsibilities for crime prevention in a book chapter (Laycock, 2004), which focussed on car crime but made a number of more general points about the locus of responsibility for various actions in the crime control context. Briefly, it was suggested that it is every individual's responsibility to contribute to the control of crime by: taking sensible precautions to protect themselves, their families, friends and communities against crime; not committing offences themselves; not buying stolen goods; and ensuring that their children are safe and are not themselves offending. They should also support the criminal justice process by reporting crimes to the police and standing as victims or witnesses in court where appropriate. Of course the list could be extended and the point was made that the responsibilities needed to be seen in some sense as "reasonable" and achieving some community or citizen consensus. What is seen as acceptable at community level might well vary by area. In some areas, particularly those with high crime rates, there may be considerable disagreement about the extent to which the police should be involved in conflict resolution for example. And that might be part of the problem of crime control in those areas.

It would also be important to guard against the notion of victim blaming. If people do not, for example, take care of their personal safety, does that mean that they are culpable if victimised? It is easy to argue at the extremes that this is unacceptable. A young woman out at night in a Western democracy, and wearing a short skirt, should not be seen as inviting rape (although in some societies that is what would be inferred). If she were also alone and drunk then there is certainly a heightened risk of such an attack but if attacked it would not be acceptable in our culture to "blame" her. Lower down the crime scale it becomes less clear cut. If, living in a high-crime area, you leave your unlocked car parked on the street with a laptop on the seat, then some might say you should expect a theft. In general circumstances then, if "reasonable" precautions are not taken, perhaps in some (but not all) circumstances you should, as a victim, share some of the responsibility for what may follow. This is a highly contentious issue and needs much fuller discussion and consideration than can be done here; it raises fundamental questions on the definition of "reasonable" and on the notions of guilt, mitigation, punishment and justice. For the purposes of this chapter it is sufficient to state that individuals are assigned some responsibility for their own safety etc. as outlined above. The default is not a simple implication of total culpability.

I further suggested that in addition to individuals, other agencies and organisations shared responsibilities for crime prevention. For example, in the U.K. the Crime and Disorder Act requires the police and local authorities to develop strategies for crime control at the local level, which combine prevention and detection, and which are based on a local crime audit. It is these agencies' responsibility to do this and it should also be within their competency to do so, although it has been argued that there is a significant training need if they are to achieve as much as has been hoped in this area (Goldstein, 2003).

In the 2004 chapter I also considered two other groups – "industry and commerce" and local, state and central governments. It was suggested that in the crime prevention area a socially responsible company would design goods, services and policies with "crime in mind," understanding that goods fitting the acronym "CRAVED" are at greater risk of being stolen and need extra protection. They would also resist marketing their goods in ways which risk drawing young people into crime, and take some responsibility for the threat of theft, attack and other offences being directed at customers. A responsible company would similarly care for its staff and take reasonable measures to protect them from victimisation through thoughtful policies, practices and training programmes.

It was seen as a responsibility of government to create a context within which these various responsibilities could be safely taken. It really amounts to changing the way in which crime is discussed and encouraging the idea that we *all* can and should take responsibility for crime reduction, as individuals, as members of communities as directors of commerce and industry. This message is, it seems, particularly problematic: To quote Garland, the approach is "politically difficult and institutionally radical" (Garland, 2000, page 348). There is the risk, for example, that it can be interpreted as blaming the potential victim, which it is not. But neither does it play to the traditional assumption that the CJS is the primary control mechanism for crime, an assumption with which the general public is particularly comfortable. Getting this message across would not be the only responsibility of government of course. Additionally, it might mean providing an efficient and effective criminal justice system; encouraging the reporting of crime and the attendance in court of victims and witnesses (and providing protection to do so if that were needed); and particularly for this chapter, ensuring that all those with the *competency* to contribute to crime prevention do so. In other words, in some way levering action from those with the competency to redesign goods, systems or services is the responsibility and within the competency of government.

This is a complex picture of inter-related rights, responsibilities and vulnerabilities, but it is even more complex than the earlier picture which I described allows. As is set out in the next section, it is not only individuals who are crime victims, it can be companies. And it is not always within the competency of any one company to protect itself. Other companies may be contributing, either wittingly or not, to the problem. If it is necessary to apply leverage to those companies, perhaps ultimately in the form of legislation, then that is a task for the central government, which has other pressures and considerations to take into account and may, therefore, not be so inclined. It is then for the victimised company to consider how it is to persuade the government itself to apply pressure. Many of these pressures are illustrated in the following section, which presents as a case study an ongoing problem for British Telecom Payphones.

REDUCING "CARDING" IN
BRITISH TELECOM PAYPHONES:
AN ONGOING IMPLEMENTATION CASE STUDY

British Telecom (BT) is the major telephone operator in the U.K. It has, amongst other things, a substantial network of public payphones on the streets and in commercial premises, for which it is responsible and which raise revenue for the company. These payphones are a "public face" of BT. They are widely distributed throughout the U.K., and BT is required by the telecommunications regulatory system to ensure that the general public has access to these phones, even in areas which may not be financially viable. Although this part of BT's business is conducted by BT Payphones, which is a separate part of the major company, in this chapter we will refer to BT for the sake of brevity.

Since the 1980s some BT payphone kiosks have been increasingly used to advertise the services of prostitutes. For some reason, which is not entirely clear, this practice is most common in the Westminster area of central London, in Brighton, a seaside town on the South coast, and in Norwich, a seaport on the eastern side of the country. By far the greatest concentration is, however, in Westminster where it is a concern of the local council as well as BT. The practice of putting prostitute cards in kiosks is known as "carding," and BT took particular exception to it since they felt, with some justification, that it degraded their kiosks, worried the public (their potential customers), and was unattractive to tourists. To make matters worse, and contrary to the views of the English Collective of Prostitutes (1992), many cards are now obscene (although they may not have been in 1992, when the English Collective of Prostitutes expressed their view). Without doubt BT "owned" the problem and felt itself to be a "victim."

Fundamentally BT has this problem because prostitutes need to advertise their services to potential clients and there are few legitimate ways in which they can do this. Accepting that prostitution is not going to go away, indeed in the U.K. it is not in itself illegal, is the start of the problem. This is an issue for the government and in the U.K. a consultation paper on prostitution was published in July 2004 (Home Office, 2004). As comes across clearly from this consultation exercise, there are complex and conflicting interests involved. The paper records that some communities take exception to the presence of prostitutes on their streets or in their community; observes that vulnerable people are drawn into prostitution from an early age; and notes the involvement of drugs, violence, illegal immigration and pimping as part of the scene. On the other hand the prostitutes argue that they are providing a service which has been in demand for millennia. They regard the consultation paper as biased, prejudiced, partial, poorly argued and taking an exceptionally punitive and enforcement-oriented approach to disadvantaged women trying to earn a legitimate living (English Collective of Prostitutes, 2004). Meanwhile BT wants clean phone boxes.

It is obviously way beyond the remit of a phone company to tackle the issue of prostitution. BT has instead concentrated on developing means of removing the cards from their kiosks. They have introduced targeted cleaning programmes, co-operated with the police when they run occasional operations against the brothels and individual prostitutes who were advertising their phone numbers in kiosks, and successfully lobbied for a change in the legislation to make carding a criminal offence. This gave the police powers of arrest over "carders," which they from time to time use as part of their operations against prostitution. The police have, for example, identified brothels using under-aged prostitutes or illegal immigrants in the course of operations against carding, although the sex workers themselves regard many of these eventualities as exaggerated and used to justify a punitive approach.

Most of the BT actions against carding have been ineffective, or had a short-term effect only. Arresting carders, for example, is particularly ineffectual since the fines are low, and there is no shortage of replacement carders. It is an example of substitution or perpetrator displacement as described by Barr and Pease (1990), where a crime opportunity is so compelling (and in this case so inconsequential at the point of sentence) that different offenders are always available to commit the crime.

One action taken by BT was potentially effective. They began noting the phone numbers on cards and barred incoming calls to those numbers. The full effect of this procedure will be reported in due course by Laycock and Csaznomski (in preparation). The procedure involved BT noting the phone numbers that were advertised on the call boxes and checking to see which numbers were BT's. If they were, BT then notified the owners of the number of their intention to block the incoming calls to the line (outgoing calls could still be made so as to protect the phone owner in emergencies). We were told by BT, in the course of a research project on this process, that they began blocking calls in this way in 1996 and that the process was declared illegal by the telecommunications regulator. In fact, the English Collective of Prostitutes has on their website a press release dating back to 1992, in which they report that this BT process was challenged by them, and the telecommunication regulator (then known as Oftel – or Office of Telecommunications – but since the end of 2003 merged into Ofcom, the Office of Communications) upheld the complaint and required BT to reinstate the lines. The press release noted:

> Preventing women from advertising in phone boxes would force *more women and young people onto the streets where they will face increased poverty, arrests, violence and persecution.* The prostitution laws make it illegal to advertise and many magazines, newspapers, newsagents, etc refuse to take ads for massage or other-services. Cards in phone boxes are a major way in which prostitute women advertise in order to stay off the streets. Women whose phones are cut off will no longer be able to work from premises." (Emphasis in the original; English Collective of Prostitutes, 1992)

What *appears* to have happened is that, as is typical in a large organization, staff move on. In 1996 staff new to the problem in BT decided to bar the relevant BT lines and did so. They were then told by the regulator that this was in breach of the trading laws (as had been established by the earlier challenge from the English Collective of Prostitutes). BT had to reconnect the lines. On this iteration, however, BT took steps to comply with the regulator's objections, and by 1999 the company was able to reinstate call barring. The effect of this was to cause or speed up the transfer of prostitute and brothel custom from BT to other telephony service providers – both landline and mobile. In contrast to the early 1990s a wide range of alternative telephony service providers are now available and there is a healthy competitive market for customers. What had started out as a potentially effective means for BT to disrupt the trade of prostitutes by barring calls when the numbers were advertised in BT call boxes (but not, significantly, otherwise), was rendered ineffectual by the growing number of alternative sources of service.

BT and Westminster City Council are at one in agreeing that the cards remain unacceptable, and they see themselves as "victims" of the carding process in that they have to: clean up the litter (this is currently estimated by BT at £250,000 per annum for removing cards alone); worry about the effect on citizens (there are occasional complaints and local surveys, commissioned by BT, show that up to 33% of respondents find the cards objectionable); and concern themselves with what are increasingly obscene pictures on public display. BT is particularly concerned with its public image and what is sees as the damage being done to it through carding.

Both BT and Westminster have asked the other operators to collaborate in the call barring scheme. A simple request is one of the first and least confrontational steps on the Goldstein (1997) hierarchy of levers aimed at provoking preventive action. Moving up the hierarchy we find "targeted confrontational requests" and "public shaming," both of which were used in 2004 by Westminster City Council in an attempt to force the mobile phone operators to join the BT scheme. In August 2004 the City Council issued a press release naming those mobile phone and landline operators which it held responsible for the continuing problem and named all their chief executives on mock prostitutes' calling cards. The Council created and circulated 20,000 such cards to passers-by in Oxford Street, a main shopping area. The Council threatened that if action were not taken to bar the numbers then the next run of cards would include the chief executives' home addresses and phone numbers.

There are a number of reasons why nothing seems to have happened. First, not all the operators were causing a problem and quite reasonably may not have seen why they should be required to do anything (although it is doubtful that they would have known that). Table 2 shows, for the landline operators, their percentage of national market share and their percentage of individual lines advertised on kiosks (note this is not the percentage of cards advertising phone numbers; some phone numbers have a large quantity of associated cards). Table 3 shows similar figures for the mobile operators. Although not ideal in making the point, the two sets of data have to be shown separately because the national figures are only available for comparison when split by landline and mobile operator.

Table 2: Percentage of National Line Ownership and Percentage of Different Lines Advertised on Kiosks for Landline Operators

Company	Percentage of national line ownership[a]	Percentage of different lines[b] advertised on kiosks (number of lines)
BT	83	12 (33)
Telewest/NTL	13	68 (180)
Other operators	4	19 (51)

[a]Data from Office of Communications (2004).
[b]Data provided by BT (see Laycock and Csaznomski [in preparation], for details).

Table 3: Percentage of National Line Ownership and Percentage of Different Lines Advertised on Kiosks for Mobile Operators

Company	Percentage of national line ownership[a]	Percentage of different lines advertised on kiosks[b] (number of lines)	National percentage of pre-pay customers[a]
T-Mobile UK Ltd	24	52 (189)	29
Vodaphone	24	25 (88)	20
O² UK Ltd	24	14 (49)	24
Orange	26	9 (33)	26

[a]Data from Office of Telecommunications (2003).
[b]These figures are based on the four main operators to enable comparison with the national picture; Ofcom do not provide details of market share for all operators. Figures were provided by BT following a special card collection exercise in March 2004.

There are a number of points to be made about these figures. First, BT has a much smaller share of the kiosk landlines, at 12%, than might have been assumed on the basis of their national market share at 83%. This is presumably a consequence of their persistent call barring of lines advertised on prostitute cards. They are, therefore, losing market share as a consequence of trying to protect their kiosks from carding. Looking at the mobile operators, T-Mobile has twice the expected market share while Orange, on the other hand, has a much smaller share, as does O². One plausible reason for the high share of T-Mobile is that they have a higher percentage of pre-pay customers. It is a feature of pre-pay that there are fewer controls on customers and the phones. Although required, details on home address, for example, are not always rigorously collected by the phone operators. This might suit a brothel operator or prostitute operating independently.

Returning to the implementation issue, with which both BT and Westminster are struggling, their first problem is that as the tables above show, not all operators are culpable. Telewest and NTL, as alternative landline operators, are in positive discussions about what might be done, but the mobile operators are not. Second, many of the alternative operators are benefiting financially, albeit marginally, from BT's present policy, so why would they want to co-operate? Third, some of the mobile operators are reported as saying that the prostitutes could simply switch to pre-pay SIM cards which can be bought for as little as £10 (*Daily Telegraph*, 27/08/2004). Furthermore, in the same newspaper article, a Vodaphone representative was reported as saying that they "do not get involved in making judgements about the nature of calls, or interpreting the legality of issues which are in the realms of the law enforcement agencies." In other words it is not our problem; it is a matter for the police. They also pointed out that the safety of prostitutes was an issue and numbers that had no connection with prostitution might be barred. So some of the operators at least, could produce reasons for inaction, and although BT disagrees with many of them, there is something of an impasse – and the cards remain in the kiosks.

One proposal is that the phone operators might be required by legislation to bar calls to numbers advertising prostitution. BT would be prepared to provide lists of numbers that were advertising in this way, and they argue that constant switching of numbers from one pre-pay to another as the numbers were barred would be sufficiently disruptive to the brothels and prostitutes as to encourage them to find another method of advertising. This notion is still under discussion.

To summarise the position, which has been going on for the order of 20 years: we start with prostitutes wanting to contact clients in what for them is a competitive market, so their cards, which are blu-tacked onto BT Payphone kiosks, become more numerous, more sexually explicit and less acceptable to BT, the local council and the general public. When BT was the main provider of telephony services, in a virtual monopoly position, the idea of call barring might have worked. The market is now much more open however, and call barring has led to a switch to other providers including pre-pay, which is much less easy to regulate. Neither BT nor Westminster City Council seems to have sufficient leverage over the other payphone operators to persuade them to bar lines (although Westminster is working its way up the Goldstein hierarchy at quite a rate!). We are left with the possibility that the government might legislate to force the barring of lines by all operators in the hope that even switching to pre-pay could be sufficiently disruptive to the advertising of the numbers that the brothels and prostitutes would find other methods of advertising. Although it is difficult to see what those other methods might be, it is worth making the point that prostitutes in other parts of the U.K. seem to function without resorting to advertising in this way. For some reason, as was mentioned earlier, it is a particular feature of the operation in Westminster and a very few other places.

This case study has been presented as illustrative of a complex social issue (prostitution), that has led to a particular problem for a commercial company (BT) and the associated local authority (Westminster), neither of which has the competency to address the problem. Over time they have tried cleaning the kiosks, enforcing a law (a ban on carding), which they themselves had to have created and which relies on the CJS for its effect, and encouraging police operations against brothels in the area – all with little or no effect on the volume of cards, which continues to increase. At the time of writing their attempts to exert leverage over the other service providers has proved limited. This is a complex problem and is by no means unique in this respect. It illustrates, amongst other things, the difficulties faced at the local level in trying to deal with problems which fundamentally need to be dealt with effectively at governmental level.

Lessons for Implementation

From an implementation perspective, the case study described above illustrates some key features that are of more general relevance. Perhaps the first is *problem definition*. It is doubtful that the full extent and complexity of the problem of carding was recognised by BT as they began their search for a solution. It looks like a simple problem – getting rid of some cards in phone boxes. As one energetic senior civil servant was quoted as saying in the *Guardian* newspaper (February 26, 2004):

> Some central areas in big towns have got prostitutes' cards in phone-boxes. What is the response of one area I was in? To pay for someone to audit the number of cards. This is the sort of thing that sends me over the edge. I have to control myself in meetings, still look calm and smile afterwards with a cup of tea and not go, "Are you crazy, have you lost your mind?" By all means count them, but take the effing things down at the same time.

As the discussion above makes clear, the effing things are taken down, repeatedly, but they keep coming back! The problem is not simple and there needs to be an early decision about where effort should most appropriately be targeted – which facet of the problem is most amenable to modification. Is it a matter of getting the law on prostitution sorted out? Or would effort be better directed at the prostitutes, the carders or the kiosks? If, for example, a rigorous and targeted cleaning programme were to be implemented (as BT are doing), then it might be necessary to determine when, exactly, the cards were being placed in the kiosks. Timing a cleaning programme just after cards were placed there would make sense, but if the carders were capable of replacing cards rapidly (as it appears they are – but that is another story), then there might well be prohibitive costs associated with this approach.

The second issue is *financial*. Starting with the prostitutes, they feel that advertising in kiosks is an important way of reaching their customers whilst avoiding street prostitution, which they regard as riskier. In the absence of an equally viable alternative they are simply not going to stop carding. A law against it is irrelevant.

BT is concerned with its public image and feels that the cards, which as noted above are increasing sexually explicit to the point of being porno-graphic, damage that image and offend the customer base. So there is a commercial interest, but the company is also mindful of the impression given of the broader area within which the payphones are located, many of which are tourist areas in a high-profile area of London. This, of course, is the concern of Westminster City Council, which can also be seen to have a financial interest in maintaining the appearance of the city centre and encouraging tourism (notwithstanding the fact that some of the tourists are the clients of the prostitutes). There is also the considerable financial cost of cleaning the cards from kiosks, mostly borne by BT but also shared by the city council.

After numerous attempts to deal with the problem by BT and West-minster, it is now fairly clear that one of the few viable options is call barring on a wider scale. But this would require co-operation from a whole range of other telephony service providers and there is no doubt that it would cost them money to apply the scheme as BT would wish. To complicate matters further some operators are actually profiting from BT's attempts to deal with the problem and increasing their market share as a byproduct of the problem. Fundamentally, it is "not their problem," and furthermore they can make the case that the police or, to quote the Voda-phone spokesperson "the law enforcement agencies," need to deal with it (the fact that the agencies can't do this in a cost-effective manner is also not the companies' problem).

The third issue is that of *identifying effective leverage*. So far this has not been a success. BT began by trying to exert leverage over the prostitutes and their carders by cleaning cards off regularly and by supporting legisla-tion that made the practice illegal. They also supported the police in targeted operations against brothels, but these do not happen with suffi-cient regularity to constitute a sufficient disincentive to the brothel. Moving to call barring, the pressure being brought to bear on the other operators, particularly the most relevant mobile operators, is largely being ignored. The steps taken by the City Council so far could be described as high risk and personal. They are targeting the chief executives of the phone companies rather than the companies themselves. They might try to direct public attention to the extent to which the companies could be held responsible for carding, but if they do that they will need to draw on the research, available to BT and some of which is reported above, which shows that by no means all companies are involved. This is an ongoing issue which in an ideal world would be sorted out by central government perhaps dealing with prostitution in a more radical manner and with local agencies (police and local councils) supporting alternative methods by which prostitutes might contact their clients and vice versa.

The fourth issue that comes from this discussion is the importance of *identifying the victim*. This can be complex and there may be degrees of victimisation that need to be considered. For example, in the case under discussion it is clear that the prostitutes feel quite heavily victimised and have no sympathy with the notion that BT or Westminster feel put upon. They also argue that the offence caused to the public is exaggerated. What is fairly clear is that with the exception of BT, the operators who have the competency to bar the lines are not in any way the victims of the behaviour. Indeed they may profit from it.

The fifth issue, which does not come across quite so clearly from the case study, is *continuity of staff*. Although this topic does not seem to have been widely researched, the lack of continuity in senior and for that matter more junior staff appears to be a serious impediment to efficient implementation. This is probably even more of an issue if the area under consideration is complex and involves a multitude of agencies and potential victims, and competency is not contiguous with victimisation. By the time clarification is determined on what needs to be done, when and by whom, all the major players have moved. The bureaucratic answer to this problem is appropriate meeting management, with agreed agendas, minutes, targets and "relentless follow-up" (Bratton and Knobler, 1998). Taking care to ensure that local partnership meetings (which are a particular characteristic of the U.K. crime reduction scene) do not degenerate into talking shops seems particularly important in this context.

A related notion is *project management*, which is discussed fully by Rick Brown in his chapter of this volume. He notes the generally poor project management associated with the implementation of community safety initiatives and presents a model of the "dynamic project lifecycle" as a means of identifying how projects evolve and ways in which common problems might be resolved.

Sixth, and this is perhaps an overriding issue that is not often addressed, *who is in the driving seat*? Who is the person or agency that is taking responsibility for the implementation of a preventive programme? If the victims are individual members of the community and are diffuse, as might be the case with domestic burglary, then it is generally assumed that the police or some partnership involving police, the local authority and maybe the community itself will take on the task of tackling the problem. (Interestingly, when dealing with domestic burglary in low-crime areas it is usually the victim who takes protective action in improving security. It is discussed as more of a "community" issue in higher-crime areas.) How this locally based group responsibility is organised would depend upon the structures and characteristics of the crime prevention set-up in the relevant jurisdiction. But for many other problems, and the case study described here is an illustration, it is not clear who is responsible. Passing the problem to the police, given the competing priorities under which they operate, is unlikely to achieve much. In the example discussed in this chapter the responsible party has largely been BT, with Westminster City Council playing a part from time to time. There can be no prescription here – someone or some body needs to emerge with sufficient commitment to sorting out the problem or sufficient concern for the costs being borne by the agency to deal with it. In well-organised major companies, for example, there might be a whole department of people with responsibility to maintain the internal security of the organisation and address threats from outside, but they would not normally be involved in the resolution of the kinds of threat directed at BT in the case study described.

Finally, a related and equally important point to that discussed above, is who should assign responsibility and identify competency, and on what basis? The implication from an early section of this paper is that it generally falls within the political competency of governments to at least think through some of these processes. There are a number of principles that might be considered relevant:[3]

- Victims should not be expected to bear disproportionate preventive costs to protect themselves from crime.

- No one should profit from the creation of criminal opportunities.

- Those who "own" solutions, i.e., those that have the competency to change the opportunity structure, should avoid negligence in creating opportunities.

- If it is not justifiable to place responsibility on a competent third party, then perhaps some consideration should be given to compensating them for taking action to reduce the opportunities that they may have inadvertently created.

This is the start of a list, which needs further development, elaboration and discussion. It begs the question, for example, of what constitutes *disproportionate preventive costs*. On the whole we tend to see protection taken by householders to the threat of burglary in proportion to their perceived risk and resources. So, for example, celebrities with high value assets and large estates spend considerable sums on the protection of their property, themselves and their families. The average member of the community spends in proportion with deadlocks on doors and windows. Some may invest in a burglar alarm and others in neighbourhood watch schemes. What constitutes proportionate cost is relative to assets and risk.

It also leaves in the air *who* should determine the extent to which companies may be profiting from the development of criminogenic products, and what should be done about those who do so. Stimulating industrialist and commercial organisations to think about the ways in which their products contribute to the crime problem is now being addressed by the European Union in its funding of a programme of work on the design of goods and legislation. This work is still ongoing and is being overseen by Ernesto Savona and colleagues at the University of Trento, Italy. The EU is acting on this issue without the full understanding of many of its member states, the vast majority of which do not take similar action at the level of the nation-state. We discussed above the role of governments in crime control, but similar responsibilities might be said to apply at supra-national level. The EU (to take Europe as the example) and the UN at the global level may be said to have a role in addressing crime control in this way. They are all the more important and significant as multi-national companies proliferate.

Returning to the community level at which much of the crime and disorder game is played out, Table 4 below is intended to assist the thinking of the local community activist who might wish to tackle a crime or disorder problem, but it applies equally well to any organisation wishing to deal with a presenting problem and get something done about it. Sometimes, as we noted above, this is easy – if the victim and competent agency overlap

Table 4: An Aide Memoire for the Local Practitioner

What *exactly* is the problem?	1. Can you describe the *behaviour* that is the problem? 2. When does it happen? 3. What facilitates it? 4. Who benefits (think broadly)?
Who is the victim?	1. Are the victims individuals, companies, or groups of householders? 2. Are they likely to know about each other? (Burglary victims probably won't, but shops' personnel in the same chain might.) 3. Are they likely to work together? 4. If not, who will act on their behalf?
Who is responsible for local action?	1. Does the victim need to do something differently (e.g., lock their doors, not leave goods in cars)? 2. Who is going to make sure something happens to address this problem? (E.g., is it the local partnership, the police, the local government?)
Who is competent to implement preventive action?	1. Can you identify a body or agency that needs to take action to change the opportunity structure for crime? 2. Are they locally, regionally, nationally or even internationally-based?
What levers can be identified and who can pull them?	1. Can you identify ways of persuading those competent to change the situation to do so? 2. Is it more a matter for central, regional or national government? In which case how can it be brought to their attention?
Who profits or loses by the offending?	1. Who gains from the offending (again thinking broadly)? 2. Is it only the offender? 3. Who loses? What do they lose?
Are key staff moving or likely to move?	1. Do your solutions rely on particular individuals remaining in post? 2. If so, how can you guard against implementation failure if they move?

– but in other circumstances the picture is much more complex, and being aware of the complexity can reduce wasted time and resources.

Address correspondence to: Professor Gloria Laycock, UCL Jill Dando Institute of Crime Science, University College London, Brook House, 2-16 Torrington Place, London WC1E 7HN; e-mail g.laycock@ucl.ac.uk

Acknowledgments: I am grateful to Professor Ron Clarke, Sarah Czarnomski and Dr Michael Townsley for their contribution to the consultancy report for British Telecom Payphones from which the example discussed in this chapter draws. BT Payphones were generous in their time and resources in supporting the work. I am also indebted to Professor Mike Hough for his valuable comments on an earlier draft.

NOTES

1. "Prostitute" is used throughout this chapter, as being in general usage, although "sex worker" is the preferred term both amongst many prostitutes and the agencies that have regular contact with them.
2. Crime and Disorder Partnerships in the U.K. were established following the Crime and Disorder Act (1998), which required local governments to work with the local police and establish partnerships to assess and respond to problems of crime and disorder in their communities.
3. I am grateful to Professor Mike Hough for his contribution to this discussion.

REFERENCES

Barr, R., & Pease, K. (1990). Crime placement, displacement, and deflection. In M. Tonry & N. Morris (Eds.), *Crime and justice: A review of research*, vol. 12. Chicago and London: University of Chicago Press.

Bratton, W., & Knobler, P. (1998). *The turnaround*. New York: Random House.

Clarke, R. V. (1999). *Hot products: Understanding, anticipating and reducing demand for stolen goods*. Police Research Series Paper 112. London: Home Office Research Development and Statistics Directorate

Clarke, R. V., Kemper, R., & Wyckoff, L. (2001). Controlling cell phone fraud in the US: Lessons for the UK "Foresight" Prevention Initiative. *Security Journal*, *14*(1), 7–22.

Clarke, R. V., & Eck, J. (2003). *Become a problem-solving crime analyst*. London: Jill Dando Institute of Crime Science, University College London. Available from Willan Publishing, Devon, UK.

English Collective of Prostitutes (1992). Press release retrieved July, 24, 2005 from: http://www.allwomencount.net/EWC%20Sex%20Workers/BTPR.htm

English Collective of Prostitutes (2004). *Criminalisation: The price women and children pay. The English Collective of Prostitute's response to the government's review of the prostitution laws.* Presented at the Conference "No Bad Women, No Bad Children, Just Bad Laws," London 4 December 2004. Available from Crossroads Books, Box 287 London NW6 5QU England.

Engstad, P., & Evans, J. L. (1980). Responsibility, competence and police effectiveness in crime control. In R. V. Clarke & J. M. Hough (Eds.), *The effectiveness of policing.* Farnborough, Hants: Gower.

Garland, D. (1996). The limits of the sovereign state: Strategies of crime control in contemporary society. *British Journal of Criminology, 36,* 445–471.

Garland, D., & Sparks, R. (2000). Criminology, social theory and the challenge of our times. *British Journal of Criminology, 40,* 189–204.

Goldstein, H. (1997). *The pattern of emerging tactics for shifting ownership of prevention strategies in the current wave of change in policing: Their implications for both environmental criminology and the police.* Paper presented at the 6th International Seminar of Environmental Criminology and Crime Analysis, Oslo, Norway. Download from: www.popcenter.org

Goldstein, H. (2003). On further developing problem oriented policing: The most critical need, the major impediments, and a proposal. In J. Knutsson (Ed.), *Problem-oriented policing: From innovation to mainstream.* Crime Prevention Studies, vol. 15. Monsey, NY: Criminal Justice Press.

Harrington, V., & Mayhew, P. (2001). *Mobile phone theft.* Home Office research Study 235. London: Home Office Research, Development and Statistics Directorate.

Home Office (2004). *Paying the price: A consultation paper on prostitution.* London: Home Office Communications Directorate.

Laycock, G. (2004). The UK Car Theft Index: An example of government leverage. In M. Maxfield & R. V. Clarke (Eds.), *Understanding and preventing car theft.* Crime Prevention Studies, vol. 17. Devon, UK: Willan Publishing.

Laycock, G., & Csaznomski, S. (in preparation). Engineering out crime. *BT Technology Journal* (forthcoming).

Morgan, R., & Clarke, R. V. (2003). *Government regulations and their unintended consequences for crime: A project to develop risk indicators.* Downloadable from: http://www.jdi.ucl.ac.uk/publications/adhoc_publications/index.ph p (accessed 10 August 2005.)

Nicholas, S., & Walker, A. (Eds.). (2004). *Crime in England and Wales 2002/2003: Supplementary Volume 2: Crime, disorder and the Criminal Justice 02/04 System – public attitudes and perceptions.* London: Home Office. Downloadable from: http://www.homeoffice.gov.uk/rds/index.htm

Office of Communications (Ofcom). (2004). *The communications market 2004: Telecoms appendix.* Published August 2004 and available from: http://www.ofcom.org.uk/research/telecoms/data/ (accessed 7 March 2006) or from Ofcom, Riverside House, 2a Southwark Bridge Road, London SE1 9HA, UK.

Office of Telecommunications (Oftel). (2003). *Market information: Mobile update. December 2003 Q2 2003/04 (July to September 2003).* Available from Office of Telecommunications, Ludgate Hill, London EC4M 7JJ, UK.

Rosenbaum, D. P., Lewis, D. A., & Grant, J. A. (1986). Neighbourhood-based crime prevention: Assessing the efficacy of community organising in Chicago. In D. Rosenbaum (Ed.), *Community crime prevention: Does it work?* Thousand Oaks, CA: Sage Criminal Justice System Annuals.

Webb, B., & Marshall, B. (2004). *A problem-oriented approach to fly-tipping.* A report for the Environment Agency. London: Jill Dando Institute, University College London. Available from the JDI website www.jdi.ucl.ac.uk (accessed 10 August 2005).

What is there to Gain?
A Case Study in Implementing
without Self-interest

by

Johannes Knutsson
Norwegian Police University College

Abstract: *Organizations or persons with the power to affect the opportunity structure for crime are not always ready to act. One should be prepared to encounter little enthusiasm and, in some instances, even open resistance. Given these negative expectations, the process of implementation went surprisingly smoothly in one case involving the practice of problem-oriented policing in a small town in Norway, and the project was successfully implemented. A more detailed examination shows that the organization of the project, the choice of measures and the process of putting them into practice were all carried out in an efficient way, thus explaining the success.*

INTRODUCTION

Over the last few decades our knowledge about what works and what does not in the field of crime prevention has improved considerably. It is fair to say that, among a number of different approaches, situational crime prevention has proved to be successful and is now well established (Clarke, 1997; Hopkins Burke, 2001). Furthermore, situational crime prevention has become an integral part of the philosophy of problem-oriented policing

(POP), and there is substantial evidence that, when properly conducted, POP is effective in preventing crime and disorder (Clarke and Eck, 2003; Knutsson, 2003; Weisburd and Eck, 2004).

Our theoretical understanding of why situational crime prevention works and of the operating mechanisms involved, has also been enhanced (Cornish and Clarke, 1985, 2004; Clarke and Felson, 1993; Pawson and Tilley, 1997; Clarke and Cornish, 2000). However, there are still some areas that need to be examined. Our learning has to a large extent been based on positive and successful examples. There are probably quite a few cases where crime preventive projects have come to naught, or virtually naught, as a result of obstacles encountered during different stages of the process of putting these measures into practice.

Since crime prevention is a politically attractive concept, it is fairly easy to get funding for projects or programs of this kind. Sometimes there seems to be a confusion of intention and effect. There are at least two examples from Sweden of reasonably well documented and well funded projects with the aim of preventing crime, but where neither of the projects achieved its explicit goal of crime reduction. Both were organized by the Swedish National Council for Crime Prevention. The projects were carried out according to the principles of action research: they began with descriptions and analyses of causes of crime, which were in turn supposed to lay the ground for the implementation of measures, which would then be evaluated. In the most ambitious of these endeavors – the Stockholm project – a large number of reports were produced covering vast fields of research (e.g. Dolmén and Lindström, 1991; Wikström, 1991; Martens, 1992). However, both projects more or less faded away to nothing – in the case of the Stockholm project, no efforts were made even to suggest substantive practical measures, and in the other, the Fisksätra project, huge problems arose both during the phase in which crime preventive measures were devised and also in the course of their implementation (Ringman, 1997).

Why these projects failed is not altogether clear. One probable reason is that the design of the projects was not altogether realistic; things do not come about in the simple and rational way that was presupposed (Moore, 1995). My own belief is that, from the beginning, they were not sufficiently focused on particular crimes or problems.

In these cases, one of the major problems was a lack of practical ideas – there was not much to implement in the first place, which means that the examples represent a failure of theory. The issue examined in this chapter, however is not the lack of ideas or theory. Rather, the focus is directed at obstacles – or the absence of obstacles – when it comes to implementing opportunity-reducing crime preventive measures. The question addressed is that of what can happen to reasonable, practical crime preventive measures and their realization when they are presented to those who are in a position, and have the competence, to affect the opportunities for crime – i.e., the owners of the solution. Our knowledge of what enhances or decreases the probabilities that crime preventive measures will be implemented is somewhat limited since this issue is often neglected in evaluation studies or is at least treated in a rather superficial way.

The chapter will build upon experiences from crime preventive projects that have been carried out in Sweden and Norway. It draws to a large extent on projects in which the author has been involved. Inside knowledge of this kind is often not included in the reports, but it is of relevance in this connection. The reason this specific kind of experience is omitted is probably because it is considered irrelevant. The focus is usually directed at the problem, the measures taken and the effects produced. Difficulties encountered in the course of the implementation process may furthermore cast a shadow on the organizations or the individuals involved, which may also help to explain why this information is omitted. Experience of this kind is valuable, however, since it leads to more realistic expectations regarding likely reactions to proposals to participate in crime preventive endeavors, and thus implicitly it also provides information as to how best to act in order to circumvent these problems. Since these understandings are not usually explicitly accounted for, they may represent an example of what is referred to as tacit knowledge.

The text begins by presenting an account of some early experiences from the field of crime prevention in Sweden. These provide a clear indication that implementation may constitute a difficult and tiring task. An example from Norway is then discussed. In this instance the implementation of the measures went unexpectedly smoothly and furthermore the measures proved to be effective. Given the rather common experience of problems and even of failure to implement crime preventive measures, this outcome is somewhat unexpected. What factors were associated with the successful implementation of the measures in this case?

EARLY SWEDISH EXPERIENCES

The introduction of the check as a common means of payment at the beginning of the 1960s was followed by a wave of frauds as the new system signified a new opportunity for crime. Criminal Investigation Division fraud squads were soon overburdened with cases to be investigated, particularly in the larger cities. The newly appointed National Police Commissioner took a personal interest and in 1965 started negotiations with the trade associations representing banks and retailers in order to halt this rapidly increasing form of crime (Persson, 1991).

The cause was soon diagnosed to be located in the lax routines associated with the use of checks as a means of payment. Retailers accepting false checks were refunded by the so-called bank guarantee from the banks, and as a consequence there was no interest in controlling checks or the persons presenting them. In order to prevent check frauds, the police wanted the banks to abolish the guarantee, to employ more secure routines in the handling of checks, and also to conduct identity checks of the persons making payments in this way.

Both associations refused to accept the proposed measures. During the prolonged discussions, which went on for years, frauds continued to increase. Finally in 1970, after a four fold increase in crime, and, certainly more importantly, following a threat of legislation to make identity controls mandatory, the banks and the retailers gave up their resistance and accepted the introduction of the proposed measures. Crime rates for check fraud immediately decreased and the feared negative side effects of a displacement to other types of crime failed to materialize (Knutsson and Kühlhorn, 1980, 1997).

It is obvious that the resistance in this case was primarily motivated purely by economic self-interest. In economic terms, the loss incurred by the banks was almost negligible by comparison with the profits the system produced. An easy and smooth process for payment by check was preferred. The costs of investigating the crimes and punishing the check forgers were ultimately paid by the taxpayer.

About ten years later the story was repeated. The introduction of new technology made checks obsolete as a common means of payment. They were replaced by credit cards, and then card frauds soon began to appear and to increase rapidly. This time, in order to base their case on better arguments, the police employed a researcher (the author of this chapter) to investigate ways to prevent this new type of crime and to formulate arguments that could be presented to the credit card companies. The parallels with check frauds were striking. The main cause of these crimes was found in the lax routines employed for controlling the identity of persons using cards (Knutsson and Kühlhorn, 1980, pp. 75–95). Armed with their experiences of check frauds and this new study, the National Police Board had a good case – or at least they thought they did.

This time there was only one meeting with the retailers' association and representatives of the credit card companies. A proposal from the National Police Board to introduce identity controls for card holders was immediately rejected. The patience of the police was shorter this time and the discussions ended. A few years later, however, stricter controls were introduced. When sums exceeded a maximum amount, identity checks became mandatory, just as the police had proposed they should. The subsequent trend in card frauds clearly suggests that this measure was effective and halted a feared increase (Ahlberg, 1992).

In this case, the reason underlying the introduction of the measures is not clear. It might be that the frauds became too costly. Another possible explanation is that the police did not give priority to these crimes, since from the police point of view it was the credit card companies who were to blame for making these offences possible. The companies were more or less forced to do something on their own account.

Both these cases were played out at the national level, with central associations representing the different organizations involved. The fact that problems can also occur at the local level is evident from next example, which concerns the prevention of collective public order disturbances.

For a substantial number of years, the police force in a little town on an island in the Baltic Sea had experienced tremendous problems with unruly and drunken youths in connection with the celebration of Midsummer's Eve. In order to cope with the situation, local police had to be reinforced with large numbers of police officers from other police districts.

Following several years of serious disturbances, during which the police had tried to control the event using conventional police methods, the police wanted a solution to the problem. At a meeting with all the parties involved, the police suggested substantial preventive measures. By not admitting youths to the surrounding camp sites during the Midsummer holiday, and by temporarily closing down a parking lot where some of those participating in the celebrations stayed, it would become much harder for them to get to the city center, where the celebration occurred. After initially having accepted the measures, opinion shifted. The argument was that the problem was not such a major one after all. The police, in their turn, then argued that if this was the case, there was no need for them to be there at all. The meeting ended with an agreement to accept the proposals presented by the police.

In this instance, prior to the meeting, the National Council for Crime Prevention had published a study in which the disturbances were described in detail (Knutsson, 1987). The study and its results had previously been presented to members of the group. It strengthened the position of the police and made their definition of the event more credible, thereby helping them to convince the other parties of the necessity of introducing the proposed measures.[1]

A subsequent evaluation showed that the implemented measures improved the situation considerably (Björ et al., 1992). However, in the follow-up interviews, those representing local business claimed that the police went too far in their endeavors to decrease the problem. The profit made from the visitors evidently weighed more heavily than the consequences of their degenerate behavior.

THE USE OF LEVERAGE

These experiences suggest that it may take hard work and tiring negotiations to get measures implemented. Herman Goldstein has suggested a hierarchy of leverage that can be used to make those in a position to affect the opportunity structure take action and assume responsibility (Goldstein, 1997). The hierarchy is stated in ten steps with the forms of leverage increasing in strength, depending on the degree of cooperation involved:

1. Educational programmes

2. Straightforward informal requests

3. Targeted confrontational requests

4. Engaging another existing organization

5. Pressing for the creation of a new organization to assume ownership

6. Public shaming

7. Withdrawing police service

8. Charging a fee for police service

9. Legislation mandating the adoption of prevention

10. Bringing of a civil action.

The hierarchy should not be perceived in absolute terms, but more as providing examples of different levers and their relative strength. It is reasonable to assume that better information is needed to substantiate a case for the more coercive forms of leverage.

According to Goldstein's hierarchy, the cases described above ended at a fairly high stage of the leverage hierarchy – the threat of legislation and the threat of withdrawing police service were among the arguments used. The evidence presented as to the reasons for showing reluctance and for the subsequent surrender is admittedly rather vague and circumstantial. But these accounts are very much in line with what we have learnt from other experiences. Those who are in a position to contribute to the reduction of opportunities for crime are often unwilling to do so. One common reason seems to involve a combination of the attitude that it is the responsibility of the police to deal with the offenders, and an unwillingness to take measures that could decrease the gains made by the actors involved (see Clarke and Eck, 2003, step 38).

Since the situational approach involves an assumption that human beings are rational self-serving creatures, this outcome ought not to come as a surprise among the adherents of this approach. The assumption, of course, is not only valid for criminals and for normally law abiding persons, but also for the owners of the solution. A critical question then becomes – what is in it for them?

THE CASE – A LOCAL PROBLEM-ORIENTED POLICING PROJECT

The aim of the problem-oriented policing project was to reduce illegal taxicab activities in Tønsberg, a small town in Norway. The SARA model, which involves scanning, analysis, response and assessment phases, was applied to the problem. Here the focus is on the response phase, which consists of two elements: (1) coming up with credible crime preventive measures that are feasible and preferably sustainable; and (2) getting them implemented. The second element often involves negotiations with persons representing organizations other than the police.

The set of measures that was proposed was primarily aimed at reducing the opportunities for the illegal cabs to operate and increasing the availability of legal means of transport. Other measures were intended to increase the moral costs for both illegal cab drivers and their passengers. These measures later proved to considerably reduce the problem (Vestfold Police District, 2004; Knutsson and Søvik, 2005). In fact, it is fair to say that the whole project was a success.[2]

To get the measures implemented a number of organizations had to be approached (Table 1). As can be seen from the table, there were quite a few parties involved. Some organizations were involved in more than one of the measures.

The process in the response phase went rather smoothly and once the negotiations ended, the actual implementation of the measures was

Table 1: Proposed Measures and Organizations Involved

Measure	Organization
Blocking off pick-up areas used by illegal cabs.	Tønsberg City Council
	The National Road Authority
	The Tønsberg Engineers' Service
	Tønsberg Car Parking and Europark
Making buses and taxis more accessible by moving the bus stand to a more centrally situated location and by creating a new taxi cab stand closer to the entertainment area.	Tønsberg City Council
	The Tønsberg Engineers' Service
	The Tønsberg Taxi Association
	Norway Bus and Nettbus
Introduction of a night-bus service on Friday nights.	Norway Bus and Nettbus
	Vestfold County Council
Improved cooperation between local taxi cab services and other providers of taxi services for a more optimal use of taxi cab transport capacity.	The Tønsberg Taxi Association
Introduction of stiffer consequences for those caught driving illegal cabs.	Vestfold police lawyers
Informing suspected illegal cab drivers about possible consequences of providing illegal taxi services.	Vestfold police force uniformed branch
	The Tønsberg Social Welfare and Immigrant Offices
Informing the public about the risks involved and about legal alternatives.	Vestfold police force uniformed branch
	Tønsberg City Council
	The Tønsberg Taxi Association
	Norway Bus and Nettbus

unexpectedly swift. The whole response process, from the formulation of the ideas through the negotiations and the implementation of the measures, took a total of three months.

Interviews with Key Persons

In order to gain some insight into the implementation process, interviews were conducted with some of the key persons involved. These interviews took place almost two years after the project was carried out. Those interviewed were the chief of police, the project manager, the city council chairman, an agent representing the National Road Authority, the leader of the local engineers' service, an agent representing one of the bus companies and the chairman of the local taxi cab drivers' association.

The Chief of Police

When the chief of police took up his position he decided that one goal for the police should be to carry out a problem-oriented policing project in a proper way. The projects that had been carried out prior to his appointment did not meet an acceptable standard to be properly called problem-oriented. He soon realized that illegal cab driving had been considered a real problem in his district for a long period of time. The police had tried to deal with the problem using conventional methods, by means of targeted actions using overtime money, seemingly without any effect. The cab drivers' association in particular complained bitterly. When the project started, the available information relating to the problem was vague and was to a large extent based on impressions. One of the success factors was the appointment of the project manager – an able young police officer. According to the police chief, another factor was the support provided by a senior researcher (the author of this chapter). The chief of police was continually informed about the progress of the project during meetings of the steering group. If required, he was prepared to provide support in the negotiation process, something which he did by talking to the county administration to persuade them to come up with money, if needed, to subsidize a night-bus service on Friday nights. Contacts with the local administration, which in the chief's opinion constitute a prerequisite for projects of this type, were good to begin with, and improved over time. According to the chief's experience, projects of this kind are vulnerable and there is definitely no guarantee of success. This is why it is important to carefully organize them, with a budget, a good structure and follow-up routines.

Project Manager

The project manager was a rather young police officer, who normally worked in the uniformed branch. Among his merits was that of having formerly been leader of the students' union whilst at police college. He was also completing his law studies at the University of Oslo. Most of the tasks were carried out by the project manager, including the major parts of the negotiating process during the response phase. He had been taught the basic principles of the philosophy of problem-oriented policing at the Police Academy. But he was not really prepared for the effort and the rigor involved in such an undertaking. As to the response phase, the difficult part was not in formulating possible measures, but rather in the negotiations that needed to be conducted. These were more demanding and more time consuming than he had anticipated. Extending the tempo-rarily closed-off section of the highway required cooperation from the National Road Authority. This particular measure was crucial for the whole project. However, it took a large number of meetings to convince the Road Authority to take part. The Authority appeared to have difficulty relating to the reasons for introducing the measure – preventing illegal cab services. But after several discussions and meetings, the police argued that there was also a traffic safety issue involved. This appeared to create an opening for the Road Authority and they decided to reserve the necessary funding and to make the suggested changes by moving the relevant barriers, thus increasing the stretch of the highway that was temporarily closed. Only one group showed a complete lack of interest. These represented the owners of the local licensed establishments, who had at first shown enthusiasm in the context of the initial contact. However, when it came to actual negotiations, they were not interested. This was a real disappoint-ment for the project manager. The opposite could be said about the reaction to the presentation of the project at the city council. The project manager was somewhat surprised by the positive reception the proposals received. When the decisions were subsequently taken, cooperation with the different units went smoothly and the measures were swiftly imple-mented. Another surprise was the willingness to cooperate shown by the private companies in charge of parking lots that the police wanted to close down during the critical hours. They promptly accepted the suggestion made by the police. One reason may be that they did not make much money during these hours and they disliked their lots being used for illegal purposes.

Chairman of City Council

The chairman of the city council had some prior knowledge about the illegal cab operations, but had not considered them harmful. His opinion changed however, and he accepted the description conveyed by the police in a meeting where the project was presented to the council. In order to get support for the proposed measures from politicians representing the other parties, he invited them to a special meeting. Even though the most important measure – temporarily closing off part of the city from car traffic – was considered rather drastic, it was nonetheless accepted. The next step was to organize a meeting with the leaders of the local administration. The message was that they should cooperate and assist the police. The chairman learnt about the success of the project at later meetings with the police. He also spent some time with the police in the field to gain first hand knowledge. On the whole, he is positive towards taking part in crime preventive endeavors of this kind, but feels each initiative should be judged according to its own merits.

The Agent Representing the National Road Authority

Before he was approached by the project manager, the agent knew of the problem mainly through the local newspaper. As a father he had also warned his daughter about using illegal cabs and, as a precaution, he had offered to come and fetch her when needed. He thought that the police had difficulties in managing the problem by themselves, and reacted favorably when the project manager phoned him. But he wanted a description of the problem in writing. There were some internal discussions and disagreements as to whether the Road Authority should take part, but he argued that the Authority had an overall responsibility for the safety of all those using the roads. Getting rid of or decreasing the extent of illegal cab activities would serve to increase overall road safety. He was impressed by the presentation of the problem and by the measures suggested to reach a solution, although he thought that the initial proposal was too far-reaching. The Road Authority also had to consider the flow of traffic passing through the city. In the agent's opinion, the cooperation with the police and the local engineer's service functioned well when the actual measures were implemented.

Leader of the Local Engineers' Service

The leader had regular discussions with the local police to exchange information and to solve possible problems. He knew about the POP-project before he was called to the meeting by the chairman of the city council. The engineers were asked to contribute but also to come up with counter arguments – if there were any. There were some costs involved in putting up signs and barriers in order to close off the streets, but he managed to cover these costs from within his own budget. He also joined some of the discussions with the National Road Authority, and before they finally agreed to take action, was somewhat disturbed by what he considered their initially not very helpful attitude.

The Agent Representing the Bus Company

The agent from the bus company primarily knew about the problem through information he received from the bus drivers. They had seen a lot of activity by illegal cab drivers in the area. However, it was not a problem for the drivers or the bus company. The police had repeatedly tried to do something about it, but in his opinion, had failed since the means available to them were not adequate. He reacted positively when he was approached by the project manager. The problem was greater and more severe than he had realized. He was impressed by the thoroughness of the work and responded favorably to the suggestions of involving the bus companies in the solution to the problem. To move the bus stand to the centrally situated location was something they had wanted for a long time. And it was a good idea to start with a night-bus service on Friday nights, but it had to be profitable. The money that was put up by the county administration to cover potential losses made it possible for them to introduce a night-bus service for a trial period. The company had been forced to accept that there were not enough customers, however, which meant that they had to close down this particular service at the end of the trial period.

Chairman of the Local Taxi Drivers Association

The problem of illegal taxicabs had been present for a considerable period of time and had gotten worse over the last few years. The association had complained to the police on several occasions, but was disappointed by the lack of response and results. The contact taken by the project manager signified something new and positive. He was impressed by the thoroughness of the description of the problem and the ensuing analysis. Their own contribution consisted in making taxi services more readily available. The situation improved dramatically following the implementation of the measures, which is something the taxi cab drivers can still experience when working weekend nights. The chairman praised the police for what they had achieved.

The way things developed within the National Road Authority is a good illustration of one of Ken Pease's (this volume) main points. In order to get the intended implementer to cooperate, it is imperative for them to find reasons for taking action that are within their range of activities. Once this occurred in the current instance, the doubts about participating vanished.

Factors Supporting Problem-oriented Initiatives

The key question in this context is: given the less-than-encouraging experiences, how is it that the process of implementation was so successful in this case? Scott (this volume) has suggested a number of factors that characterize successful problem-oriented policing projects. These factors and the form they took in this particular project are described below and summarized in Table 2.

1. *Characteristics, skills, and actions of project managers*

   The ultimate initiative for starting the project was taken by the commissioner. An able project manager was appointed, known to be ambitious in his work and with an open and outgoing style. A senior researcher was engaged as an advisor. The commissioner took a strong personal interest and was continually informed of progress. The advisor chose to work closely with the project manager, but only to provide active support and advice when he felt these to be necessary.

2. *Resources*

   Following a recommendation from the advisor, resources were allocated to the project to ensure that the project manager would have enough time to work with the project. A steering group was appointed in which the commissioner and his deputy were members. Developments within the project were reported to the steering group and proposals for measures were explained to and decided upon by them.

Table 2: Factors Associated with Implementation Success

1.	Characteristics, skills, and actions of project managers	• Project manager was outgoing, confident and ambitious. • The chief of police was personally involved in the project. • Project manager had experienced researcher as advisor.
2.	Resources	• Internal resources in police budget were set aside to ensure that project manager could devote time needed to fulfill all tasks in SARA-process. • The project manager was responsible for the success of the project and reported to a steering group in which the chief of police and his deputy were members. Important decisions were taken in the group.
3.	Support and cooperation external to the police agency	• Local mass media covered the project positively. • Proposal for measures was presented to and positively received by city council. • Existing organizations had capacity and mandate to implement proposed measures and reacted favorable to these proposals.
4.	Evidence	• Great efforts were put into the scanning phase in particular, to produce compelling evidence about the problem, creating a foundation for the analysis and proposed measures.
5.	Complexity of implementation	• Even though many organizations were involved, the implementation of each measure was not complicated.

3. Support and cooperation external to the police agency

One reason for starting the project was a local mass media report of a serious crime committed during a ride provided by an illegal cab driver. The local police chief informed a journalist about the plans for a problem-oriented project aimed at reducing illegal cab activities. A favorable article was published in the local newspaper. The project manager and the police chief were also given the opportunity to present the project and the proposed measures to a meeting of the city council. The response was appreciative and the positive reception was transmitted to the relevant bodies within the local administration, implying that they should be supportive. On the whole, the proposals lay within the organizations' mandates and with one exception they were not costly. This exception involved subsidies from the county council to the bus companies to start night-bus operations on Friday nights. This part of the negotiation process was conducted by the police chief.

4. *Evidence*

   In order to create a firm foundation for the whole project, particular care had been put into the scanning phase. A variety of methods were used to collect data to identify, specify and describe the problems resulting from the phenomenon at issue. This resulted in a thorough description of the problem, which simplified both the analysis and the search for effective measures. The consequence was that there was a solid case to present.

5. *Complexity of implementation*

   Seen as a whole the set of measures introduced appear rather complex. However, when broken down into individual measures, most were in fact rather simple to implement for each of the organizations involved.

Thus, when looked at from an organizational perspective, most of the factors associated with a positive outcome for a problem-oriented project were present.

Other aspects are more associated with the measures per se. The characteristics of measures associated with successful implementation are described by Clarke and Eck (2003, step 39). They argue that the probability of getting measures implemented is higher when measures:

- Are aimed at close causes, rather than distant.

- Use mechanisms that are clearly stated.

- Are sustainable and don't require supervision.

- Are not costly.

- Are not technically complex.

- Do not take much coordination between organizations.

The correspondence of these characteristics with the measures employed in the project is shown in Table 3 and discussed below.

Table 3: Characterization of the Measures Employed in Terms of Factors Affecting the Likelihood of Implementation

Measure	Distance to cause	Mechanism	Sustainable	Costs	Technical complexity	Coordination between organizations
Blocking off pick-up areas used by illegal cabs.	Close	Clear	Yes	Moderate	Small	Little
Making buses and taxis more accessible.	Close	Clear	Yes	Small	Small	Little
Introducing night-bus service on Friday nights.	Close	Clear	No	Large	Not relevant	Little
Introducing stiffer consequences for those caught driving illegal cabs.	Distant	Clear	Yes	Small	Not relevant	Not relevant
Informing suspected illegal cab drivers about possible consequences of providing illegal taxi services.	Distant	Clear	No	Small	Small	Little
Informing the public about the risks involved and about legal alternatives.	Distant	Clear	No	Small	Small	Little

Distance to Cause

The measures "Blocking off pick-up areas used by illegal cabs," "Making buses and taxis more accessible," and "Introducing night-bus service on Friday nights" are close to the "cause" in both a temporal and spatial sense. In the analysis of the problem, the imbalance between the availability of illegal versus legal means of transport was considered to be one of the main causes of the illegal taxicab activity. The reason that the measures "Introducing stiffer consequences for those caught driving illegal cabs," "Informing suspected illegal cab drivers about possible consequences of providing illegal taxi services," and "Informing the public about the risks involved and about legal alternatives" were classified as being distant from the cause, is that punishment and measures aiming at changing attitudes produce their effects indirectly through the fear of future negative consequences associated with the illegal acts or via a change of mind-set.

Mechanisms

All the mechanisms that are supposed to produce the desired outcome are clear cut and it is easy to see the links between the measures and the desired results. Even so, their possible effectiveness is another and, ultimately, an empirical question.

Sustainability

"Blocking off pick-up areas used by illegal cabs" and "Making buses and taxis more accessible" are sustainable since these measures were results of physical changes (moving barriers and signs, creating a new taxicab stand). The introduction of a night-bus service on Friday nights was dependent upon subsidies from the county administration for a trial period. When this period ended, the service would have continued if there had been enough passengers to make the service cost-effective. The demand for this particular service was not sufficient, however, and it was terminated after the trial period. The need for this service had been overestimated. The leaflets and some of the other printed information that were used to inform potential passengers and suspected illegal cab drivers were supposed to be distributed by uniformed police in the field when they encountered suspect activities or when they were asked about means of transport. With measures of this kind, the interest will usually fade once the novelty of a project wanes. (This suspicion was confirmed during follow-up field observations.

The material that had been produced was not used.) This is why these measures have been classified as not sustainable. The same holds for posters that were put up. After a while they disappeared.

Costs

The costs of "Blocking off pick-up areas used by illegal cabs" and "Making buses and taxis more accessible" were considered moderate, since they could be accommodated within the budgets of the respective organizations. To organize the night-bus service on Friday nights, the bus companies asked for subsidies to cover possible losses. The county administration set aside the equivalent of about $40,000 (USD) – a sum which in this context is considered to be relatively large – for the trial period. When this money was used up, the service was terminated. The costs for administering the stiffer penalties are regarded as small. When the police officers encountered a case of illegal taxicab driving, it did not take much longer to put these penalties into effect. And the penalties did not involve much more paperwork for the police lawyers to administer. The translation of information aimed at suspected foreign illegal cab drivers was undertaken free of charge by a cab driver with language skills. The costs for printing the informational material were shared between the organizations involved, resulting in a low level of costs for each partner.

Technical Complexity

The level of technical complexity was low for the measures that had a physical character – making and moving signs and barriers. The leaflets and the other printed matter were produced by the project manager more or less by himself. He used widely available, user friendly software and equipment that the police already had at their disposal. In sum, the measures were not very technically complex or complicated.

Cooperation among Organizations

Some of the measures were carried out by organizations that were used to carrying out similar activities. The implementation occurred with advice and cooperation from the police. For other measures, a number of meetings were required to reach agreement, but once these measures were decided upon, no further cooperation was needed. None of the measures required continuous collaboration between different organizations in order to be put into effect.

On the whole, on the basis of these criteria, most of the measures end up on the positive side of the scales in relation to the question of effective implementation.

CONCLUSION

There is no single factor that might explain why the process of implementation was successful in this particular case. However, there are a number of coinciding factors that in all likelihood are crucial. The first set of factors is connected to the project, the way it was organized and how it was carried out. One vital element was the substantial interest shown by the police chief. An able and motivated project manager with time enough to concentrate on the tasks was also a key factor. Even if he was inexperienced in the practise of problem-oriented policing, given guidance from the advisor, he was able to present a solid case. Right from the start, there was a spirit of cooperation between the police and the local community – a spirit which was strengthened as a consequence of the success of the project. To achieve acceptance for the more far-reaching measures, both local politicians and the local administration were informed by the chairman of the city council, and the administration was encouraged to cooperate. Most of the discussions relating to the measures and the negotiations about their implementation went well. When it comes to use of leverage, the forms of leverage employed were on the mild side. The use of more or less formal requests, based on the scanning and analysis phases, proved sufficient. With only minor exceptions the measures fell within the repertoires of the routine activities of the organizations involved. One crucial exception was the cooperation required from a national organization, and it took several meetings and discussions to get this actor to accept the proposals. But once the person representing this organization found a suitable motive that could be made to fit within their specific agenda, they too joined in. Furthermore, and again with just one exception, the measures were not costly. The mechanisms utilized were logical, easy to understand and, arguably, the most effective ones, sustainable and close to the causes of the problem. Taken together, most of theses factors are favourable for successful implementation and could thus explain the success of the case discussed.

To end by stating the obvious, namely that there is absolutely no way of guaranteeing the successful implementation of crime preventive measures, and that there are seldom any short cuts, is not very helpful. As in most other cases, getting things done requires hard and well planned work in combination with insights into the working psyche of persons operating within the organizations involved.

Address correspondence to: Professor Johannes Knutsson, Norwegian Police University College, Pb 5027 Majorstua, 0301 Oslo, Norway; e-mail: johannes.knutsson@phs.no

NOTES

1. The account is based on personal communications from a representative of the police and an employee from the local city administration who attended the meeting.
2. It is difficult to provide a fair opinion about projects one has been involved in oneself. The project became one of the Herman Goldstein Award finalists in 2004, which suggests that it was a properly conducted problem-oriented policing project.

REFERENCES

Ahlberg, J. (1992). Bedrägeri. In J. Ahlberg (Ed.) *Brottsutvecklingen 1991*. Brottsförebyggande rådet. Brå-rapport 1992:2. Stockholm: Allmänna förlaget.

Björ, J., Knutsson, J., & Kühlhorn, E. (1992). The celebration of Midsummer Eve in Sweden – A study in the art of preventing collective disorder. *Security Journal*, 3(3), 169–174.

Clarke, R. V. G. (1997). *Situational crime prevention: Successful case studies, 2nd ed.* Monsey, NY: Criminal Justice Press.

Clarke, R. V. G., & Cornish, D. (2000). Rational choice. In R. Paternoster & R. Bachman (Eds.), *Explaining crime and criminals: Essays in contemporary criminological theory*. Los Angeles: Roxbury.

Clarke, R. V. G., & Eck, J. (2003). *Become a problem-solving analyst*. London: Jill Dando Institute of Crime Science.

Clarke, R. V. G., & Felson, M. (1993). Introduction: Criminology, routine activity and rational choice. In R. V. G. Clarke & M. Felson (Eds.), *Routine activity and rational choice*. Advances in Criminological Theory, vol. 5. New Brunswick: Transaction Publishers.

Cornish, D. B., & Clarke, R. V. G. (1985). Modeling offenders' decisions: A framework for research and policy. In M. Tonry & N. Morris (Eds.), *Crime and justice: An annual review of research*, vol. 6. Chicago: University of Chicago Press.

Cornish, D. B., & Clarke, R. V. G. (2004). Opportunities, precipitators and criminal decisions: A reply to Wortley's critique of situational prevention. In M. J. Smith & D. B. Cornish (Eds.), *Theory for practice in situational crime prevention*, vol. 16. Crime Prevention Studies. Monsey: Criminal Justice Press.

Dolmén, L., & Lindström, P. (1991). *Skola, livsstil och brott – Ungdomar i åtta Stockholmsskolor*. Brå-rapport 1991:3. Stockholm: Allmänna förlaget.

Goldstein, H. (1997). The pattern of emerging tactics for shifting the ownership of prevention strategies in the current wave of change in policing: Their implications for both environmental criminology and the police. Paper presented at 6th ECCA seminar, Oslo, Norway.

Hopkins Burke, R. (2001). *An introduction to criminological theory*. Uffculme, Devon, UK: Willan Publishing.

Knutsson, J. (Ed.). (2003). *Problem-oriented policing: From innovation to mainstream*. Crime Prevention Studies, vol. 15. Monsey, NY: Criminal Justice Press.

Knutsson, J. (1987). Midsommarfirandet på Öland 1987. *Brottsförebyggande rådets tidskrift Apropå*. 4:9-20.

Knutsson, J., & Kühlhorn, E. (1980). *När checkbedrägerierna försvann*. Brottsförebyggande rådet. Rapport 1980:4. Stockholm: Liber förlag.

Knutsson, J., & Kühlhorn, E. (1997). Macro measures against crime. The example of check forgeries. In R. V. G. Clarke (Ed.), *Situational crime prevention. Successful case studies* (2nd ed., pp. 113–121). Monsey, NY: Criminal Justice Press.

Knutsson, J., & Søvik, K-E. (2005). *Problemorienterat polisarbete i teori och praktik*. Polishögskolan 2005:1. Solna: Polishögskolan.

Martens, P. (1992). *Familj uppväxt och brott*. Brottsförebyggande rådet. Brå-rapport 1992:1. Stockholm: Allmänna förlaget.

Moore, M. (1995). Learning while doing. Linking knowledge to policy in the development of community policing and violence prevention in the United States. In P-O. Wikström, R. V. G. Clarke & J. McCord (Eds.), *Integrating crime preventive strategies: Propensity and opportunity*. BRÅ-report 1995:5. Stockholm: National Council for Crime Prevention Sweden. Allmänna förlaget.

Pawson, R., & Tilley, N. (1997). *Realistic evaluation*. London: SAGE.

Persson, C. (1991). *Utan omsvep*. Stockholm: Norstedt.

Ringman, K. (1997). *Brottsförebyggande åtgärder i en förort – teori och praktik*. Stockholm: Kriminologiska institutionen.

Vestfold Police District (2004). *Gypsy cabs in Tønsberg – a case for Problem Oriented Policing*. Accessed Nov. 28, 2005 at: http://www.popcenter.org/Library/Goldstein/2004/04-35(F).pdf

Weisburd, D., & Eck, J. (2004). What can police do to reduce crime, disorder, and fear? *The Annals of the American Academy of Political and Social Science, 594*, 42–65.

Wikström, P-O. (1991). *Sociala problem och trygghet*. Brottsförebyggande rådet. Brå-rapport 1991:5. Stockholm: Allmänna förlaget.

Joining up the Pieces: What Central Agencies Need to Do to Support Effective Local Crime Prevention

by

Peter Homel
Australian Institute of Criminology[1]

Abstract: *An analysis of the processes used for implementing the U.K.'s Crime Reduction Programme, together with some recent crime prevention efforts in Australia and New Zealand, demonstrates that many of the problems found in the implementation of local crime prevention projects are the result of a number of common and frequently repeated errors in the way that central and local agencies relate to each other in the planning, delivery and evaluation of initiatives. Some of these errors include the use of centrally defined crime targets to establish priorities; short-term, non-recurrent project funding; project management failure resulting from too many simultaneous interventions; a failure to identify and plug gaps in implementation skill and capacity; and a "hands-off" approach to implementation support. It is argued that a stronger process of active and ongoing engagement between central and local agencies is necessary to overcome this problem. The model proposed treats the policy and program delivery chain as a single integrated system rather than a fragmented process with disconnected ownership and responsibility. In other words, it promotes the equal importance of vertical policy and service delivery integration and support (i.e., through all layers of government and the community) as well as the more common horizontal cross-agency integration (e.g., at the local, regional or central levels).*

Crime Prevention Studies, volume 20 (2006), pp. 111–138.

FINDING THE PIECES

"In recent years we (i.e., Government agencies) have proceeded to raise the program delivery standard and then put amateurs in charge of delivery (i.e.,, local community partnerships)."

These are the words of a senior policy and research manager involved in the development and implementation of a number of major British initiatives directed at the reduction and prevention of crime. He was responding to questions about why one of the best formulated and well resourced efforts for achieving a significant and sustained reduction in crime, the British Crime Reduction Programme, had encountered such enormous implementation problems – to the point that it was on the verge of being considered a failure.

His perspective is that of a person working in a head office or a "central agency" as they are often known. However, his remark reflects a strong insight into the practical challenges of local program implementation. What his comment highlights is the level of disconnect between the expectations, capacities and skills of people designing programs at the central level and those involved in program management and delivery at the local or regional level. Centrally, researchers and policy makers are working to develop ever more sophisticated policies and program initiatives based on the principles of "joined-up" governance (explained below) and evidence-based policy, while those at the local and regional level are struggling to put these initiatives into practice in frequently fragmented and resource poor communities with a minimum of training and support in the new disciplines of performance-based management and accountability.

Unfortunately, the insight apparent in his remark continues to prove elusive to many of those at the central agency level with responsibility for the development of policies and programs for the prevention and reduction of crime. As will be seen, crime prevention programs from London to Los Angeles or in Sydney or Wellington consistently report remarkably similar problems with local implementation.

The purpose of this chapter is to look behind this experience in order to find solutions that can be used to overcome these difficulties with future local crime prevention programs. However, the focus is not exclusively on local initiatives. Nor does it focus on initiatives that address single crime types (e.g., gun-related violence, burglary or fraud) or particular strategic approaches (e.g., community based or situational crime prevention).

Rather, it chooses to look at the systems and processes that are employed to design and implement crime prevention programs as a whole. This means examining the roles and functions fulfilled by central agencies and all the intermediate policy and program layers through to the local level – and back again. The focus is on the way that crime prevention work is transacted at different levels of the program delivery chain and how these processes can be improved.

Particular attention is given to the recent experience of the U.K.'s Crime Reduction Programme (Homel et al., 2004a). However, examples are also drawn from crime prevention initiatives and programs in the USA, Australia and New Zealand. Furthermore, the practical examples discussed are not limited to crime prevention alone. Illustrations are also drawn from the community based drug harm prevention field as well as urban and community renewal.

But before we can turn to generating the sorts of solutions that are needed, we have to make sure that we find all the pieces. Or, in terms of the opening observation: what level has the program delivery bar been raised to, why this has happened and what does it mean for program delivery, particularly at the local level?

The first part of this task is to develop an understanding of some of the new forms of governance that now apply to program design and management. In particular, what is meant by the notion of "joined-up" or "whole-of-community/government" programs? Then there is a need to appreciate the practical implications of the modern commitment to the use of "partnership" arrangements for the achievement of shared outcomes, particularly in terms of project and resource management and questions of accountability and attributing multiple outcomes to mixed sector interventions. The third element is coming to grips with the challenges involved in the process of translating the growing bodies of research evidence about effective crime practice into effective on ground action.

Overarching all of this is a need to design policies and programs that are able to support a process for ongoing organisational and individual learning and change as well as the adoption of new and innovative practices so that lessons about "what works" are able to be effectively identified and incorporated into new initiatives.

But this is getting too far ahead. First let us turn to the environment in which crime prevention work occurs and the new standards of governance that are being applied.

WHAT IS THE MODERN ENVIRONMENT FOR CRIME PREVENTION?

There now exists a much better understanding of the causes of criminal behaviour. In particular we have been able to develop some better insights into the interactions among the social, developmental, situational and opportunistic aspect of crime. For example, while social deprivation is recognised as potentially contributing to the likelihood of crime involvement as young people develop, we also recognise that socially deprived communities can also generate greater opportunities to offend. So opportunity-reduction measures alone are likely to be less effective alone than if they are combined with effective and social-developmental interventions, and vice-versa (Homel, 2005).

With this better understanding of the causes of crime we have also been able improve our appreciation of the type and mix of measures that can be used to bring about sustained reduction and long-term prevention of crime, particularly in the use of situational crime prevention measures.

Furthermore, we also have come to recognise that the interventions that make up these new programs are likely to have a greater chance of success if they are designed and undertaken as a package of closely linked and coordinated measures. In this way the possible perverse or contradictory effects of separate single measures can be planned for and designed out prior to implementation.

A number of examples of how this sort of approach can operate effectively can be found around public health partnerships directed at violence reduction (Roussos and Fawcett, 2000). By way of illustration: health workers, police, local government authorities, bar managers and the wider community all have an interest in reducing and preventing the incidence of alcohol-related violence around licensed premises. Health agencies will be concerned at a number of negative health outcomes, including the need to treat injury resulting from alcohol-fuelled violence; police will want it reduced because they inevitably get called in to break up the fights involving intoxicated bar patrons; the local government authority will have public amenity and planning concerns related to the impact on neighbouring business and residents; and the concerns of bar managers will include impacts on business profitability, potential liability associated with injury to staff and other patrons, as well as the risk of action by liquor regulatory authorities if problems persist.

As can be seen, each interested party will have different motivations for seeking to reduce and prevent the problem. They will also have a different view about what measures will be acceptable and/or effective. So any effective action needs a consensus view about the nature of the problem and the range of possible solutions. Typically a viable response strategy will entail a mix of situational and social responses, frequently built around the use of the regulatory measures controlling the overall context for the sale of liquor in bars. So, for example, responses may include the training of staff in the responsible service of alcohol, changes to policing practice such that they take a more problem-oriented approach, the education by health authorities of patrons regarding their risks and responsibilities through signage etc., and variations in planning and business operation controls, such as restricting opening hours in order to limit the potential for problems at peak times.

But unless these measures are introduced in a collaborative and joined up way, each has the potential to exacerbate rather than fix the problem. For example, more aggressive policing in the absence of patron education or responsible service measures may result in more frequent confrontation between police and intoxicated patrons and/or liquor outlet managers, leading to more incidents of violence, and so on. Education in the absence of regulatory enforcement will be less effective.

This understanding of the need for collaborative policy development and program planning and delivery has now become a key feature of the way crime reduction and prevention efforts are organised.

However, this collaborative approach is not unique to crime prevention. Rather, it is an example of a more general shift in public administration away from a command and control mode of governance and towards governance through multiple stakeholders working together to deliver integrated solutions to social problems across sectors and tiers of government. Within Australia this sort of approach is most commonly described as the "whole of government" or "whole of community" approach to crime prevention. In parts of the U.S.A. it is known as "networked government," while in the U.K. the approach is popularly known as "joined-up government" (Lee and Woodward, 2002).

These joined-up government approaches require a high level of policy, program and organisational integration to the point of joint or collective action and shared or mutual responsibility for performance and outcomes. In a recent report by the Institute of Public Affairs Australia (IPAA) this situation was described as "organisational fusion" (IPAA, 2002).

Because the logic of the joined-up approach is built on the recognition that the causes of crime and their solutions are complex and multi-faceted, the joined-up approach also requires that crime prevention action be a coordinated effort of many agencies in partnership with community and business groups.

Organising to implement a joined-up program has significant practical implications for how normal business is transacted. Many existing processes may need to be changed, or at least adapted. Some important areas can include:

- Pooled budgets need to be established. Often in this situation one agency will become the designated "banker" for a program;

- Partnership arrangements need to be negotiated and established. They do not just happen automatically. For example, non-government/voluntary sector, private sector, other levels of government such as local government may come together in a collaborative arrangement to share expertise, skills and resources as well as sharing the risk associated with implementing an innovative program;

- Relationships between the service provider and client will often need to be revised. Many conventional program delivery models conceive of the client as a passive recipient of services. Joined-up or whole of community models generally seek to establish a relationship with the client that sees them defining priorities for action and resource deployment;

- Co-ordination of service delivery and tendering with partner criteria may need to be developed. Conventional business models for service delivery operate most comfortably with single service agencies clearly identified for the delivery of specific services. Partnership models recognise the economic value in different agencies coming together to coordinate and share the delivery of services that might, for example, be directed to a single family unit or community as a way of improving both effectiveness and efficiency;

- Addressing integrated planning and triple bottom line analysis (i.e., assessing economic, environmental and social impacts). A simple example of this for crime prevention is the use of a measure designed to improve natural surveillance of a location or site by clearing foliage and vegetation around a dwelling or public space. However, while the crime prevention outcome may be achieved by clearing the foliage, the overall social amenity of a location may be reduced and the environmental qualities may also be degraded;

- The undertaking of innovative community consultation, engagement and joint management arrangements;

- The development and implementation of joint databases and customer intake and referral mechanisms; and,

- Coming up with viable and meaningful joint performance measures and indicators (IPAA, 2002).

All of this implies that the adoption of a joined-up approach to crime prevention requires thorough on going planning across the entire program delivery process. It also means that the policy development and program implementation process must be seen as a single integrated system rather than a series of discrete or loosely connected parts able to operate in isolation.

WORKING IN "PARTNERSHIP"

As suggested above, the use of "partnership" arrangements is frequently seen as an integral component of the operation of joined-up approaches. Under the partnership model, service provision is not viewed in terms of the core functions and responsibilities of separate agencies and interest groups, but in terms of how to best organise and run services to achieve those goals, regardless of where the service is sourced from, in order to achieve shared goals outcomes.

However there is a great deal of confusion over what the term "partnership" means in practice. The term is used widely to describe local structures such as for planning, coordinating and delivering local crime prevention initiatives. But there is no one form that is seen as being most effective or appropriate in all circumstances (e.g., see a recent report by the Joseph Rountree Foundation, 2003).

Numerous definitions exist regarding what it means to be in a "partnership" arrangement within the public sector. For example, Bennington and Cummane (1999) list a number of elements that will be present in a successful partnership arrangement. These will include commitment; equity; trust; mutual goals/objectives; collaboration over implementation; continuous evaluation; and timely communication and responsiveness. Brinkerhoff (2002) emphasises the need for a balance between mutuality (e.g., equality in decision making, joint accountability, mutual trust and respect, as well as jointly agreed purposes and values) and the specific organisational identity and features of partner agencies that both add value to the process and make each agency indispensable to others.

The bulk of attention in how to get partnership models operational has focused on the co-ordination and collaboration of local services within a regional and local context. As has been pointed out in a recent review of the experience of integrated governance approaches in Australia (IPAA, 2002:13), improved *co-ordination* is often regarded as the prime solution to government problems.

However, other research has demonstrated that without a clear and coherent plan and capacity for active technical support at the central level even the best local action is likely to fall short of the goal (Homel et al., 2004a). As well as this, it is clear that functional inter-agency agreements among central agencies are also necessary in order to maximise local and regional collaboration. These partnership arrangements need to flow both horizontally (i.e., across agencies) and vertically (i.e., from the centre to the local and regional level) if they are to be effective at promoting joined-up action in practice.

This does not mean that the relationships within any partnership arrangements will always be equal. The nature of the power relationships among each agency involved in the partnership will be a product of what value they can add to the achievement of the joint outcomes. For example, at times it may be appropriate for a regional manager to assume leadership of an initiative, as a result of being best placed to lever the necessary resources or most effectively to influence the policy process. In other circumstances, a local authority may be most appropriate as it has access to the most relevant resources. In other situations it may be the police, a community or voluntary organisation, a local business group, or another government agency.

However, without a functioning partnership arrangement based on the principles of integrated governance, this form of flexible organisation will not be able to occur.

ATTEMPTING TO JOIN UP THE PIECES

The British Crime Reduction Programme

> *"The design of programs like the Crime Reduction Programme is based on wrong assumptions about how business is transacted at a*

> *local level and leads to excessively high estimations of the general sophistication of local project managers."* Key stakeholder interview comment from Crime Reduction Program review (Homel et al., 2004)

Crime Reduction Programme (CRP) was a three-year £400 million cross-government commitment to achieving a sustained reduction in crime. It was described as "the biggest single investment in an evidence-based approach to crime reduction which has ever taken place in any country" (Home Office, 1999:3). Mind you, this needs to be seen in the context of criminal justice system that was already expending around $13 billion per year on existing services. However, while other countries were still largely focusing on pilot projects and fragmented crime reduction efforts, the U.K. did attempt to convert many years of accumulated crime reduction evidence into a program to trial some potentially innovative new practices (Goldblatt and Lewis, 1998).

The CRP was to be an investment in crime reduction initiatives that showed promise (based on existing evidence), with subsequent evaluation of these initiatives to determine whether that promise was realised in fact. Successful initiatives were to become part of mainstream practice. Research and evaluation personnel were to work hand-in-glove with policy and resource managers to ensure that successful initiatives flourished and that necessary changes were made to those programs that were shown to be less effective. As a result, crime would be reduced along with the estimated £50 billion annual cost of crime to the U.K. community.

The objectives of the CRP were to achieve a sustained reduction in crime, improve and mainstream knowledge of best practice, and maximise the implementation of cost-effective crime reduction activity. The program was intended to contribute to crime reduction by ensuring that resources were allocated to where they would achieve greatest impact.

The program was developed as 20 specific, but linked, initiatives of varying scale organised around five broad themes:

1. Working with families, children and schools to prevent young people becoming offenders of the future;

2. Tackling crime in communities, particularly high-volume crime such as domestic burglary;

3. Developing products and systems that are resistant to crime;

4. More effective sentencing practices; and,

5. Working with offenders to ensure that they do not re-offend.

These themes involved innovative action by all parts of the criminal justice system as well as the development of new modes of operation and partnership working. The CRP was designed to operate within a multi-agency, mixed-service sector framework across every level of government in England and Wales. This meant encompassing action at a national, regional and local level. The initiatives that made up the program ranged from broad-based issues of community concern (e.g., violence against women, youth inclusion), to specific types of crime (e.g., domestic burglary), and to special and difficult populations (e.g., offenders). The variety of strategies employed was quite extensive, ranging from situational measures (particularly for addressing outcomes such as reducing burglary and developing crime-resistant products), to developmental and early intervention measures, as would obviously be most appropriate for the first theme.

By the end of its three year cycle in 2002, the CRP had implemented more than 1,500 separate initiatives that were managed by a variety of agencies at all levels of government, from Whitehall to local government and community-level partnerships.

The Home Office was the lead agency for the program as a whole, but funding was not provided to the Home Office purely for its own discretionary purposes. It was to act as a "banker" for the other government agencies who were also participating in the CRP.

There were very clear ideas from the outset about how the CRP should work. It was to accumulate the best available research-based evidence for approaches to "what works" from any area that might contribute to the achievement of crime reduction outcomes. This knowledge was to be organised in terms of whether the initiatives were: (a) promising but so far unproven; (b) based on stronger evidence, but confined to limited research settings or derived from non-criminal justice areas (e.g., health or education); or (c) proven in terms of small-scale initiatives and therefore ready for larger-scale implementation. On the basis of this knowledge, a portfolio of viable evidence-based initiatives was to be developed, with sufficient resources budgeted for the effective implementation and evaluation of these.

Apart from the Home Office, a wide range of other government agencies was to be engaged in the delivery of these initiatives. Additionally, much of the delivery of local level CRP sub-programs was to be undertaken by other agencies via a competitive bidding process for CRP program monies. Alongside the bidding process, a comprehensive evaluation and assessment strategy was to be developed.

It was intended that the implementation of initiatives would occur progressively via a series of funding rounds. The initiatives would be reviewed, refined and further developed during implementation using program evaluation feedback. The overall learning from the initial (three-year) implementation phase would be accumulated and disseminated, with successful initiatives moved into mainstream funding, while unsupported or cost-ineffective strategies would be withdrawn.

As can be seen from this program logic, the CRP was attempting simultaneously to implement and review a complex array of initiatives with varying levels of evidence to support them. Further, it was seeking to determine which initiatives were individually strong and cost-effective as well as assessing the best mix of strategies for maximising crime reduction impacts. It was also aiming to learn about sustainability, both in terms of the impact of initiatives and how they might be transferred to mainstream programs and continued over time.

Most importantly, the CRP was also designed to operate in a joined up way across government agencies at the central and regional level and in partnership with local government and community groups at the local level. In other words, it was attempting to manage the implementation of a complex innovative program with multiple interventions and outcomes simultaneously in a vertical direction (i.e., from a central policy level through a regional structure to local delivery) and horizontally (i.e., across diverse central agencies).

Given these ambitious aims and the need to implement new forms of governance, it is unsurprising that from the outset the CRP experienced a range of implementation challenges. For example, by the end of the CRP's first three years the program's implementation experience was one of significant program delays, underspending of funds and other frustrations that had impacted on the program's overall viability and capacity to meet its stated goals. Seventeen percent of the allocated budget remained unspent and some program areas had still not started or were only just commencing.

Within one program area it was found that nearly half of the projects had experienced some significant implementation problems. Of these, a third could be said to have experienced very serious problems – to the point that the money had been spent and the programs had not occurred (Homel et al., 2004a).

The report on the review of the implementation of the CRP prepared for the Home Office provides a detailed set of explanations for why these problems occurred (Homel et al., 2004a). However, some of the most important included:

- Difficulties in finding, recruiting and retaining suitably qualified and skilled staff;

- Generally inadequate technical and strategic advice and guidance from the centre (i.e., the Home Office) and the regions; and,

- Inadequate levels of project management competence and skill, particularly in financial and resource management.

The point is that even with a significant financial and political commitment, in combination with a well developed evidence base about what works best for crime reduction, only relatively modest innovation and change was achieved.

HOW THE CRIME REDUCTION PROGRAMME MANAGED LOCAL DELIVERY

Structurally, the CRP was a centrally designed and managed initiative. While it was expected to contribute significantly to the achievement of a series of national crime reduction targets, as spelled out in the Home Office's Public Sector Agreement (PSA), delivery was predominantly focused on local initiatives (Homel et al., 2004b).

The CRP operated within a multi-agency mixed service sector framework across every level of government in England and Wales. The program itself worked through a comprehensive array of separate but linked crime reduction initiatives, most of which were designed to be delivered locally.

However, the original design for the Crime Reduction Programme did not anticipate a major role for regional management. Rather, its business model reflected what could be described as a "franchise" approach. The concept of a "franchise" is most often associated with modern retailing. It is where a local retail or service outlet is individually owned (or owned by a separate company), but the product sold, the look and feel of the outlet, and the basic standards of service are centrally defined and complied with by the local outlet owner (i.e., franchisee). Obvious examples are small chain stores found in major shopping centres.

What is most important about the "franchise" model is that while some regional relationships may exist (and these are most often in the context of large transnational organisations), the strongest relationship is direct from the centre to the local service provider rather than through any regional management structure (Homel et al., 2004b).

However, the environment into which the CRP was launched was one in which improving local area and regional program delivery and policy co-ordination was a significant government priority. Key strategies of significance to the CRP included the strengthening of the Government Regional Offices in England (Cabinet Office 2000), the establishment of a Regional Co-ordination Unit within the Cabinet Office, and the continued development of the Local Strategic Partnerships structure (Johnson and Osborne, 2003).

Nine Regional Government Offices (RGOs) for England were first set up in 1994. Their purpose was to ensure coherence and add value to the policy development and delivery process. They brought together the English regional services for the following departments: Office of the Deputy Prime Minister; Department of Trade and Industry; Department for Education and Skills; Department for Transport; Department for Environment, Food and Rural Affairs; Home Office; Department for Culture, Media and Sport; Department of Health; and Department for Work and Pensions, as they were then known.

The Home Office had Directors in each of the RGOs. These Directors were responsible for crime reduction, drugs misuse, active community and race equality issues within their regions.

The Drugs Teams in RGOs were set up by the Home Office to support the delivery of the Government's drugs strategy at a regional level. The nine teams provided direct support and advice to all Drug Action Teams (DATs) in England. They worked with regional and sub-regional bodies to integrate issues into broader social programs.

The Home Office also had a Crime Reduction Team in each of the RGOs and the National Assembly for Wales. Each team was responsible for improving the performance of Crime and Disorder Reduction Partnerships (CDRPs) and administering Home Office funding programs in line with guidance and ensuring delivery of targets. They also promoted effective joint working of CDRPs and DATs to raise and improve joint delivery of crime and disorder and drugs agenda.

The government had also established the Regional Co-ordination Unit (RCU) as the corporate centre of the Government Office network in 2000, as an interdepartmental unit located in the Office of the Deputy Prime Minister. Together the RCU and RGOs aimed to simplify bureaucratic processes and add value to delivery through shared experience and best practice, bringing together key stakeholders and local partners, and providing a high quality service by combining skills in the RGOs at the local level with the co-ordination role of the RCU.

Local Strategic Partnerships (LSP) had been set up as a single non-statutory, multi-agency body, which matched local authority boundaries, with the aim of bringing together at a local level the different parts of the public, private, community and voluntary sectors. LSPs addressed deep-seated, multifaceted problems, requiring a range of responses from different bodies. Local partners working through a LSP were expected to take many of the major decisions about priorities and funding for their local area (DETR, 2001).

In addition, the passing of the Crime and Disorder Act (1998) formalised the establishment of local crime and disorder reduction partnerships among local government authorities, the police and other local agencies. This Act required the local crime and disorder reduction partnerships to undertake a local crime audit and to develop a strategic plan for reducing and preventing crime in their local communities. The Crime and Disorder Act, however, envisaged that resources for the implementation of these local crime reduction strategies would be found through the redirection and redeployment of existing resources. In other words, no additional resources (either financial or otherwise) were specifically directed towards supporting the implementation of the initiatives that were meant to flow from the local crime audits and strategic plans.

As can be seen, it was a complex bureaucratic and administrative environment in which the CRP was meant to operate. Not surprisingly, as the program began in April 1998, there was still quite a deal of confusion about who was responsible for what and how business was meant to be transacted.

THE CRP'S REGIONAL EXPERIENCE

> *"There were far too few people working centrally on the project's development and implementation and no consistent project management approach."* Key stakeholder interview comment from Crime Reduction Programme review (Homel et al., 2004)

The on-ground experience of the CRP's implementation was very mixed. In the early stages of the program's implementation, significant problems arose in relation to the differing expectations of the centre, the regional offices and local partnerships about a wide range of program management and implementation issues.

Critically, one of the most consistent references to program implementation problems was to the way in which the centre itself failed to develop an adequate capacity to recognise and support the ongoing and evolving needs of regional and local program implementation. This observation was a consistent one, regardless of whether they themselves were located centrally, regionally or locally (Homel et al., 2004b:12).

For example, debate quickly emerged about how long the project development and funding application processes could be expected to take and whose responsibility it was to overcome any difficulties. The evidence available through the CRP review suggests that much of this debate focused on whether the role of the Regional Crime Reduction Directors, and the regional teams that were developing under their management, was a purely administrative role or more of a support and development role (Homel et al., 2004a).

It appears that there was considerable confusion about the division of responsibilities for ensuring these difficulties were overcome. A number of interim and process reports from specific program evaluators also point to confusion over administrative, project management and accountability responsibilities.

This carried over into conflicts associated with project commencement delays once funding was provided. For example, in the case of the Round Two of the Reducing Burglary Initiative (a central CRP initiative), funding meant to be available for 12 months became available with only eight or nine months of the program funding period remaining. Local projects were then expected to telescope the complex development and staff recruitment processes into this truncated time frame.

Yet at the centre, the perception was that local projects were simply being slow in the uptake of the initiative and that regional staff were not acting quickly enough to intervene to support them. Regional teams, on the other hand, were unclear about whether they were in fact responsible for providing this assistance, as a separate support program contract had already been let with two non-government organisations, Crime Concern and National Association for the Care and Resettlement of Offenders (NA-CRO).

Another illustration of this confusion and frustration involved the management of bid processes over short periods interrupted by major public holidays (e.g., Targeted Policing Initiative Round 1 bids being called over the Christmas period). Many of these difficulties related as much to the inefficiencies inherent in a competitive bidding process being employed by the CRP, as inefficiencies in the way the processes were managed. However, they illustrate the sorts of conflicts and inefficiencies that inhibited the CRP's optimum performance.

The key stakeholder interviews and the survey of people involved in the CRP at the centre, regionally and locally, identified a variety of other sources of implementation difficulty.

All of this suggests that those at the centre (i.e., Home Office HQ) were largely "disengaged" from the reality of the implementation process. Centrally, staff numbers were small (initially only one senior civil servant and two policy staff were assigned directly to manage the implementation process),[2] and so the capacity to extend beyond a basic funding-management relationship was very limited. This lack of capacity proceeded to manifest itself in an increasing focus on the program's financial expenditure patterns at the expense of measuring outputs and performance and identifying emerging problems and responses.[3]

However, some specific sub-programs did receive significant development assistance while others did not (e.g., the Reducing Burglary Initiative benefited from a major development workshop held in late 1998). Unfortunately, this inconsistency of approach and lack of capacity to provide important ongoing support contributed to the development of a "support gap" in the implementation scheme that the regional offices increasingly came to be expected to fill. At the same time, the Regional Crime Reduction Directors and their teams had not been established with this role as a specific part of their brief, so the "support gap" effectively flowed further downstream to the local level.

Over all, what is particularly important about the above observations is that they run directly contrary to a long held view of conventional centre-regional-local relationships. This view argues that what is required for effective local delivery is minimal direct involvement from the centre. Under this conventional approach, it is the role of the centre to accumulate the evidence, formulate the policy (usually in the form of a broad strategic framework or guidance), and organise the necessary resources for action that are then passed to local or regional agencies for implementation and the delivery of outcomes. The centre then resumes a monitoring and reviewing role that may ultimately result in a revised policy or strategic framework, but never providing any direct assistance or other forms of intervention (see Lee and Woodward, 2002, for a discussion of these models.)

The experience of the Crime Reduction Programme has shown that this approach was inadequate. As one highly experienced person working closely with local communities put it: "the emphasis of Government on empowering local communities has led to a possible contradiction of messages and neglected the fact that local communities need to be assisted to make informed local decisions."

HAVE THE CRIME REDUCTION PROGRAMME'S IMPLEMENTATION PROBLEMS OCCURRED ELSEWHERE?

While the Crime Reduction Programme was clearly unique in many ways, it was not the only attempt at building an integrated whole of government approach to reducing and preventing significant community problems going on in the U.K. at the same time.

For example, similar themes of local implementation problems and performance failure also emerge in recent reviews of Local Strategic Partnerships (LSPs) and Neighbourhood Renewal programs in the U.K. (Geddes, 2003; Johnson and Osborne, 2003). More particularly, many of the CRP's experiences are echoed in the National Audit Office's review of the early experience of the New Deal for Communities program[4] (NAO, 2004).

These reviews highlight the range of significant difficulties in bridging the gap between a centrally designed and driven initiative and the new models of governance required effectively to implement these initiatives at a local and regional level. In other words, the CRP's difficulties were not unique.

However, while the review of the implementation of the CRP argues that it may have been possible to anticipate them and plan to overcome them within the British context (Homel et al., 2004), a bigger question is whether these experiences and problems are echoed in equivalent programs around the world.

The short answer is "yes," they are. One very instructive example comes from a comprehensive review of a key component of the New Zealand crime prevention program, the Safer Community Council (SCC) Network (NZ Ministry of Justice, 2003). This review reported that in spite a ten-year implementation experience "there is no discernible evidence that the SCCs are making a strong contribution to reducing crime in local communities" (p. 4). The explanation for this apparent failure was a lack of specific crime prevention expertise at the local level, inappropriate local co-ordination, and a breakdown of the relationship between central government and local stakeholders.

The report's recommendations for how the New Zealand Crime Prevention Unit (NZ CPU) should refocus its approach to working with communities to improve the effectiveness of crime prevention delivery at the local level echoes parallels many of the findings from the CRP implementation review. In particular, the report recommended that the NZ CPU should be able to offer communities the following services:

- *Leadership* – by setting the national crime prevention policy direction and effectively managing partnerships;

- *Operational support* – including facilitating access to appropriate crime prevention training, coaching, and contract management;

- *Resources* – funding, expertise, knowledge transfer and capacity building in the areas of crime prevention program management and governance;

- *Information* – provision of timely, accurate and relevant information on policy [through the Crime Reduction Strategy], crime data analysis, problem identification, program planning, and best practices; and,

- *Marketing* – advocacy to [Government] Ministers on behalf of SCCs. (NZ Ministry of Justice, 2003:7).

Across the Tasman Sea, the Australian experience of local crime prevention implementation has been remarkably similar, although unlike New Zealand and Britain, Australia's federal system has meant that the bulk of program delivery has been the responsibility of state and territory governments.

The existence of this third layer of government, between the national and local government structures, has had an interesting impact on the development and delivery of crime prevention work in Australia. One effect has been to shorten the distance between the policy and program development process being undertaken by the central agencies and the local delivery agencies, which are typically regional branches of government authorities or community-based agencies. However, in practice this potential benefit has been largely negated by the existence of overly complex bureaucratic processes and a lack of consistent policy and strategic direction, both at the state/territory and federal level (Homel, 2005).

As observed by Cameron and Laycock (2002:330), while the rhetoric of local delivery is consistent with best practice, the reality of what actually occurs does not support this rhetoric. They go on to comment on the general lack of a professional capacity at the local level as well as the absence of consistent and effective support from the central agencies to the program delivery process. This is something exacerbated by the tendency to use short-term project based funding arrangements to support individual initiatives rather than supporting ongoing programs of work.

Cameron and Laycock (2002) also point to the absence of any significant body of Australian crime prevention program evaluation literature upon which to draw as a resource for ongoing program improvement. This has had the effect of creating a sort of knowledge void similar to that observed in New Zealand, where local practical experience and research have been unable to be effectively shared and learning to occur. However, where these evaluations have been undertaken (and published) they reveal problems and difficulties remarkably similar to the U.K.'s experience with the Crime Reduction programme.

For example, in a review of the Safer Cities and Shires program developed and implemented by the Victorian state government during the late 1990s, Cherney (2004) attributes many of the program's implementation flaws to a lack of commitment by the central agencies responsible for leading the initiative to the establishment of adequate support and collaborative program delivery mechanisms. He also identified as a key problem a lack of consistent leadership and an unwillingness to devolve resources, authority and decision-making powers to the local inter-agency partnerships responsible for actually implementing the local level initiatives.

The sort of difficulties experienced in the implementation of Australian local crime prevention programs also highlights many of the difficulties inherent in the use of highly articulated policy and program management strategies. Australia, with a relatively small population (around 20 million), a huge physical area (larger than Europe) and federal system of government has a long history of using highly devolved and regionally-based service delivery models. However, because of the political tensions inherent in a federal system of government, where local government vies with state and federal government for resources and influence, regional management systems have generally been tightly managed by central government, of whatever level. This has led to a strong interest in joined-up or whole-of-government models that are built around regional coordination systems that attempt to maximise the efficient delivery of services, frequently with the participation of local government (Homel, 2005; IPAA, 2002).

Interestingly, all levels of government promote and maintain separate forms of regional structures, even at the local government level where distances may be large.

But reviews of the operation of these regional systems regularly report significant deficiencies and problems (O'Faircheallaigh et al., 1999; IPAA, 2002), regardless of the type of service being delivered. For example, a recent review of the implementation of the New South Wales (NSW) Drugs and Community Action Strategy, a community development initiative aimed at enhancing the capacity of NSW communities and agencies to deal with illicit drug issues, reported that while the program was able to report a number of significant successes, the regional coordination elements of the program had not been effective and were in need of significant reform (NSW Premier's Department, 2004). The report recommended the establishment of new more effective structures for regional management and coordination that would be better able to promote better participation and ownership by local agencies. Again, a factor identified as a key deficit in the program was inadequate central leadership and engagement with local delivery agencies.

This failure to establish adequate mechanisms to achieve local "buy-in" to centrally defined and managed policy initiatives echoes the U.K. experience with the Crime Reduction Programme. It also parallels the New Zealand crime prevention experience. And it repeats almost word for word the core problems experienced by the RAND Corporation in its replication in Los Angeles of a successful gun violence reduction initiative that was originally undertaken in Boston.

The Boston project had been designed to tackle the problem of gun violence among youth gang members through the application of the principles of Problem-oriented Policing (Goldstein, 1990) and deterrence theory through the applied use of a collaborative partnership approach among federal, state and local criminal justice, health, education and welfare agencies and community-based groups (Kennedy, 1997; Kennedy et al., 2001).

The Boston project could be described as an organically developed theory-driven strategy rooted heavily in the local community in which it was implemented. The RAND project in Los Angeles was one of a number of U.S. Department of Justice sponsored attempts at replicating the key features of the Boston initiative in other locales suffering high rates of gun related violence. In the words of the RAND researchers:

> ... the intervention was not implemented as designed, and it never developed dynamically or in response to changing needs. Part of

> the reason stems from the reorganization of the LAPD gang crime units in response to a scandal involving some gang unit officers who planted evidence and used excessive force. Also, the project did not succeed in getting working group participants, who referred to it as the "RAND study" or the "RAND project," to view it as their own and seek to continue it. No single agency emerged to take charge of the project and carry it forward, perhaps because of limited resources for the work. (Tita et al., 2003:12)

In other words it seems as though there was a reluctance to own a new initiative that was not really seen as locally appropriate or developed. Further, there was evidence that the systemic changes that were required to implement such an innovative program were not supported, either politically or financially.

So it would seem that the difficulties the Crime Reduction Programme experienced in achieving local delivery have certainly not been unique. More significant, however, is the realisation that these other initiatives have been reporting such similar implementation problems over many years and the possibility has also existed for some time to consolidate the lessons that they have been providing.

So what is to be done?

JOINING UP THE PIECES TO IMPROVE LOCAL IMPLEMENTATION

The key point is that many of the problems of local crime prevention implementation arise from a failure by central agencies to invest adequate effort in understanding the internal capability of a community to take the necessary crime prevention action. In effect, an inadequate joining-up process occurs.

This was a problem that was particularly apparent in the U.K.'s Crime Reduction Programme. What was presented was a template of well-evidenced crime prevention based initiatives without a mechanism for assessing their specific appropriateness in different contexts, nor a way of determining which communities would be best able to pick them up and implement them. Yet, as has been demonstrated, the CRP was not uniquely guilty of this tendency to present partial solutions to the prevention of crime.

Bearing this in mind, it is possible to develop a table of generic implementation problems that will typically be associated with local crime prevention programs, as well as a set of possible solutions for overcoming the problem. These are presented in Table 1. Note that the proposals outlined in this table are written primarily from the perspective of redefining the role central agencies need to fulfil to enhance their capacity to properly support local program delivery.

Inevitably such a process of role and process redefinition has implications for how other parts of the crime prevention program delivery stream operate, particularly in relation to assuming more responsibility and new forms of accountability. Some of these new relationships are illustrated in the table below.

So what does this all mean for the organisation of future the centre-regional-local crime prevention delivery processes?

First, the experience of implementing the British Crime Reduction Programme and the other programs discussed has shown that to achieve effective local crime reduction program delivery, all levels of the program implementation process need to be treated as a single integrated system. Even where regional management is employed, the central agency must be an active part of a delivery process.

This means that the centre itself must be appropriately staffed and adequately resourced if it is to contribute positively to the delivery process. "Appropriate" does not mean large or expensive. It means "effective" in the sense of being able to provide the type of support required to improve program implementation. This can include support to budget development and reporting tasks, training and other forms of passing on best practice knowledge and skills, etc.

Similarly, the regional offices and local implementation teams must be staffed by technically competent and policy-literate people who are capable of providing direct support (such as the analytical skills needed to interpret and apply research findings, as well as project management guidance and training) to individual projects. There must also be process for assisting the centre to remain actively informed of progress towards targets and where and in what form strategic and technical assistance to address emerging deficits is required.

It also means that those at the centre must be in a position to properly assess the appropriateness of particular strategies and interventions for specific communities. To do this they must have ways and means of properly communicating with and learning from the communities the crime prevention strategies that are directed at and being implemented within. The sort of partnership approach that is currently advocated for working

Table 1: Generic Problem/Solution for Joining-up Local Crime Prevention Implementation

Typical Implementation Problem	Proposed Solution
1. The central agency often operates as a "hands-off" provider of resources, target setter, and passive monitor of progress, in circumstances when capacity for local delivery is poor.	• Establish a pro-active adequately informed central agency willing and able to participate directly in the partnership process and technical support arrangements at the regional and local level.
2. There is an inadequate local supply of people with the necessary skills to develop and implement sound and well thought through projects.	• Develop and implement human resource recruitment and staff development strategies to accompany program implementation plans • An adequately resourced and easily accessible training and development program specifically targeted at known deficit areas at central, regional and local levels, including project and resource management as well as education in effective crime prevention practice. • Inclusion of training and knowledge development strategies as core components within plans for program delivery.
3. A lack of leadership with the required qualities to conceive and operate a crime prevention program or its constituent parts across all levels of the delivery process. This is often associated with poor role delineation and a lack of capacity for effective problem solving and for strategic thinking.	• Promote the routine use of a form of "logic model" analysis for designing programs as well as their constituent projects. This will provide a rational, outcome-focused framework for analysing problems and managing initiatives • Close cooperation between central, regional and local staff to forge effective, *collaborative* ways of working.

(continued)

Table 1: *(continued)*

Typical Implementation Problem	Proposed Solution
4. Ineffective program performance monitoring. This is important for feedback on program performance in order that adjustments can be made when necessary throughout the life of the program, not just after it has finished. Adequate tools for basic program performance monitoring are often not available.	• Development of a comprehensive program management information system, extending well beyond the monitoring of simple measures such as financial performance. • Application of program performance monitoring processes as an integrated part of program management and as an ongoing component of program development and evaluation.
5. Past lessons are not heeded. Many programs often fail to take advantage of the experience of previous crime prevention programs and available research. As a result many avoidable errors are reproduced.	• Development, implementation and use of a working knowledge management system and good practice tools to aid program implementation and avoid repeating past errors.
6. While a program may aspire to be an evidence-using and evidence-generating program, this goal is often not translated into supportive, practical on-the-ground activities.	• Establishment of adequately resourced and appropriately skilled central teams to work with regional staff in transferring the specialist technical and program design and management skills needed to initiate and sustain effective local delivery. • The application of an approach to program development and delivery that will enhance the systematic flow of knowledge, adoption of innovation, effective learning and organisational change.
7. Programs are always subject to many external pressures (such as political or bureaucratic imperatives) that may impact on their integrity and capacity for effective implementation.	• Development of an applied risk management approach to program development and implementation at central, regional and local levels, since not all influences on crime prevention policy, projects and programs will always be within the direct control of policy and program managers.

in this area and was discussed above allows an ability to effectively achieve this sort of communication. But it also must not be allowed to overwhelm the implementation process. As demonstrated by some of the work in New Zealand and Australia, the maintenance of the cordial and viable partnership arrangements can become very costly and distract from the direct delivery of effective programs on the ground.

Therefore, the model that is to be employed in managing this process must be clearly articulated, well communicated and understood. In practice, it must be a negotiated relationship that recognises and responds to the full range of roles, specialties and responsibilities of all the parties involved.

To help maximise effective delivery through the sort of collaborative joined-up approaches now routinely expected of crime prevention programs, an appropriate investment in adequate resources and staff competencies at every level is required. In particular, the centre and the regional offices, where present, need to be capable of providing well-supported strategic guidance and technical assistance to local services that are both flexible and responsive to local needs and capable of learning from successful innovations.

In adopting this approach, program implementation becomes a dynamic process by which new knowledge is cultivated and constantly reapplied to produce innovative policies and programs. New skills will be effectively acquired and transferred across the management layers to be applied where and when they are required. This also means a commitment to a continually evolving management system that will adapt to meet the different requirements of the changing crime reduction environment and needs of partners.

Action to achieve such a system goes beyond conventional planning and funding processes. It encompasses a range of capacity-building actions to enhance skills and knowledge.

The implementation of a "partnership" management model requires a commitment to an open approach to centre/region/local relations that is structured, nurturing, sustaining and consistent. The process will be a dynamic one; changing according to the requirements of a developing program moving progressively towards the achievement of defined a diverse set of crime prevention outcomes.

◆

Address correspondence to: Peter Homel, Australian Institute of Criminology, GPO Box 2944, Canberra, ACT 2601, Australia; e-mail: Peter.Homel@aic.gov.au

NOTES

1. The opinions expressed in this paper do not necessarily reflect the views of the Australian Institute of Criminology or the Australian government.
2. This appears to be partly explained by a staffing recruitment freeze that had been applied across the Home Office and other civil service agencies in late 1998. Documents suggest that although the need for additional staff was recognised by some senior Home Office officials, the special needs associated with the implementation of the CRP were not acknowledged and so it was not exempted (Homet et al., 2004a).
3. Minutes of the meeting of the Home Office's Crime Reduction Programme Board for the periods 1999–2001 provide evidence of this increasing focus. However, also note that there was increasing external pressure from HM Treasury on the Home Office centrally to improve its financial roll-out processes and increasing demands for detailed accounting on expenditure (Homel et al., 2004a).
4. The New Deal for Communities (NDC) program is one of the latest efforts to tackle social and economic deprivation. Its mandate is to "narrow the gap" between deprived communities and the national average in five "theme" areas of employment, education, health, crime, and the physical environment. Over a ten-year period, more than £2 billion will be invested in 39 of the most deprived communities in England. The NDC program marks a departure from previous area-based initiatives in terms of the significant level of funding involved, the length of the initiative, and the involvement of community residents.

REFERENCES

Bennington, L., & Cummane, J. (1999). Partnering relationships in the public sector. *The Quality Magazine*, August, 8–15.
Brinkerhoff, J. M. (2002). Assessing and improving partnership relationships and outcomes: A proposed framework. *Evaluation and Program Planning, 25*, 215–231.
Cabinet Office (2000). *Reaching Out: The role of central government at regional and local level.* Performance and Innovation Unit. London: Cabinet Office.

Cameron, M., & Laycock, G. (2003). Crime prevention in Australia. In A. Graycar & P. Grabosky (Eds.), *The Cambridge handbook of Australian criminology* (pp. 313–331). Cambridge: Cambridge University Press.

Cherney, A. (2004). Crime prevention/community safety partnerships in action: Victorian experience. *Current Issues in Criminal Justice, 15*(3), 237–252.

Department of Education Training and the Regions (DETR). (2001). *Local strategic partnerships: Government guidance*. London, DETR.

Farland, T. (2002). *Regions, agencies, results: A review of the NSW Regional Co-ordination Program*. Sydney, Australia: NSW Premiers Department.

Geddes, M. (2003). *Limits to local governance: Recent experience in the UK*. Paper for seminar at the Centre for Public Policy, University of Melbourne, Victoria, Australia, 19 September 2003.

Goldblatt, P., & Lewis, C. (1998). *Reducing offending: An assessment of research evidence on ways of dealing with offending behaviour*. Home Office Research Study 187. London: Home Office.

Goldstein, H. (1990). *Problem oriented policing*. New York: McGraw Hill Inc.

Home Office (1999). *Reducing crime and tackling its causes: A briefing note on the Crime Reduction Programme*. London: Home Office.

Homel, P. (2005). A short history of crime prevention in Australia. *Canadian Criminal Journal of Criminology and Criminal Justice, 47*(2), 355–368.

Homel, P., Nutley, N. S., Tilley, N., & Webb, B. (2004a). *Investing to deliver. Reviewing the implementation of the UK Crime Reduction Programme*. Home Office Research Study 281. London: Home Office.

Homel, P., Nutley, N. S., Tilley, N., & Webb, B. (2004b). *Making it happen from the centre: Managing for the regional delivery of local crime reduction outcomes*. Home Office Online Report 54/04. London: Home Office.

Homel, R. (2004). Developmental crime prevention. In N. Tilley (Ed.), *Handbook of crime prevention and community safety* (pp. 71–106). Cullumpton, Devon, UK: Willan.

IPAA – Institute of Public Affairs Australia (2002). *Working together – Integrated governance: Final report*. http://www.ipaa.org.au/12_pdf/national_research_final.pdf

Johnson, C., & Osborne, S. P. (2003). Local strategic partnerships, neighbourhood renewal, and the limits to co-governance. *Public Money and Management*, July, 147–154.

Joseph Rountree Foundation (2003). *Developing people – regenerating place: Achieving greater integration for local area regeneration*. York, UK: http://www.jrf.org.uk

Kennedy, D. M. (1997). *Juvenile gun violence and gun markets in Boston*. Washington, DC: U.S. National Institute of Justice.

Kennedy, D. M., Braga, A. M., & Piehl, A. M. (2001). Developing and implementing Operation Ceasefire. In *Reducing gun violence: The Boston Gun Project's Operation Ceasefire*. Washington, DC: U.S. National Institute of Justice (NCJ 188741).

Lee, S., & Woodward, R. (2002). Implementing the Third Way: The delivery of public services under the Blair Government. *Public Money and Management* October-December, 49–56.

Mant, J. (1998). *Place management: Why it works and how to do it*. Broadway, NSW: University of Technology Sydney.

National Audit Office (2004). *An early progress report on the New Deal for Communities*. London: The Stationery Office.

New South Wales Premier's Department (2004). *NSW drugs and community action strategy evaluation report*. Sydney.

New Zealand Ministry of Justice (2003). *Review of the Safer Community Council network: future directions*. Wellington, New Zealand.

O'Faircheallaigh, C., Wanna, J., & Weller, P. (1999). *Public sector management in Australia: New challenges, new directions*. South Yarra, VIC: Macmillan Education.

Roussos, S. T., & Fawcett, S. B. (2000). A review of collaborative partnerships as a strategy for improving community health. *Annual Review of Public Health, 21*, 369–402.

Tita, G., Riley, K. J., Ridgeway, G., Grammich, C., Abrahamse, A. F., & Greenwood, P. W. (2003). *Reducing gun violence. Results from an intervention in East Los Angeles*. Santa Monica, CA: RAND.

Wilson, J. Q., & Kelling, G. L. (1982). Broken windows. *The Atlantic Monthly, 249*(3), 29–38.

Not Seeing the Wood for the Trees: Mistaking Tactics for Strategy in Crime Reduction Initiatives

by

Mike Hough
Institute for Criminal Policy Research, King's College London

Abstract: *This paper advances an explanation for the very widespread implementation failure that has been seen in British initiatives to reduce crime through partnership work. It suggests that a narrow form of rationalism has been applied to crime problems that oversimplifies the nature of these problems and misidentifies priorities for action. This reductionist process is the consequence of the interaction between "managerialist" methods associated with the reform or "modernisation" of public services and a theory of knowledge which admits a narrow range of "evidence" about what works. The various crime reduction partners have not seriously engaged with crime reduction efforts, because this rationalist perspective has privileged tactical solutions of a particular sort at the expense of strategic solutions with which senior managers in partner agencies are actually preoccupied.*

INTRODUCTION

This chapter examines reasons for the underachievement of a crime reduction strategy involving local partnerships that was introduced into England

and Wales by the incoming New Labour government shortly after winning power in 1997. This was one of the new administration's most welcomed crime reduction measures. The 1998 Crime and Disorder Act required local police and councils to set up Crime and Disorder Reduction Partnerships (CDRPs). They were required to be in place in 1999. They were intended to be coalitions of senior managers from:

- Local authorities[1]
- Local police
- Local Health authorities (now Primary Care Trusts)
- Probation
- Fire service
- And other relevant statutory, voluntary and commercial bodies.

The underlying principle in establishing CDRPs was that the criminal justice system can exercise little direct control over many of the main "drivers" of crime, and that other parts of the local state are better placed to do so. For example, local planning, housing and regeneration departments can steer the development of the land-use and housing mix in specific high-crime areas. Health authorities can tackle problems associated with substance misuse, and are also well place to take action against some forms of violent crime, such as domestic abuse. Local education authorities and youth services and leisure departments have an obvious role to play in preventing youth crime, through their policies for handling misbehaviour in schools and truancy, for example. The Crime and Disorder Act requires CDRPs to pursue a cyclical triennial process involving: the auditing problems of crime and disorder, the validation of the results through consultation, and the construction and implementation of a strategy for tackling the problems.

Many, including myself, felt that the introduction of CDRPs would turn out to be a landmark in crime reduction policy. It promised to bring substantial new resources and energy to crime control. Seven years on, there is a widespread sense that CDRPs have failed to live up to their promise.[2] This paper includes some evidence in support of this pessimistic view, but essentially, I have offered a judgement on the issue. Others will have reached different judgements – though the government itself was reviewing the provisions of the 1998 Crime and Disorder Act at the time of writing. Those who feel that I have sold CDRPs short will find little of value in the rest of the paper. Its main purpose is not to document CDRPs' underperformance, but to offer an explanation for it, and some may feel that there is no underperformance to explain.

The paper is written from the viewpoint of someone who has spent several years offering encouragement and support from the sidelines to central and local government efforts to reduce crime through partnership-working. I was involved in the preparation of government guidance for CDRPs (Hough and Tilley, 1998), and in the training of CDRP staff when the measure was introduced. I was a member of an inner London CDRP for several years, and currently provide research-based advice to one of the ten regional government teams responsible for "performance managing" CDRPs. With colleagues, I have evaluated many crime reduction projects that were initiated by CDRPs. I offer these biographical details not just to establish my credentials, but to indicate that I really wanted the initiative to work, and have tried, where I can, to make them work. In other words, I have reached somewhat pessimistic conclusions about the achievements of CDRPs from a starting point of prejudice in favour of them.

There is a growing literature on partnership-working, both within the field of crime reduction and elsewhere (e.g., Pearson et al., 1992; Tilley, 1992; Gilling, 1994, 1997; Liddle and Gelsthorpe, 1994; Crawford and Jones, 1995; Hughes, 1996; Crawford, 1997; Bowling, 1998). There is a consensus that it is hard to do well. Obstacles include:

- Mismatches between partner organisations' values and working cultures

- The resultant mutual suspicion and distrust

- Difficulties in persuading people within one organisation to undertake work whose short-term benefits accrue only to their partner organisations

- The greater priority given to organisations' core functions over partnership work

- The competing demands of other partnerships[3]

- Rapid staff turnover at senior management level

- Limited capacity in analysing problems effectively and identifying solutions

- Lack of project management skills.

All of these factors have affected crime reduction partnerships, and I do not wish to underplay their importance. What I want to do in this paper is to highlight a further factor which to date has attracted insufficient attention. This relates to the way in which current approaches to public sector reform in Britain tend to oversimplify crime reduction issues, with two important consequences:

- Crime reduction issues are cast in terms which privilege a narrow range of tactical solutions, whilst ignoring various crucial strategic approaches.

- This narrowing of potential solutions discourages the engagement of those agencies that lie beyond the perimeter of the criminal justice system.

The argument that I propose to develop is not intended to be an exhaustive explanation of CDRPs' underperformance. It is intended as an additional explanation to those listed above. However, it is of particular importance right now, because, as I shall discuss at the end of the paper, the response to date of central government to CDRPs' underperformance has been to increase the intensity of focus on their performance management systems which I would argue are part of the problem, and not the solution.

The lessons that can be learnt from the English and Welsh experience with CDRPs will be more appropriate for some countries than for others. Despite its three tiers of government, there is a relatively centralised political system. The *central* tier is by far the most important. Although there is a *regional* tier of government in England, this largely serves as the delivery arm of central government policy. It lacks political representation, and has little autonomy.[4] Historically, the lower tier of *local* government has been important, with political representation and the power to raise taxes. Over time, however, local government has becoming increasingly dependent on central government grants, and this financial dependence has progressively eroded the importance of the local tier. Those countries with federal systems may find it hard to recognise the "new governance" that characterises British political administration, with centralised performance management. On the other hand, the broader lessons about the risks of target-setting by higher tiers of government on lower ones may have general applicability

CDRPS' PERFORMANCE - A BALANCE SHEET

Any assessment of CDRPs needs to take a long view, and in particular needs to remember the almost total breakdown of relationships that had occurred in the 1980s in Britain between many urban local authorities and local police.[5] There have been considerable improvements since 1998. New structures are in place, and new relationships have been built among the police, probation and local authority departments. An optimist would – probably wrongly – also point to the significant falls in crime that have occurred since then, and attribute them to new partnership work.

On the other hand, gloomier commentators would draw attention to the widespread implementation failure in partnership work, the pervasive experience of CDRPs as "talking shops" (coupled with the suspicion that the real decisions were made elsewhere), the limited analytic purchase displayed in crime audits, and the way in which crime reduction strategies tend to dress up pre-existing programmes of single-agency work as partnership work. There have also been some consistent absences from the partnership table: the most notable absentees are health authorities, staff from local authority planning departments, regeneration departments and even local education authorities. Probation staff have played a significant part in some CDRPs and a marginal part in others. Experience in involving the voluntary sector, businesses and local residents has also been patchy.

These weaknesses in partnership structures are part of the explanation for the high rate of implementation failure amongst CDRP-led projects. There is no shortage of examples. By way of illustration, I shall present some findings from an evaluation my unit undertook of 20 burglary projects in the South of England between 1999 and 2002. Table 1 describes how well the 20 CDRPs in five different police forces implemented the burglary reduction programme for which each of them had been funded. Each programme had several elements, often led by different agencies within the partnership. The table shows the number of elements planned for each project, and the number actually implemented.

It can be seen that well under half of the total number of programme components were fully implemented as part of the 20 programmes. Bearing in mind that these were highly visible "flagship" projects exposed to scrutiny through a national evaluation, the level of implementation failure is striking. The reasons for this are discussed in detail elsewhere (Hough et al., 2005). For our purposes, however, the table illustrates that CDRPs clearly find it difficult to deliver on some projects.

I do not propose to document further the extent of CDRPs' underperformance. Clearly there are hard questions to be asked: were expectations over-inflated? Did people underestimate the time needed for new structures to bed in? But I hope that I have said enough to establish that there

Table 1: Levels of Implementation in 20 Burglary Projects in Southern England and Wales

SDP	Number of elements planned	Elements fully completed	Elements partially completed	Elements not attempted
Project 1	5	1	1	3
Project 2	5	2	2	1
Project 3	9	3	6	0
Project 4	8	3	0	5
Project 5	6	1	2	3
Project 6	7	3	4	0
Project 7	5	4	1	0
Force A	**45**	**17**	**16**	**12**
Project 8	6	3	3	0
Project 9	7	4	1	2
Force B	**13**	**7**	**4**	**2**
Project 10	12	2	4	6
Project 11	7	7	0	0
Project 12	1	1	0	0
Project 13	5	2	1	2
Project 14	4	4	0	0
Project 15	1	0	1	0
Project 16	9	2	3	4
Project 17	10	4	6	0
Force C	**49**	**22**	**15**	**12**
Project 18	5	4	1	0
Project 19	3	2	1	0
Force D	**8**	**6**	**2**	**0**
Project 20	7	0	0	7
Force E	**7**	**0**	**0**	**7**
Total	**122**	**52**	**37**	**33**

Source: Hough et al., 2005.

has been a degree of underperformance, and that this needs explaining. I now propose to trace the way in which the "modernisation" agenda has contributed to this underperformance.

MODERNISATION

Over the last 25 years Conservative and Labour governments in Britain have shared a "modernisation" agenda for public services. From 1979 onward the Conservative government aimed to get better "value for money" out of the public sector, through a mixture of "modern" management methods and downward pressure on budgets. The favoured solutions included budgetary cuts, applying private sector management methods to the public sector, the introduction of purchaser/provider splits (or quasi-markets) within bureaucracies, and the introduction of new providers, usually from the private sector, to compete with existing ones.

Many aspects of this approach were retained – indeed developed and extended – by New Labour from 1997 onward. Reform of public services is now a key Government priority, as reflected by the establishment of the Prime Minister's Delivery Unit and the Office of Public Services Reform. As with the previous Conservative administration, their basic approach has been to secure greater accountability through performance management regimes that rely on quantitative performance indicators and target-setting. The concept of competition as a lever on performance has been retained, though the language of privatisation and "market testing" has now been replaced by that of "contestability."[6]

This new form of public sector governance – "New Public Management" – emerged in the late 20th century in many developed countries (see McLaughlin et al., 2001, for an account of its development within criminal justice in Britain). Under some administrations, there was a strong ideological commitment to paring down the public sector, which can be traced to neo-liberal political philosophies about the virtues of small government (see e.g., Wilson, 1990). Others have judged pragmatically that the best way to drive up public sector performance is for central government to set broad objectives and for local agencies to have the freedom to choose how best they should set about achieving the nationally set objectives. In other words, there is tight central control over the *ends* to be pursued by public services, but local control over the *means* by which the ends are achieved. One of the defining metaphors of modernisation was introduced by the management theorists Osborne and Gaebler (1992), who are associated with the emergence of New Public Management in the United States. They suggested that the job of government is not to *row* but to *steer*. In other words, government should ensure that public services are provided, but should not necessarily aim to provide these services directly themselves. The metaphor was taken up with enthusiasm by central government politicians and administrators in Britain – but appreciated less by their local government counterparts – who were usually cast in the role of rowers. This model of governance is often supported by reference to private sector organisations whose success is built on radically decentralised decision making to local managers, within a central framework of simple performance targets.[7]

Stated in these terms, the new governance has plenty to capture the imaginations not only of central government but also those entrepreneurial local providers to whom "earned autonomy" is attractive.[8] As I shall argue, however, in politically sensitive policy areas such as law and order, central government finds it hard in practice to set coherent targets.[9] It also finds it hard to risk loosening its control over local delivery. The promise of localism in principle tends to be negated by forms of centralised micro-management in practice: the centre not only "steers" policy but succumbs to the temptation of "rowing," in the hope of speeding things on a little, and securing some visible and electorally important successes. There are obvious tensions between a centralised system of target-setting and the "local problem solving" model that is embedded in the statutory require-ments on CDRPs to auditing their local crime problems and to tailor their responses accordingly – a point to which I shall return.

The new governance emerged not by accident but in response to real problems in conventional post-World War II public administration. As the size of both the central and local state grew in the second half of the 20th century, monolithic public service bureaucracies in many industrialised countries grew into powerful, slow-moving, self-serving bodies that could define the terms of their own success. Not surprisingly, some developed inflexibilities both in their management and their workforces, and the rigidities of public bureaucracies became increasingly obvious when they were unable to respond to the increasingly rapid rate of social change. The limitations of public bureaucracies began to emerge at the same time as new technologies which promised to solve them: the new style of governance was made possible by considerable advances in information technology, without which quantitative performance management from "the centre" would be impossible, even as an aspiration.

If the key feature of the modernisation agenda is the centralised definition of ends and the decentralisation of decisions about means, vari-ous further features emerge as a consequence. The linking of funding to performance is an important one, providing the incentive to agencies to achieve targets – or a disincentive to miss them. A corollary of this is the splitting of monolithic bureaucracies into purchasers and providers, to allow greater "incentivisation" within the agency. This simplifies the introduction of competition or "contestability," both among public, voluntary and private sectors, and within sectors, through competitive bidding for "challenge funds."

These features of modernisation relate to the nature of funding. Modernisation's logic also points inevitably to a particular emphasis on processes of *prioritisation*. It is hard to quarrel with the basic principle that organisations should identify their key priorities and focus their energies on them. The risk is that systematic and focussed action against *misidentified* or *poorly identified* priorities can have worse consequences than poorly marshalled and ineptly implemented action against well-specified priorities.

To anticipate arguments that I shall develop later in the paper, there are features of "law and order" politics that tend to produce over-simplified or mis-specified priorities. The factors that lead people to treat each other badly are complex; political and media debate cannot handle this complexity, and thus uses an oversimplified discourse about crime. The modernisation agenda feeds on this simplified discourse to develop and impose inappropriate targets on the public services that it seeks to improve. Senior managers at local level understand their organisations well, and are well aware of this reductionist process. Of particular importance in explaining the lack of engagement of key CDRP partners from outside the criminal justice system is the tendency for crime problems (and solutions) to become framed in ways that are largely irrelevant for all except the police.

REDUCTIONIST KNOWLEDGE MANAGEMENT

Those pursuing the modernisation agenda tend towards scepticism about the capacity of local agencies to do their jobs properly. Poor local performance is thought to be a consequence more of incompetence than of resource shortages.[10] The solution is for the "steerers" to point the "rowers" in the right direction, tell them where to focus their efforts, and give them the right tools (or right oars?) to do the job. (The tool-kit metaphor is pervasive in the crime-reduction world, and indicative of a systematic misjudgement about the complexity of the enterprise: plumbers have tool-kits; social engineers do not.) In the case of crime reduction, the task of identifying "what works" and filling appropriate tool-kits with this knowledge has fallen to Home Office research teams.

Just as it is hard to argue with the overarching principles of priority-setting, it would be hard to take issue with the principle that implementation of any form of social policy should be firmly grounded on evidence about effectiveness. There are important questions about the admissibility of different sorts of evidence, however, and some approaches to knowledge management risk skewing social policy. I shall argue that criminal policy is currently exposed to exactly this risk.

Over the last five years, however, there has been increasing enthusiasm within government in Britain, including the Home Office, for forms of systematic research reviews associated with the Cochrane collaboration in the field of healthcare, and with the Campbell Collaboration in criminal policy.[11] These systematic reviews exclude all studies that fail to reach a level of methodological quality – the threshold being set individually for each review. For example, the Maryland Scale of Scientific Methods is often used as a filtering device.[12] One of the most influential international reviews of effective practice in criminal justice, conducted by Sherman and colleagues (1997), adopted systematic review principles identifying:

- What is known to work
- What is promising
- What does not work
- What is not known.

For the purposes of the review, "known to work" meant "established as effective by at least two high quality evaluations."[13] In fields of study which lend themselves readily to evaluation through randomised controlled trials (RCTs) or to other forms of tightly designed quantitative evaluation, the Campbell/Cochrane approach is clearly appropriate. We can reasonably expect our doctors to base their prescribing decisions on evidence that is filtered to remove all studies of poor quality. This is because pharmaceutical evaluations are relatively straightforward: there is usually little implementation failure – in that people in drug trials tend to take their medicine as required – and clearly measurable outcomes. Also important is the fact that pharmaceutical interventions are not usually dependent for their effectiveness on the social meaning that the recipients attach to them (though there are obviously placebo effects). Evaluating strategies for crime reduction usually tends to be more complex, and it is especially challenging when it is addressing various forms of "social crime prevention."

As general rule, simple interventions that target large numbers of people or neighbourhoods in the pursuit of a single, easily measured, objective can be readily evaluated to a high standard. More complex interventions with multiple objectives are much harder to evaluate. The more aggressively that modernizers pursue the Campbell/Cochrane approach, the less they will encourage these more complex forms of crime reduction. To put this another way, the "tool-kits" offered by central government to CDRPs will be filled piecemeal with pieces of tactical knowledge, but will have little to offer by way of strategic knowledge.

Strategic and tactical knowledge are obviously concepts that need to be defined in relation to one another, as tactics are by definition sub-components of strategies. Tactical knowledge in this field can be exemplified by the answers to questions such as:

- Is investment in CCTV a better way of reducing vehicle crime than investment in DNA analysis?

- Are "boot camps" effective in deterring or rehabilitating young offenders?

- Does methadone prescribing reduce drug-related crime?

Examples of what I mean by strategic knowledge are to be found in answers to questions such as:

- What principles should be followed in securing the legitimacy of local agencies in the eyes of their publics?

- What are effective principles for reducing social exclusion and promoting civil renewal?

- What principles should one follow in dividing resources between primary and secondary prevention?

Strategic knowledge thus comprises high-level principles about crime control and order maintenance, whilst tactical knowledge comprises the answers to much more specific and detailed questions. Empirical or evaluative research tends to answer – with greater or lesser precision – tactical questions fairly directly. Research can also provide answers to strategic questions, but this is rarely done exclusively or even largely though tightly controlled evaluations. It makes more sense to think in terms of research *cumulatively* constructing and testing strategic *principles* – or middle-range theories – about crime reduction. One of the weaknesses of the U.K. government's current approach to providing "tool-kits" is that too much attention is paid to identifying tactics that "work," and too little attention is paid to discussion of principles of crime control.[14]

THE UNINTENDED CONSEQUENCES OF THE MODERNISATION AGENDA

Let us now turn to an examination of some of the unintended consequences of the modernisation agenda on the operation of CDRPs and the way in which a deficient approach to knowledge management has compounded these consequences. In essence the argument is that:

- Order maintenance is a highly complex process,

- but the populist nature of debate about crime precludes recognition of this complexity,

- and results in a performance management system based on "common-sense" notions of crime control.

- These "common-sense" notions are reinforced by the central government's approach to knowledge management, which offers tools consistent with this common sense understanding of crime control,

- and precisely those priorities and preventive options that CDRPs could effectively champion are relegated to the sidelines,

- so that key partners fail to engage with, or disengage from, CDRPs.

Complexity

Systems of crime control and order maintenance have some important institutional characteristics. Two sorts of institutional feature are worth emphasising. First, such systems work well only when they can command institutional legitimacy. For the institutions of justice, the building blocks of legitimacy are:

- Fair procedures (or procedural justice)

- Fair outcomes (or outcome justice)

- Helpfulness and concern for victims and offenders

- Civil and even-handed treatment.

The factors that corrode legitimacy are, of course, the obverse of these: lack of respect for those passing through the system; arbitrariness, unfairness, high-handedness, rudeness and corruption. Whilst the importance of institutional legitimacy is obvious in relation to formal policing,

I would argue that the policing functions discharged by the broader local state – often through CDRPs – are also likely to work best when the agencies involved have the respect and confidence of the population.

The second institutional feature worth emphasising is the way in which systems of crime control have the capacity to communicate social meaning – to symbolise characteristics of the state and the level and nature of security that it offers (cf., Manning, 1977; Loader and Walker, 2001). Precisely what is symbolised, and how this is done, will vary from country to country, and over different historical periods. It is clear that the police – or "the Law," as they are often called in the U.K. – do indeed symbolise the criminal law. The police are the most central and most visible component of our formal systems of social control, but the capacity of a private security company or a local authority body to control citizens' behaviour will depend in part on public attitudes towards those bodies. Any analysis of social control that ignores this symbolic function will be a very partial one. Any theory about order maintenance that takes a narrowly instrumental view about controlling criminal behaviour will mislead.

The modernisation project is ill-equipped to handle complexity of this sort. It is not that any competent politician or civil servant would deny that the system displays these forms of complexity. It is just that they are on the one hand locked into the pressures of the "here-and-now" to get *some* form of performance management system in place,[15] and on the other hand, they are progressively locked into a simplified and populist discourse about law and order, to which we shall now turn.

Pressures to Populism

The increasingly populist nature of law-and-order politics (cf., Beckett, 1997; Roberts and Hough, 2002; Roberts et al., 2003) is the second feature of policing that subverts scientific rationalism when it is applied to policing. There are several possible renditions of this process.[16] The first is that in an era of mass-media communication the electoral system serves to select politicians whose understanding of complex social issues is about as subtle as the coverage of these issues in tabloid newspapers. This can and does occur,[17] but to date, it remains the exception rather than the rule in British politics. The second is that politicians exploit the possibilities offered by the mass media to frame policy issues in ways that suit their political agenda (cf., Beckett, 1977). In other words, politicians lead the mass media to present policy issues in particular ways.[18] The third is that the media exert such power in the politics of late-modern societies that politicians have little alternative except to engage publicly with complex social issues in media-defined terms.

In a complex world all three of these interpretations of populist processes carry some force. In particular, politicians can exercise a degree of control over the way that the mass media present events and issues – and *vice versa*. The end product is that – whether by design or constraint – politicians simplify the policy issues with which they grapple, both in their public statements and – as a consequence – in the performance management systems that they construct.

Performance Management Based on Common-sense Notions of Crime Control

The upshot of these pressures is that the performance management systems to which the criminal justice system is exposed are based on simple – and I would argue simplistic – notions of crime control. Those responsible for the system may recognise the over-simplification, and regard it as representing a provisional "holding position" which may be improved in the passage of time, but this does not alter the fact that complexity is being ignored. The present system of performance management has tended to:

- Over-emphasise crime control as a primary police function in contrast to order maintenance[19]

- Over-emphasise deterrent threat as the main lever for securing compliance with the law

- Over-claim on central government capacity to exercise control over crime

- Over-promise on crime control targets

- Over-claim on target achievements.

Criminal justice elites – chief constables, senior judges and other senior staff in the criminal justice system – are in a position to challenge political representations of crime and disorder problems, but rarely do so. At one level, this is because they are expected and sometimes required not to stray too far, in their public pronouncements, into politically sensitive territory. But at the same time, they often tend to judge it to be in their organisational interests to acquiesce to the political rhetoric about crime fighting. Politicians control purse-strings and can exercise powerful patronage. Leaving this aside, statements by senior CJS figures about the complexity of their task will appear self-serving and will resonate less well with the public than ones which stress the urgency and importance of tackling crime.

Another feature of the CJS performance management systems is that they focus on crime *events* rather than on *perpetrators*.[20] This is partly a reflection of the available statistics: we know how many burglaries are recorded by the police in the country, or in a police force, or in any Basic Command Unit (BCU, what used to be called a police division), for example, but it is much harder to say how many active burglars are known to the authorities. But it is also likely in practice that targets requiring CDRPs to reduce the number of crime events will impel CDRPs to crime-specific approaches that ignore options such as long-term offender-based prevention, which are not offence-specific. This has important consequences for engaging in CDRP work those agencies such as education and health authorities, whose orientation is towards the processing of *people* rather than *events*.

The Government Approach to Knowledge Management

These pressures on CDRPs to pursue a particular range of offence-specific tactics are amplified by the nature of the tool-kits provided for them by central government. I suggested above that some forms of prevention are more amenable to evaluation than others, and that our knowledge is soundest about some types of offender-based secondary prevention (such as cognitive behavioural programmes for offenders) and some types of place-based primary prevention (such as crime-specific situational prevention measures). It is hard to *demonstrate* that the content of the Home Office tool-kits artificially narrows the range of preventive options considered by CDRPs. However the likelihood is that it does so.

Marginalized Preventive Options

The upshot of the combined impact of the modernisation agenda and the government's approach to knowledge management is a narrowing of the range of preventive options considered by CDRPs. Crime reduction issues are cast in terms which favour subsets of tactical preventive options associated with specific categories of crime, whilst ignoring various broader strategic approaches that on the one hand are unlikely to contribute to target-hitting in the short term, and on the other hand are very difficult to evaluate.

This process of marginalisation reveals itself in the absence of discussion in CDRPs, or in the regional government departments with a watching brief over them, of various key issues:

- Issues of broad policing *style* are totally ignored.[21]

- *Sensitive* issues such as the use of police stop-and-search tactics are avoided.

- Issues about *confidence* in local agencies, and the *legitimacy* of local agencies, are ignored.

- Issues to do with primary prevention (e.g., SureStart programmes) are considered in other local arenas.[22]

- Local authority plans for *regeneration* and economic *redevelopment* are rarely scrutinised for their criminogenic or preventive capacity.

- This is especially true of plans to stimulate the *late-night economy* in large cities.[23]

Disengaging Partners

This artificial narrowing of preventive options discourages the engagement of agencies in CDRP business. Senior managers in health and education authorities or in regeneration or planning departments will, of course, notice that the government modernisation agenda has had the effect of oversimplifying crime problems and solutions, and of framing them in a way that minimizes any role for their own agency.

It also seems likely that these partners will disengage from CDRPs if the key strategic issues for their colleagues in criminal justice agencies are ruled "out of bounds." One might expect a local partnership that was genuinely committed to maximizing compliance with the law to collectively assess, as a matter of priority, how "the Law" in their area was perceived by its citizenry. If issues about police legitimacy and confidence in the police are sidestepped by CDRPs, the other partners will realise – with greater or lesser clarity – that the real issues in crime control are being avoided.

A further important factor behind partners' disengagement is to be found not in the *content* of targets, but in the *control* of the process. It will be remembered that CDRPs are statutorily bound to a triennial problem-solving process, where they audit crime problems, identify priority problems and develop a strategy to address these problems. This presupposes that they control the targets for local crime control. The reality now is that the content of their performance management systems has been increasingly determined by central government. This process of centralisation removes much of the rationale of the CDRPs' statutory obligations.

THE GOVERNMENT'S SOLUTION TO UNDERPERFORMING CDRPS

The government solution to CDRPs' perceived underperformance has been to construct a performance management system that runs in parallel to the system to which the police are exposed. Crime reduction targets have been negotiated between CDRP members and regional government officials, within a framework set by central government. The aim is that in aggregate, CDRPs' targets will sum to the 15% reduction in recorded crime to which the Home Office is committed over the coming three years.

The strategy would be a high-risk one – if it were not for the fact that the underlying trend in crime as measured by the BCS is still a downward one.[24] The regional government officials have no statutory powers to impose targets on CDRPs, and no powers to impose sanctions on "failing" CDRPs. Neither CDRPs nor regional officials really have any idea of what is driving crime trends downward, and what level of investment in what activities is needed to guarantee that targets are met. Nor is there any clarity about the division of responsibility between CDRPs and local police BCUs for hitting the targets that they broadly share.[25] Many participants within the system recognise its frailties. Some regard the declaratory value of setting aspirational or "stretch" targets as offsetting any problems inherent in the system;[26] others regard it as an elaborate form of shadow-boxing with which they must engage if they are to secure their survival within the organisation. The most likely consequences of the system are that:

- CDRPs will continue to be constrained by an over-simple model of order maintenance.

- Formal strategies will remain focussed on achieving crime-specific targets.

- Issues of real strategic importance will be ignored.

- Cynicism within CDRPs will grow, as will distrust of regional and central government officials.

- Disengagement of "peripheral" partners will grow.

ALTERNATIVE APPROACHES

As it settles into its third term of office, it seems unlikely that the U.K. government will turn its back on its preferred means of pubic sector reform. The safest prediction is that it will retain or extend its system of accountability to central government through centrally- or regionally-set targets. There are signs that central government is beginning to withdraw from the role of tight performance management. At the time of writing, a system of Local Area Agreements was being piloted, whereby previously fragmented government grants for neighbourhood development in deprived local authorities were being aggregated into a single "pot" of money; local authorities were given great autonomy over priority setting, and were exposed to a simpler form of performance management.[27] However, in parallel with this development, the Home Office was continuing to develop what local authorities were experiencing as a more aggressive form of performance management over CDRPs.

There are things that could be done to improve the coherence of the system as it impacts CDRPs. Perhaps the first step is to ensure that the system has some legislative coherence. There is no point in pretending that CDRPs are somehow accountable to regional and central government, and that the latter have powers to set targets for the former when in statute they do not.

The precise shape of this legislative accountability depends on the extent to which a centralised system is favoured. There is a strong argument for more decentralised performance management systems, which abandon centrally-set targets that specify a given percentage reduction in crime. National crime reduction targets have little integrity, partly because recorded crime statistics are an unreliable measure of crime, and partly because we have very little knowledge about the means of driving local crime down, or of the resources needed to do this. The difficulties in relying on a target that uses recorded crime figures (the PSA1 target to reduce crime by 15% over three years) are likely to become clear if and when the recorded crime trend is shown to be at odds with the BCS trend.[28]

The government's recent strategy on prolific and priority offenders might present an opportunity to take a new approach to performance targets that could at the same time engage – or re-engage – missing CDRP partners.[29] This strategy is premised on the assumptions that a small minority of offenders account for a large amount of crime; these offenders typically come from problem families living in areas of intense social deprivation. They and their families are likely to be known not only to the police, but to all the partner agencies – the probation service, social services, health services, education welfare officers and so on. Partnership work using "people-based" strategies is the obvious way of tackling this particularly difficult and disadvantaged group.

The more that central and local government share a vision of CDRPs as partnerships designed to tackle the small number of persistent offenders coming from very troubled families, the more likely it is that the "people-processing" agencies that are currently reluctant to engage in CDRP work might see the logic in doing so.[30] Targets relating to work with these groups could be designed in such a way that they complemented, rather than competed with, the targets set for these agencies by *other* government departments.

A More Radical Option

By way of conclusion it is worth sketching a more radical decentralising option – though I recognise that there are obvious risks to any government in loosening its control over a policy area that is highly politicised.

In some areas of policy, particularly health and education, there is a groundswell of opinion that the unintended consequences of the modernisation strategy are outweighing the gains. To flog the metaphor to death, the central government "steerers" have overestimated their navigational capacity, and keep on directing their "rowers" onto unforeseen rocks. There are calls from the two main opposition parties to abandon national targets altogether, which are actually consistent with New Labour's ambitions for localism and civil renewal. As discussed above, the government is itself experimenting with a simpler and more decentralised form of dispensing grants and managing performance, through the Local Area Agreement system.

One can envisage a system of performance management for CDRPs in which they were required by statute not only to prepare three-year strategies, but also to set explicit targets for themselves within their strategy. In other words, central government would establish a performance management framework for CDRPs, whose precise targets would be populated at local level. Central and regional government might have a responsibility to ensure that CDRPs complied with this process, and would need reserve powers to intervene where partnerships were demonstrably failing. But normally, CDRPs would be accountable for their performance to local politicians rather than national ones.

The advantages of such a system would become clearer with the passage of time. If responsibility for crime control were seen to be a genuinely local responsibility, we might on the one hand avoid the perversity of penal populism that dogs our current justice system; and on the other, we might begin to see some truly innovative solutions that were properly tailored to local problems.

Address correspondence to: Professor Mike Hough, Director, Institute for Criminal Policy Research, 4th Floor-King's College London, 26-29 Drury Lane, London WC2B 5RL, UK; e-mail: mike.hough@kcl.ac.uk

Acknowledgements: I would like to thank Gloria Laycock, Mike Maguire and Layla Skinns for comments on earlier drafts.

NOTES

1. Usually at district or borough level – an administrative unit whose population is rarely under 100,000, and rarely larger than 500,000.
2. This view was already emerging in 2002. The Audit Commission (2002) concluded that CDRPs had yet to demonstrate any significant impact.
3. Senior managers in local agencies are now required to engage in a wide range of partnerships: the overarching Local Strategic Partnership; the CDRP; the Drug Action Team; partnerships concerned with child welfare; those concerned with mental health issues; etc.
4. The equivalent of the regional tier in Wales is provided by the Welsh Assembly, which is a much more significant body.
5. For example, many local authorities in London boroughs set up Police Monitoring Units which pursued an aggressively oppositional approach to police reform.

6. See for example the Carter Review of the correctional services (Home Office, 2003).

7. For example, some companies let local managers have extensive freedom over their operations – provided that they meet a single target specified in terms of growth of profits.

8. The idea of earned autonomy is best exemplified in the system whereby hospitals can achieve foundation status if they achieve a given level of performance.

9. "Law and order" is not the only politically sensitive police area, of course. Health and education can be political mine-fields, and target-setting for these highly complex systems can have demonstrably perverse effects. However, the criminal justice system exemplifies public sector work at its most complex, reflecting the interleaving of moral and legal systems of social control.

10. This is not surprising, given the perfectly proper concern with securing better value for money. Though under-investment can be a major source of financial waste, the mind-set of modernisers is that public services generally fail to make good enough use of the resources they already have.

11. See http://www.cochrane.org for details of the Cochrane Collaboration, and http://www.aic.gov.au/campbellcj for details of the Campbell Collaboration.

12. The Maryland Scale assigns evaluative studies into one of five categories, according to the form of experimental control that is used to help to attribute causality. The highest score is reserved for studies that use randomised controlled trial methods. Systematic reviews usually exclude all studies that fall into the lowest two categories, and some include only the top, or the top two, categories.

13. Sherman et al. (1997) define programmes that work as follows: "These are programs that we are reasonably certain of preventing crime or reducing risk factors for crime in the kinds of social contexts in which they have been evaluated, and for which the findings should be *generalizable* to similar settings in other places and times. Programs coded as 'working' by this definition must have at least two level 3 evaluations with statistical significance tests showing effectiveness *and* the preponderance of all available evidence supporting the same conclusion."

14. The U.S. Department of Justice's COPS Guides (Problem-Oriented Guides for Police) pay rather more attention to issues of principle, and to the factors that underlie success or failure.

15. An important process here is the triennial Comprehensive Spending Review, where the Treasury requires spending departments to offer evidence in support of their plans, and quantitative performance indicators by which to judge success. The pressure on Home Office ministers to sign up to a "dumbed down" set of targets in exchange for budgets is overwhelming.

16. A full explanation of the pressures to populism are well beyond the scope of this paper; but it would need to take account of the shrinking capacity of the sovereign state in late-modern industrialised societies, and that paradoxical response to this process that involves reaffirmation by the state of its crime control capabilities (cf., Garland, 2001; Young, 1999).

17. The "One Nation" party in Australia under Pauline Hanson's leadership is a possible example.

18. Beckett's thesis is that the U.S. political rhetoric about criminals as outsiders was politically led, and served to support a separate neo-conservative policy agenda of paring down public expenditure on social security and welfare programmes.

19. A complicating factor in this analysis is the British government's recent rediscovery of anti-social behaviour as a policy issue. One "reading" of the emergence of current anti-social behaviour strategy is that it is a necessary corrective – both politically and substantively – to a decade of over-focussing on crime control. Another is that its origins are in government thinking about civil renewal, and that it has been only superficially integrated in crime control policy.

20. Currently the key target for local police areas and for their CDRPs (PSA 1) is to reduce the number of crimes in a specified group of crime categories by at least 15% over the coming three years. Some agencies, notably the prison and probation services, are subject to a range of offender-related targets, of course.

21. Of course it might be argued, especially by the police, that policing style is an *operational* issue for the police to grapple with by themselves. Alternatively it might be argued that policing style is a *political* issue, to be dealt with by the Home Secretary, or else by the local police authority. But if CDRPs are serious about controlling crime and disorder, they need to articulate the principles that inform their strategies, and they need to ensure that these are consistent with the policing principles of their police partners.

22. SureStart programmes are intended to provide support for families with young children at risk of social exclusion, focussing on early

education, childcare, health and family support (see: www.surestart. gov.uk).

23. Several British cities have encouraged investment in pubs, clubs and other forms of nighttime entertainment, usually involving the sale of alcohol, valuing the anticipated economic benefits more than the costs in terms of increased disorder.

24. The British Crime Survey shows that most categories of crime in England and Wales have been falling since the mid-1990s.

25. In London, CDRPs and the corresponding police command units share the same crime reduction targets. Elsewhere targets are similar, but not necessarily the same.

26. Stretch targets are those that the workforce would generally regard as unattainable, or at least very hard to attain. They probably make some sense for organisations that have gone stale, and whose performance is some way behind the "market leaders."

27. http://www.odpm.gov.uk/stellent/groups/odpm_localg ov/ documents/page/odpm_locgov_029989.hcsp

28. The 15% reduction is only for those categories of recorded crime that can also be measured by the British Crime Survey.

29. The Home Office launched a Prolific and Other Priority Offenders Strategy in July 2004 (see: http://www.crimereduction.gov.uk/ppo).

30. This is not to dismiss the difficult and complex issues about the sharing by different agencies of confidential information about these families.

REFERENCES

Audit Commission (2002). *Community Safety Partnerships*. London: Audit Commission.

Beckett, K. (1997). *Making crime pay: Law and order in contemporary American politics*. New York: Oxford University Press.

Bowling, B. (1998). *Violent racism*. Oxford: Clarendon Press.

Crawford, A. (1997). *The local governance of crime: Appeals to community and partnerships*. Oxford: Oxford University Press.

Crawford, A., & Jones, M. (1995). Inter-agency co-operation and community based crime prevention. *British Journal of Criminology, 35*(1), 17–33.

Garland, D. (2001). *The culture of control: Crime and social order in contemporary society*. Oxford: Oxford University Press.

Gilling, D. (1994). Multi-agency crime prevention: Some barriers to collaboration. *The Howard Journal, 33*(3), 246–257.

Gilling, D. (1997). *Crime prevention: Theory, policy and politics*. London: UCL Press.

Home Office (2003). Managing offenders, reducing crime – A new approach. *Correctional Services Review by Patrick Carter*. London: Prime Minister's Strategy Unit.

Hough, M., Hedderman, C., & Hamilton-Smith, N. (2005). The design and the development of the Reducing Burglary Initiative. In N. Hamilton-Smith (Ed.), *The Reducing Burglary Initiative: Design, development and delivery*. Home Office Research Study. London: Home Office.

Hough, M., & Tilley, N. (1998). *Auditing crime and disorder: Guidance for local partnerships*. No. 91. London: Home Office PRG.

Hughes, G. (1996). Strategies of multi-agency crime prevention and community safety in contemporary Britain. *Studies on Crime and Crime Prevention, 5*(2), 221–244.

Hughes, G., & Gilling, D. (2004). Mission impossible?: The habitus of the community safety manager and the new expertise in the local partnership governance of crime and safety. *Criminal Justice, 4*(2), 129–149.

Liddle, M., & Gelsthorpe, L. (1994). *Inter-agency crime prevention: Organising local delivery*. Crime Prevention Unit Paper 52. London: Home Office.

Liddle, M., & Gelsthorpe, L. (1994). *Crime prevention and inter-agency co-operation*, Crime Prevention Unit Paper 53. London: Home Office.

Loader, I., & Walker, N. (2001). Policing as a public good: Reconstituting the connections between policing and the state. *Theoretical Criminology, 5*(1), 9–35.

Manning, P. (1977). *Police work: The social organization of policing*. Cambridge, MA: MIT Press.

McLaughlin, E., Muncie, J., & Hughes, G. (2001). The permanent revolution: New labour, new public management and the modernisation of criminal justice. *Criminal Justice, 1*(3), 301–317.

Osborne, D., & Gaebler, T. (1992). *Reinventing government: How the entrepreneurial spirit is transforming the public sector*. Reading, MA: Addison-Wesley.

Pearson, G., Blagg, H., Smith, D., Sampson, A., & Stubbs, P. (1992). Crime, community and conflict: The multi-agency approach. In D. Downes (Ed.), *Unravelling criminal justice*. London: Macmillan.

Roberts, J., & Hough, M. (Eds.) (2002). *Changing attitudes to punishment: Public opinion, crime and justice*. Cullompton: Willan Publishing.

Roberts, J. V., Stalans, L. S., Indermaur, D., & Hough, M. (2003). *Penal populism and public opinion. Findings from five countries*. New York: Oxford University Press.

Tilley, N. (1992). *Safer cities and community safety strategies*. Crime Prevention Unit Paper 38. London: Home Office.

Sherman, L., Gottfredson, D., MacKenzie, D., Eck, J., Reuter, P., & Bushway, S. (1997). *Preventing crime: What works, what doesn't, what's promising: A report to the United States Congress*. Available at: http://www.ncjrs.org/works/

Wilson, J. Q. (1990). *Bureaucracy: What government agencies do and why they do it*. New York: Basic Books.

Young, J. (1999). *The exclusive society: Social exclusions, crime and difference in late modernity*. London: Sage.

Implementation Failure and Success: Some Lessons from England

by

Kate J. Bowers

and

Shane D. Johnson
Jill Dando Institute of Crime Science, University College London

Abstract: *It is of vital importance that practitioners plan ahead to help avoid future implementation problems. By thinking strategically, it should be possible to foresee at least the more common problems that might be faced. Here we attempt to assist in this process by producing a typology of schemes and discussing the elements of different sorts of scheme that both guard against and accentuate the risk of implementation failure. For example, schemes that are very specific about the crime they are targeting are likely to experience fewer problems than those with more general aims. We argue that this will generally be true even when the implementation team is less experienced and where problems arise in relation to under-resourcing or red tape. The reason for producing the typology is to help practitioners more easily identify the types of scheme which will be less risky to implement. However, it is important to consider that there is likely to be a trade-off associated with choosing to implement schemes that are likely to be easily delivered. For instance, implementing high-risk approaches can encourage innovation and generate new knowledge. Whichever the strategy taken, we recommend* *that the practitioner is at least aware of potential implementation problems prior to implementation. Consequently, we discuss approaches that can aid practitioners in considering the risk and protective features of their particular planned operation(s).*

INTRODUCTION

New crime prevention projects should be by definition a change from existing practice, and as such may require people to work in a different way (a form of organisational change) and involve the recruitment of new staff or interaction with new partners. For this reason, new projects or interventions are exposed to risks different from those of an organization or partnership's normal practice. Thus, the successful implementation of a new scheme may often hinge upon the identification and management of potential risks or threats to delivery.

Using a series of case studies, the aim of the current chapter is to illustrate some of the complexity of the implementation process and how this can impact upon the likelihood of a crime reduction scheme's success. The reason for so doing is to help practitioners anticipate problems that may arise for particular types of scheme and, in advance of implementation, consider whether they are likely to be in a position to deal with them. We suggest that where problems are likely to arise and could not easily be overcome, it would be more sensible to implement a different type of scheme, or enrol the help of the relevant actors. The latter is, of course, simply common sense, but how does one systematically and objectively ask the right questions to come to this type of decision, and how do we make sure that important but less obvious factors are not overlooked? In response to this question, we suggest one way of classifying different types of scheme and some of the factors that might usefully be considered.

To do this, a classification system will be introduced for the purposes of describing different types of intervention or scheme. As an initial step, the first element of this is fairly general and relates to what, how, and by which agents the scheme will be implemented. Associated with this is a discussion of the strengths and weakness of different types of scheme (e.g., more innovative are contrasted with tried and tested methods) in terms of the likely benefits they may generate *if* implemented successfully. This is important, as it is very unlikely to be the case that all schemes will lead to similar benefits. On the other hand, benefits need to be balanced with ease of implementation and with resilience of the plan to implementation failure. Some proposals will have relatively high resistance to failure, whereas others may be very sensitive to any impedance.

Consideration of the probable benefits of different strategies is common in many everyday life problems and made explicit in the mathematical study of game theory. To take the very simple example of gambling, we know that selecting either red or black in roulette is far more likely to yield a win than putting money on a particular number. However, we also know that a greater reward would be realised if a particular number were selected and fortune smiled upon us. The gambler in us would therefore be tempted to take the higher risk in the hope of greater rewards, even though the rational mind, aware of the laws of probability, might not. In relation to crime prevention, whilst the common aim is to reduce crime as much as is plausible, different actors may have different appreciations of the risks associated with different strategies and their own perception of what reduces crime best. Thus, implementers should explicitly weigh up the costs and benefits of a particular intervention before embarking on it. This is something that may well be done implicitly whilst planning a scheme. However, with the exception perhaps of those who use frameworks such as Ekblom's "5I's" (Ekblom, 2002), it is rare that we see this done explicitly before implementation. However, doing so can make clear the reason for a selecting a particular approach and the risks involved in alternative approaches to all actors involved. Clarity of this kind may perhaps ensure that the most appropriate scheme is implemented, or it may secure the active engagement of all those involved with their eyes wide open, and identify important partners who might otherwise not engage with a project.

To illustrate on a basic level, there will be different advantages and disadvantages to playing it safe or taking more risky strategies. A prime illustration of this is to think through the case of innovation verses a more tried and tested approach. An innovative measure has the appeal that successful implementation will help to test the impact of a new intervention and thus add to the knowledge base. If successful this could bring recognition and praise to the practitioner. However, because of its novelty and the associated limitation of directly transferable knowledge, there is likely to be (on average) an increased risk of failure. On the other hand, a tried and tested measure will be easier to implement, as more is known about how, when and where the selected measure has previously worked. And, if the intervention is wisely selected, the practitioner is also likely to have the satisfaction of a crime reduction, which might be enough of an incentive in itself. Which of these different approaches a practitioner takes will or should depend upon a number of factors. These could include the practitioner's own level of experience in the field, pressures from interested agents, and (not least) the personalities of those involved. We will turn to these issues in the following sections.

Whilst these issues, focusing on the differences between the likely crime reductive impacts of different schemes as they do, might on the face of it be seen as not integral to a chapter on implementation, we argue that implementation success, programme theory and so on are inexorably linked. One of the factors key to implementation success is a complete understanding of what is to be done, how, by who, when, in what way and why. Programme theory – the explicit specification of how a scheme is expected to impact upon crime – can help to highlight factors that otherwise might not be identified or given adequate consideration. To illustrate, consider the example of repeat victimisation (RV) prevention strategies. The rationale for such schemes is based on research (see Pease, 1998) which demonstrates that for a variety of crimes prior victimisation is one of the best predictors of future risk, and that when repeat victimisation occurs, it does so swiftly. Schemes aimed at reducing repetition typically do so by hardening the target at risk. In the case of burglary, this often involves increasing the levels of physical security. Importantly, to prevent RV the intervention must occur quickly – ahead of the time course of the phenomenon. In this way, even though a repeat victimisation prevention scheme may be implemented through the provision of enhanced security to vulnerable households, if the timing of intervention is asynchronous with that articulated in the programme theory, this would represent an example of implementation failure.

So far, the concept of implementation failure has been considered in a generic way. However, just as the process of implementation is complex so too is what constitutes failure. We might ask if a scheme is resilient to implementation failure, but resilient to what, precisely? A further purpose of this chapter therefore is to try to unpack some of the elements of implementation failure, and suggest a systematic approach to their classification. After all, in identifying regularities as it does, classification can help to further refine a problem and suggest consequent solutions to it. It should be noted that none of what follows is intended to be prescriptive. Crime prevention schemes and partnerships come in many shapes and sizes. Instead, our aim is to provide one way of looking at the problem of implementation which can be tailored by those who might use it.

We will attempt to cross-reference various elements of crime reduction schemes with tentative comments on their likely benefits and resilience to implementation failure. It is important to provide case studies to illustrate some of the points highlighted by this exercise, and hence we have selected four schemes that have a fair degree of variation in terms of their defining characteristics. All four of these interventions were evaluated by the authors and are examples of U.K. crime prevention schemes. The first is an anti-theft chair initiative with the aim of reducing bag theft in a busy bar in Westminster; the second a large-scale burglary reduction situational crime prevention initiative implemented in Liverpool; the third a Targeted Policing Initiative aimed at reducing business crime on Merseyside; and the fourth, a further burglary reduction intervention implemented elsewhere in the north of England with a focus on potential offenders.

The next sections will focus firstly on classifying schemes and secondly on a number of implementation issues that the authors consider key "make or break" factors for the case studies that follow. Typically the latter include failures in the consideration of programme theory (and associated implementation failure), misunderstanding of the demand for measures, inhibitive legal issues and staff turnover.

DIFFERENT TYPES OF SCHEME

As mentioned above, there are a number of dimensions to different schemes that can help distinguish them from each other, some of which are shown in Table 1. Each element falls into one of four general categories shown in bold type. In terms of the types of scheme, there are a number of criteria. For example, one way of distinguishing between types of scheme is to establish whether they have a situational crime prevention or a dispositional focus. The former include measures that manipulate features of the physical environment in which opportunities for crime are apparent. Examples include closed-circuit television (CCTV), target hardening and crime prevention through environmental design (e.g., Clarke, 1997). Situational schemes can also cover victim-orientated schemes that advocate or facilitate the development of security practices among those at risk. In contrast, schemes with a dispositional focus intend to get lasting changes in the behavioural dispositions of offenders and/or those at risk of offending. Thus, there is an attempt to change dispositions irrespective of the particular situation that the offender finds himself or herself in.

This should not be confused with the issue of whether schemes are people-centred or equipment-centred, which is also a classification

Table 1: A Generic Classification of Different Crime Prevention Schemes

Element of scheme

What type of scheme is it?

Innovative/tried and tested
Situational/Dispositional
Equipment centred/People centred
Crime general/Crime specific
Technology based/Non-technological

Who are the targets?

Victims (or potential victims)/Offenders
Individual recipients/Area-based measures
Randomly selected/Risk-based selection

Who is implementing?

Single agency/Multiple agencies
High/Low community involvement
Implemented by bid authors/others

How intense is the scheme?

Highly/Not people intensive
Highly/Not equipment intensive
Highly/Not training intensive
Short/Long term in effect
Low/high maintenance measures
Highly/Not focused in space
Highly/Not focused in time

criterion shown in Table 1. Some types of scheme rely more heavily on the actions of people to operate successfully on a day-to-day basis than others. For example, a neighbourhood watch scheme relies on people being available to keep an eye on other properties. In contrast, fitting a new door lock to attempt to deter crime is more reliant on the equipment doing its job than on the involvement of other people.

Concerning "who the targets of the scheme are," we need to consider whether specific targets or a wider area are to receive treatment and whether the recipients will be selected randomly or on the basis of identified vulnerability. Such specification identifies a key element of implementation that requires attention. If a scheme requires a degree of precision in relation to targeting, who will provide the relevant data and who has the skills to translate this into a format suitable for intelligent resource allocation? This is not a trivial point. Consider that many interventions have as a priority the reduction of crime within hotspots, areas where the concentration of crime is highest. Despite the regularity with which crime reduction interventions are initiated to deal with such problems, many police forces or crime reduction partners are still unable to identify such areas with much precision.[1] Nor are they able to identify victims of repeat victimisation on a routine basis. Thus, consideration of what data and analysis are required for the successful implementation of a scheme should be identified at the planning stage, rather than citing their absence as a problem after implementation has failed or becomes distorted.

Concerning "who is implementing," we distinguish between single and multiple agency responses and whether the scheme was implemented by those who first suggested it or who acquired the funding. As we will see, the latter can be particularly important because, whilst a thorough understanding of how an intervention is intended to work and who will contribute to its efficacy (and how) may be clear to those who conceived it, such knowledge does not always transfer well. This relates to a theme discussed by Nick Tilley in this volume. In that chapter he discusses how important knowledge may (or not) be communicated from those proficient at what they do to those wanting to learn. A similar message applies to the transfer of knowledge from those who conceive an intervention and those who deliver it. Where these two groups are different people, consideration needs to be given as to how this will be done without a loss of programme integrity. In relation to the number of partners involved in implementation, while multi-agency working can add an additional level of complexity, where a working infrastructure already exists, research demonstrates that this can actually aid implementation (e.g., Bowers et al., 2004).

Finally, there are elements that distinguish among levels of intensity of the scheme – including the dosage of the resources to be allocated, the level of maintenance necessary and the length of time for which the measures are expected to last. Consideration of these in relation to the theory of how the intervention is envisaged to trigger the relevant crime reductive mechanisms is essential at both the planning and implementation stages. For instance, where crime reduction relies on a particular intervention remaining potent or adapting to emerging challenges, the maintenance or shaping of the measures over time may be critical.

Different interventions will probably share certain combinations of the elements outlined above. For example, situational measures typically focus on protecting victims rather than targeting offenders.[2] Equally, those schemes that are people-intensive are more likely to also be training-intensive than those which are not. However, even where there may be a degree of overlap of features across a range of considered interventions, what the use of this classification can do is to ensure that these characteristics are explicitly considered and thus make it more likely that any problems subsequently highlighted have the potential to be addressed.

BALANCING BENEFITS AND LEVELS OF RESILIENCE

Considering the different elements of Table 1, the possible benefits of each (e.g., situational versus dispositional) will vary depending on the precise context in which a scheme is implemented and who is involved (see Pawson and Tilley, 1997). A detailed consideration of all eventualities is beyond the scope or aim of this chapter. Instead, we focus on some of the particular advantages of certain *types* of scheme. In suggesting these, we make the assumption that all other things are equal, and hence focus on the particular appeal of a limited set of possibilities. In the following paragraphs we will highlight a number of examples, but for completeness readers are referred to Table 2.

One clear benefit of situational measures is that because they deal with the immediate environment, immediate reductions in crime are more likely than in those approaches that concentrate on changing people's dispositions (Laycock, 2001). This is partly because a detailed specification of the problem and responses to it are often relatively easy to generate. This is clearly important for implementation success and the targeting of limited resources in a sensible and targeted way. We do not suggest here that offender-based interventions will fail to reduce crime, but that an understanding of how they might work is likely to be more complex, as is their implementation.

One advantage of schemes that apply technological solutions is that they can enhance knowledge about the crime reductive potential of new or existing technologies. This is an important process as adaptable offenders also find new ways of exploiting technology to their advantage, and it is therefore important to keep ahead in the "arms race" (Ekblom, 1997). Important lessons also will be learned regarding their implementation and realised application; however, on the flip side the use of some technology

Table 2: The Potential Benefits of Schemes with Different Elements

Element of scheme

What type of scheme is it?	Which option is most likely to be beneficial?
Innovative/tried and tested	Innovative – more is likely to be learnt
Situational/Dispositional	Situational – more immediate and detectable reduction effects are likely
Equipment centred/People centred	Both could be equally beneficial
Crime general/Crime specific	Interventions that really did reduce as many crimes as possible at the same time would be most beneficial
Technology based/Non-technological	Technological – more is likely to be learnt

Who are the targets?	Which option is most likely to be beneficial?
Victims (or potential victims)/Offenders	Both could be equally beneficial, although vulnerable targets may be more easily identified
Individual recipients/Area measures	Schemes that cover wider areas therefore secure a larger number of recipients
Randomly selected/Needs-based selection	To evaluators randomly selected recipients can be useful; to all other groups risk-based methods of resource allocation would be the most beneficial

Who is implementing?	Which option is most likely to be beneficial?
Single agency/Multiple agencies	Multiple agencies can provide different resources and experience. However, sometimes too many agencies can cause differences in opinion and therefore delays
High/Low community involvement	High community involvement might help with reassurance and address community concerns. However conflicts can arise between implementers and communities in terms of which problems should be addressed and how
Implemented by bid authors/others	Implemented by bidders – they have the best idea of what was originally planned

(continued)

Table 2: *(continued)*

Element of scheme

How intense is the scheme?	Which option is most likely to be beneficial?
Highly/Not people intensive	From a cost-effectiveness perspective, not people intensive
Highly/Not equipment intensive	For short-term effects and from a cost-effectiveness perspective, not equipment intensive. However, where the cost of equipment is not recurrent but impacts are sustained, expensive startup equipment costs can be easily justified
Highly/Not training intensive	From a cost-effectiveness perspective, not training-intensive
Short/Long term in effect	Long term in effect
Low/high maintenance measures	Low maintenance measures
Highly/Not focused in space	From a cost-effectiveness perspective, highly focused in space
Highly/Not focused in time	From a cost-effectiveness perspective, highly focused in time

such as CCTV can be problematic and may deliver only modest impacts (e.g., see Gill and Spriggs, 2005). Thus, although the application of new technologies can deliver new knowledge and possible reductions in crime, is the associated risk an acceptable one? Furthermore where an interface is required between a new technology and existing information systems, does there exist an appreciation of issues relating to the compatibility of the two? This is in no way to suggest that the use of different technologies should be avoided, but rather that their applications require careful planning.

In terms of the targets, schemes that target a wider area may be likely to have a greater impact than those that target a limited set of individuals.[3] Economy of scale can also mean that the cost per treated victim (potential or otherwise) may be less for a scheme delivered over a wider area. For instance, treatment may be delivered to a specific area rather than to recipients located in different areas. At the simplest level, the former can reduce the time taken to travel to and from the treatment area, thereby providing more time dedicated to the delivery of the intervention, less to travelling. However, the effective delivery of larger-scale interventions can require a different level of infrastructure, and may require the timely supply of larger quantities of appropriate materials. This can add a further level of planning to the process, and may require a different configuration of staffing than currently exists. This requires consideration from the outset, and may require adaptation during implementation.

There will inevitably be some measures that are beneficial in some ways and perhaps not in others. The degree of community involvement is an example of this. High community involvement can be beneficial in terms of helping to reassure the public that measures are being taken to reduce crime. However, sometimes such schemes can experience conflict between the implementers and the community involved in terms of the perception of the problems that should be prioritised for action. Communities, are of course influenced by what Felson (2002) refers to as the dramatic fallacy. Salient but infrequent events, often without pattern, have an intense psychological impact upon residents which can encourage a demand for intervention. However, where no "problem" (in the problem-oriented policing sense) exists, this is not a sensible course of action; but how does one explain this, particularly where anxieties are sensitised and rationality suspended? In such cases community participation may be difficult to manage and could hinder the implementation of some interventions.

Benefits also need balancing when considering intensity. In some senses, the more resource intensive a scheme, the better. Various large-scale evaluations of burglary reduction schemes demonstrate this (Ekblom et al., 1996; Bowers et al., 2004), showing a positive relation between burglary reduction and the dosage of intervention. On the other hand, it is important to consider the cost of the scheme; a more intense scheme will be more expensive, so from a cost-benefit perspective, the optimal situation may be to have a scheme that has the greatest return in terms of reduction, but with the minimal possible resources.

From this discussion, it should be apparent that an important point to consider is *who* is actually likely to benefit from the presence or absence of a particular element in the matrix shown in Table 2, and *how* they benefit. Some of the interest groups that may benefit from schemes are implementers, funders, the local community and academics/evaluators. The story is complicated further by the fact that these groups are likely to benefit from the benefit of others. In this sense, we can see that some combinations are likely to yield win-win situations. Hence, if the funders benefit (e.g., government by seeing a downwards trend in the crime rate) or academics benefit (e.g., by adding to the knowledge base in terms of new research), then the implementers are likely to benefit as they will be cited as an example of good practice. This follows on to the issue of exactly *how* they benefit. Benefits include production of new knowledge, recognition and kudos, crime reduction, and cost-beneficial crime reduction.

Discussion will now turn to some of the potential risks associated with some of the above factors in relation to implementation failure. As observed in the introduction, it seems logical that in many cases those schemes that offer the greatest potential benefits will also have associated with them the highest risks. Therefore, for each characteristic (e.g., situational versus dispositional) we tentatively assess the likelihood of implementation failure and "resilience" to it. Before discussing this table in detail, we turn to the criteria used to make the assessments provided.

There exist a number of factors that are likely to contribute to implementation failure. These include problems with staffing (particularly high staff turnover, no "champion" to take the project forward and lack of experience), problems with infrastructure (are the partners and facilities necessary to implement already in place?), theory failure (when the inputs of the scheme do not logically lead to the desired outcome; which means that even if measures are put in place, crime reduction is unlikely), legal problems and red tape, latency of implementation and, problems with the sustainability of the scheme. All of these issues, if they occur, are likely to have negative impacts on the efficient and effective implementation of a scheme. They can therefore be seen as risks that need to be guarded against. The presence of multiple risks for any one scheme is likely to have an additive or even multiplicative effect on implementation. This is especially likely to be the case where the threats to implementation success are comparatively different in nature. For example, a scheme which has staffing problems and suffers from legal issues is less likely to be successfully implemented than one that has only one type of problem.

If the primary goal of the practitioner is to ensure implementation, then the best strategy would be to choose schemes that possess elements that provide the greatest protection against implementation failure. Table 3 therefore provides a rough guide to which types of scheme are likely to be more resilient to the various implementation problems. For example, we suggest that innovative schemes are more likely to suffer from a greater

Table 3: Resilience of Different Scheme Elements to Implementation Failure

Scheme element	Lack of experience	Theory Failure	Under-resourcing	High staff turnover	No champion	Lack of infrastructure	Lack of exit strategy	Red tape	Slow Implementation	Displacement
What type of scheme is it?										
Innovative/ tried and tested	-/+	-/+	-/+	-/+	-/+	-/+	n/n	-/+	-/+	n/n
Situational/ Dispositional	+/-	n/n	+/-	+/-	n/n	n/n	+/-	+/-	+/-	-/+
Equipment centred/People centred	+/-	n/n	+/-	+/-	+/-	+/-	+/-	+/-	+/-	+/-
Crime general/ Crime specific	-/+	-/+	-/+	n/n	n/n	n/n	-/+	-/+	n/n	+/-
Technology based/Non-technological	-/+	n/n	-/+	n/n	-/+	n/n	-/+	-/+	n/n	n/n

(continued)

Table 3: *(continued)*

Scheme element	Lack of experience	Theory Failure	Under-resourcing	High staff turnover	No champion	Lack of infrastructure	Lack of exit strategy	Red tape	Slow Implementation	Displacement
Who are the targets?										
Victims (or potential victims)/Offenders	+/−	+/−	+/−	+/−	n/n	+/−	+/−	+/−	+/−	−/+
Individual recipients/Area measures	n/n	+/−	+/−	n/n	n/n	n/n	+/−	+/−	n/n	−/+
Randomly selected/Needs-based selection	−/+	n/n	−/+	n/n	−/+	n/n	n/n	−/+	n/n	n/n
Who is implementing?										
Single agency/Multiple agencies	−/+	n/n	−/+	−/+	+/−	+/−	n/n	+/−	+/−	n/n
High/Low community involvement	−/+	n/n	−/+	−/+	−/+	n/n	+/−	+/−	n/n	n/n

Table 3: *(continued)*

Scheme element	Lack of experience	Theory Failure	Under-resourcing	High staff turnover	No champion	Lack of infrastructure	Lack of exit strategy	Red tape	Slow Implementation	Displacement
Implemented by bid authors/others	+/–	+/–	n/n	n/n	+/–	+/–	n/n	n/n	n/n	n/n
How intense is the scheme?										
Highly/Not people intensive	–/+	n/n	–/+	–/+	–/+	–/+	n/n	n/n	–/+	n/n
Highly/Not equipment intensive	–/+	n/n	–/+	n/n	n/n	n/n	–/+	n/n	n/n	n/n
Highly/Not training intensive	–/+	n/n	–/+	–/+	n/n	n/n	n/n	n/n	–/+	–/+

(continued)

Table 3: *(continued)*

Scheme element	Lack of experience	Theory Failure	Under-resourcing	High staff turnover	No champion	Lack of infrastructure	Lack of exit strategy	Red tape	Slow Implementation	Displacement
Short/Long term in effect	-/+	n/n	-/+	-/+	n/n	n/n	-/+	n/n	-/+	-/+
Low/high maintenance measures	n/n	n/n	+/-	n/n	+/-	n/n	+/-	n/n	n/n	+/-
Highly/Not focused in space	n/n	n/n	+/-	n/n	n/n	+/-	+/-	n/n	+/-	-/+
Highly/Not focused in time	-/+	n/n	n/n	-/+	-/+	-/+	+/-	-/+	-/+	-/+

Key

-+ means that schemes with the first characteristic are more likely to suffer that implementation problem that those with the second.
+/- means that schemes with the second characteristic are more likely to suffer that implementation problem than those with the first.
n/n means that there is no difference in risk of implementation failure of that type between the schemes.

number of implementation problems than tried, tested and perfected ones. We see from the table that under-resourcing, having no clear "champion" and having high staff turnover are more likely to cause problems if the scheme being implemented is innovative in nature. However, innovative schemes are no more likely than tried and tested ones to suffer problems with displacement or from the lack of an exit strategy. As noted above, it is important to note that Table 3 is based on the authors' experience and general assessment of the different factors, and hence is subjective. It should be used to help guide decision making, and in particular what is considered during project planning, rather than to prescribe what is to be done. Practitioners may wish to tailor the tables contained in this chapter for use in particular contexts.

There are some types of scheme that are more resilient to some types of failure and less resilient to others. For example, targeting victims rather than offenders is likely to guard against problems with lack of experience, red tape and slow implementation, but due to the nature of the scheme, might be more open to problems of displacement. On the other hand, schemes that attempt to change the disposition of offenders are often difficult to implement, but where successful, spatial displacement should be less likely as the recipients should have reduced their overall level of offending (assuming of course, that other offenders do not take their place).

One thing immediately noticeable from Tables 2 and 3 is that for many elements, there is an obvious trade-off between the associated rewards and those factors that protect against threats to implementation success. Hence, schemes that are innovative, general in terms of the type of crime they seek to reduce, technology-based, high in levels of community involvement, or based on a random selection of targets and controls, are likely to be more beneficial in some ways, but over all are more likely to be subject to implementation problems. This illustrates one balancing act that requires consideration when choosing what to implement and how to do it.

There do appear to be some exceptions to this trade-off. For example, situational crime prevention schemes can lead to higher returns but are also often easier to implement. Likewise, schemes that are implemented by those integral to the conception of a scheme rather than others are likely to be more successful and easier to implement, as the practitioners involved will most likely have the best understanding of the original concept and the role of each of the contributing actors.

FOUR U.K. SCHEMES AT THE "CONCEPT" STAGE

The aim of the above section was to present one way of thinking about what practitioners might expect from different types of scheme, and the challenges that may arise during implementation. We will now illustrate some of the issues raised in more depth by discussing four case studies. Each of these interventions has been classified on the basis of the criteria outlined above, and the results are presented in Table 4. This reveals that all of the chosen schemes had an innovative element and were situational in nature. Two were more equipment-centred and the other two relied more heavily on human intervention. There were apparent differences in terms of who implemented the schemes and how intensive they were.

In the following section, the four example schemes will be compared in terms of the problems experienced in relation to three different implementation related issues; programme theory, legal issues and staff turnover. Before continuing, to facilitate an understanding of how each intervention changed during implementation, a brief outline of the interventions as originally conceived will be provided.

The Anti-theft Chair Intervention

The aim of the project was to reduce levels of bag theft in a bar in Westminster by providing security measures for people's possessions. The project was a pilot to test the viability of using the measures more generally. A variety of anti-theft measures were designed by the project management team at Central St Martins College (CSM), and some, such as clips of different sizes and different materials (e.g., wood and brass), were intended to be fixed to existing chairs and tables in the bar. Others measures involved the manufacture of new types of chairs which would enable people to store their bags within the structure of the chair. So, for example, a net would be placed between the legs of a chair in which a bag could be placed.

Ensuring customers' awareness of the anti-theft measures was seen as a critical element of the implementation process. The measures provided were designed to be fairly discrete and in keeping with the design scheme of the bar in general, and thus a publicity campaign was deemed necessary. Some plans for publicising the measures included general messages to alert people to the risks of bar thefts and specific publicity concerning the location of the new measures in the bar. Other brass signs, which depicted a bag, were to be manufactured to indicate that a bag hook was available under the table or on the seat.

Table 4: Elements of the Four Schemes used as Case Studies

	Anti-theft Chair	Alley-gating	Business Crime Direct	RBI
Element of scheme				
1. What type of scheme is it?				
Innovative/tried and tested	Innovative	Innovative	Innovative	Innovative
Situational/ Dispositional	Situational	Situational	Situational	Situational
Equipment centred/People centred	Equipment	Equipment	People	People
Crime general/ Crime specific	Specific	Specific	Specific	Specific
Technology based/Non-technological	Design of chairs	Design of gates	Use of call centre	Non
2. Who are the targets?				
Victims (or potential victims)/ Offenders	Victims	Victims	Victims	Offenders and victims
Individual recipients/Area measures	Individual	Area	Mix	Mix
Randomly selected/Needs-based selection	Needs	Needs	Needs	Needs
3. Who is implementing?				
Single agency/ multiple agencies	Multiple	Company – with some partners	Multiple	Multiple

(continued)

Table 4: *(continued)*

	Anti-theft Chair	Alley-gating	Business Crime Direct	RBI
High community involvement/Low community involvement	Low	High	Medium	High
Implemented by bid authors/ Implemented by others	Bid authors	Others/bid authors involved	Others	Others
4. How intense is the scheme?				
Highly people intensive/not people intensive	Not	High	Medium	High
Highly equipment intensive/not equipment intensive	Not	High	Medium	Low
Highly training intensive/not training intensive	Not	Med	Med	Med
Short term in effect/Long term in effect	Long	Long	Mix	Long
Low maintenance/high maintenance measures	Low	Med	Med	High
Highly focused in space/not focused in space	Focused	Not	Not	Focused
Highly focused in time/not focused in time	Not	Not	Not	Not

The Alley-gating Intervention

Alley-gating, the installation of security gates across footpath and alleyways, is a form of situational crime prevention that attempts to reduce the opportunity to commit crimes such as domestic burglary. The gates are nearly always fitted in the alleyways to the rear of rows of terraced housing (row homes to American readers). There is now evidence of alley-gating initiatives throughout England, but for the purposes of this chapter we will focus on the implementation challenges experienced by practitioners in Liverpool, Merseyside. The gates installed were fitted as part of the activities of the Safer Merseyside Partnership, an umbrella crime prevention organization that spanned the five districts of Merseyside. After an initial piloting phase, the day-to-day operation of the scheme was managed by Safer Terraces, at the time a new commercial organization with an infrastructure that over time evolved to match the challenge at hand.

When installed and properly used, alley-gates should control access to vulnerable locations – usually paths or alleys at the rear and to the sides of houses – and hence reduce burglary. A recent evaluation of 3,178 gates fitted in the Liverpool area shows that in terms of crime reduction, alley-gates are effective at reducing burglary (Bowers et al., 2005).

Business Crime Direct

Business Crime Direct (BCD) was an initiative funded by the Home Office's Targeted Policing Programme which aimed to reduce crime against small businesses throughout Merseyside. It was envisaged that the initiative would build on the experience of previous research, which found that it was crucial to access and provide treatment to the harder-to-reach businesses whose managers saw crime as an inevitable part of everyday life; those were often the most victimised businesses (Bowers, 2001). To maintain and extend the longevity of the crime reductive effect of any assistance given, it was also seen as important to provide a continued support service to those at greatest risk.

Using a call centre, BCD was therefore set up to manage potential recipients of security improvements and to direct grant assistance. It would do this by receiving inward enquiries from concerned businesses and by making outward contact with businesses and referring those most at risk to Security Advice Officers, who would then make site visits. This dual approach to managing the contact between businesses and crime prevention experts, along with the accurate recording of the history of this contact, was intended to provide long-term support to hard-to-reach higher risk businesses.

Reducing Burglary Initiative: Landlord and Tenant Scheme

Between 1999 and 2001, the Home Office Reducing Burglary initiative funded 63 projects aimed at reducing burglary; the example given here was from one such project in the north of England. The project was police led and involved a number of different measures, including target hardening and security surveys, household surveillance, the disruption of offending, property marking and a community radio scheme for shops. For the purposes of this chapter, we concentrate on two other associated interventions, the aim of which was to make it difficult for burglary offenders to live within the scheme area. The "passport to good housing scheme" used information generated by the local authority housing department to vet tenants. Tenants who were accredited were provided with an identification card, which could be presented to landlords of houses of multiple occupancy (HMOs) when seeking accommodation.

Implemented hand in hand with this was the "accredited properties" intervention, which encouraged landlords to register their properties under an accreditation scheme, and to increase the security of their housing. In so doing, they were to be given access to the best tenants. Thus, in addition to making it more difficult for less desirable tenants to rent property in the area, by using levers with local landlords it was intended that the security and quality of housing in the area would be improved. Note that this scheme was offender-orientated in terms of targets, but situational in nature as it did not aim to change the disposition of offenders, but to make the environment safer by displacing them.

In the following sections, some of the different implementation problems experienced by the implementers of these schemes will be discussed. For each scheme, the authors have only highlighted those threats to successful implementation where there are lessons provided by that scheme.

Programme Theory

As mentioned earlier, programme theory is strongly related to implementation success. Implementation plans will often need to change where programme theory has been poorly thought through or totally ignored. This is particularly the case with new or innovative crime prevention approaches, for which the links between the particular measures and the crime reductive mechanisms to be triggered will yet to have been demonstrated. Below are examples of a scheme in which the programme theory was straightforward and one where it was more problematic.

Anti-theft Chair: An Example of Sound Programme Theory

Table 5 shows the mechanisms through which the measures were proposed to reduce the theft problem. Whilst there are a number of different possible mechanisms, in essence, the theory was that crime would be reduced by

Table 5: Possible Mechanisms through which Anti-theft Measures Might Impact on Crime

Mechanism 1	Mechanism 2	Mechanism 3	Mechanism 4
Installation of anti-theft measure	**Installation of anti-theft measure**	**Installation of anti-theft measure**	**Installation of anti-theft measure**
↓	↓	↓	↓
Some customers notice measures and use it to secure their bags	Some customers notice measures and use it to secure their bags	Some customers notice measures	Offender notices measures
↓	↓	↓	↓
Offender attempts to steal bag(s)	Offender sees measures	Customers are more conscious of bags and secure them without using measures (e.g., wears bag across shoulder)	Offender perceives increased risk of apprehension
↓	↓	↓	↓
Customer or staff are alerted to attempt	Offender perceives increased risk of apprehension	↓	Offender decides not to take bag
↓	↓	Offender perceives increased risk/ effort involved in undertaking bag theft	↓
Offender is apprehended	Offender decides not to take bag	↓	**Bag theft is reduced in bar, but offender steals bag from unprotected licensed premises next door**
↓	↓	**Bag theft is reduced**	
Bag theft is reduced	**Bag theft is reduced**		

the facilitation of measures that patrons could use to reduce the opportunity for offending – their bags could be safely attached to their chairs, or stored within them.

RBI Landlord and Tenant Scheme: A Problem with Theory Failure

Table 6 shows that for this intervention in many situations there would be no real effect of the intervention; it relied too much on the complete participation of landlords and tenants to work effectively. In all cases except where there was complete sign-up of all parties there is the potential for a degree of leakage whereby offenders could still secure accommodation in the area. Even with complete sign up there was the possibility that this would just displace the offending problem elsewhere. The programme theory adopted also assumed that the best criterion for sifting tenants was on the basis of their past criminal record (not specific to burglary). However, many people have one-off offences on their criminal records, and many others with a criminal record may never have committed burglary specifically. A further assumption is that not being able to live in a property will prevent an offender from committing burglary at that household, or at those nearby, which is rarely likely to be the case. For instance, while offenders display a preference for committing crime within proximity to their home address, the average distance travelled is around 1.5 miles (a circular foraging area of over 7 miles) rather than a few streets. Thus, for this scheme not only was there a problem with the programme theory, but also a critical aspect (complete sign up) of the scheme was never fully achieved.

Whether an intervention works or not is not the question here. The issue of importance is of how consideration of programme theory can aid implementation, or identify problems that require attention to increase the probability of success. In the case of the second scheme, it should be evident that a full consideration of the programme theory suggests a requirement of implementation dosage that may otherwise not be made explicit.

Legal Issues

Alley-gating: An Example of Difficulties with Legal Issues

At the time of implementation, to install gates that would close access to alleyways, there was a legal "duty of care" to conduct a comprehensive

Table 6: Possible Mechanisms through which the Tenants and Landlords Registration Scheme Could Reduce Burglary

Mechanism 1	Mechanism 2	Mechanism 3	Mechanism 4
Introduction of tenants/ landlords registration scheme	**Introduction of tenants/ landlords registration scheme**	**Introduction of tenants/ landlords registration scheme**	**Introduction of tenants/ landlords registration scheme**
↓	↓	↓	↓
Full sign-up by all tenants and landlords in area	Some tenants sign-up and all landlords in area sign up	All tenants and some landlords in area sign up	Some tenants and some landlords in area sign up
↓	↓	↓	↓
Landlords only accept tenants who have cards	Landlords only accept tenants who have cards	Some landlords will accept tenants who do not have cards	Some landlords will accept tenants who do not have cards. Shortage of tenants may force some landlords to take those without cards
↓	↓	↓	↓
Tenants who do not have cards are more likely to have a criminal record and cannot find accommodation	Tenants who do not have cards cannot find accommodation	Offenders, deflected from some landlords will go to others	Offenders, deflected from some landlords will go to others
↓	↓	↓	↓
Tenants with criminal records move elsewhere	Tenants with and without criminal records move elsewhere	**No reduction in the burglary problem**	**No reduction in the burglary problem**
↓	↓		
Burglary is reduced in area but increases in other similar areas	**Burglary may be partially reduced. Some good tenants are sent elsewhere.**		

consultation with *all* residents affected by the gates, and to secure written consent from them. It was also necessary to contact all public service providers whose access to the alleyways would be affected. These included the local authority, emergency services, refuse collectors, and agencies that hold under-soil rights (electricity, water, gas, telephone and cable television companies).

This consultation process took some time to complete. Indeed, the project workers estimated that the process could take at least 12 months. One of the major issues was that residents who were reluctant to give their support had to be re-visited, which took some time. Interestingly, it was noticed that many residents in end houses were reluctant to give their support. These residents felt that having the gate attached to the sides of their houses would leave them more vulnerable to burglary. The project workers estimated that it took seven times longer to secure the consent of these residents than those who lived elsewhere along the alley. Ironically, these were actually the most vulnerable before burglary and hence potentially the most likely to benefit from intervention.

It was necessary to address some serious legal issues before it was possible to install gates along public passageways. Where the Local Authority was the primary landowner, it was necessary to apply for a closure order through the local Magistrate court. This often proved to be a long and arduous process, especially when groups in favour of open access to rights-of-way opposed the application. Furthermore, once a closure order was obtained, residents became the legal owners of the alleyway(s) and therefore became responsible for them. This had a number of practical implications. For example, arrangements for access were sometimes required by service providers who had laid pipes or cables underneath the alley. The Liverpool schemes found that they had to get agreement from all service providers for every alley that was to be gated – permission to go ahead in a general way would not be granted.

One of the main obstacles found to hinder the progress of installing alley-gates was the inability to identify the landlords and/or homeowners of the properties that will be affected by the gates. Once identified, it was not always easy to contact them. Where properties were privately rented, the landlord was not always living in the house or even the same city or country as the property. The tenants of these properties did not always feel that they could give permission for the gates to be installed without first contacting the landlord. This again illustrates the increased complexity of the implementation of some interventions, and how the number of actors involved can easily escalate. Given the associated latency of implementation associated with this type of scheme, implementers would be well advised to plan ahead, and to identify such obstacles to implementation as soon as is possible. Only through a comprehensive review of the agents involved and the programme theory can this be achieved.

Anti-theft Chair: Problems with Red Tape

As noted above, one of the original elements planned was a publicity campaign aimed at increasing general awareness of the bag theft problem and, in particular, to highlight the new anti-theft measures fitted in the bar. Following discussions with staff from the bar and others from the management company, these plans were substantially altered. This was due to the fact that there was some resistance to displaying the publicity. It was felt that posters warning customers about bag theft would give the wrong signal, and make people warier of others in the bar and less relaxed. In the worst case scenario it was felt that the publicity would possibly put people off from drinking in the bar altogether. For similar reasons, it was felt that the inclusion of publicity pointing out the measures would also lead to some unease on the part of customers. For instance, they might feel that the venue was a particularly "high risk" bar (it was!).

The publicity that had been designed for the bars was in fact fairly unobtrusive in nature. Particularly popular (with other bars in the West-minster area) were information "toblerones," so called because of their three sides, which sat on tables or bars. These were very reassurance-orientated in their message. They also gave practical advice on keeping personal belongings safe and what to do if they went missing. Other publicity included novel handbag-shaped flyers that pointed out measures installed under the tables.

Eventually, for the reasons discussed above, CSM persuaded the bar management that it would be useful to have some form of publicity. The staff did not want it on show in the bar, and additionally felt it would be at odds with the branded menus and the more general décor of the bar. Therefore, the publicity was placed on the back of toilet cubicle doors.

The downgraded publicity in the bar was potentially quite harmful to the overall effectiveness of the intervention. Table 5 above emphasises the importance of customer awareness as a first step in the effective opera-tion of the scheme. One of the most powerful ways of ensuring this would have been the use of publicity. Whilst bar staff were encouraged to ask the customers to use the measures, at certain times they were too busy to do this. Moreover, at many times of the day the throughput of clientele can be high. Results of customer feedback confirmed a significant problem with awareness of the measures, with 44% of customers sampled not noticing the measures in the first place, let alone failing to use them.

Staffing Issues

The most common form of implementation in Britain is through multi-agency partnership. Within multi-agency partnerships, conflicts and tensions can exist which are caused by the differing objectives (and "frames"; see Ken Pease's chapter in this volume) of the partnership's participants, who aim to divert the project in various different directions. This is natural, as the goals of the different organizations are likely to be different. Other staffing issues that commonly cause problems with implementation are turnover of staff and the lack of a clear scheme leader or champion.

Anti-theft Chair: Problems with Staff Turnover and Encouraging Involvement

A general implementation problem related to the continuation of a core team of individuals committed to the anti-theft chair scheme. For example, both of the key representatives from the Metropolitan Police, who helped enormously during the initial planning stage of the scheme and in securing money towards the evaluation, were transferred to other areas and/or positions within the lifetime of the scheme.

In general, the bar staff were very supportive of the scheme. They were very helpful in the process of documenting bag thefts using forms specially designed for the evaluation, and in bringing the anti-theft measures to customer's attention when possible. However, there did appear to be some incidents of bag theft that were not captured. This could have been because the customers did not bring the incident to the attention of the bar staff (although people nearly always do inform staff about this) or, alternatively, the staff turnover associated with bars may have caused a problem with awareness of the project and the recording requirements.

Business Crime Direct: Problems with a Partnership Approach

The multi-agency BCD partnership suffered some problems caused by the different objectives of partnerships. Examples of the need to meet wider objectives included the desire to further research on business crime within the university that evaluated the project; the need for the call centre to fulfil the objectives of their own training initiatives; and the desire of the Chambers of Commerce/Business Associations to increase satisfaction amongst their members by providing an effective response to the growing problem of business crime.

Tensions arose when it became apparent that the strategy was not leading to the levels of demand envisaged. The call centre was receiving an average of only nine incoming calls per week, even after the marketing campaign was implemented. The strategy had to increasingly rely on increasing the client base through outbound calling. The involved partners were quick to diagnose the cause of the problem as lying with the element of the service for which they were not responsible, and communication between the different actors worsened. Particular problems arose from the lack of clear definitions of the role of each partner. The management of the hotline, for example, were initially reluctant to return funding from which they had staffed their call centre simply because of a lack of incoming calls, when their duties had been defined as "the provision of call centre services." Having no involvement with the promotion of the hotline number, they could hardly be blamed for the phone not ringing.

The issue of accountability appeared to further frustrate partners who all had differing views on how the scheme should be implemented. The scheme was ultimately accountable to a steering group, which was not always fully attended and at times could not agree on successful ways forward. This was not only in relation to the general direction of the scheme, but also to issues which were thought to be more trivial, such as that of data collection. Once more the interaction of the different agents involved and a lack of a clear programme theory lead to an outcome that one would not necessarily anticipate.

PUTTING IT ALL TOGETHER

One way of using the classification introduced in planning future interventions is to systematically work through them for a planned intervention and context. Context here would include the organisation(s) involved and the resources available. One potentially useful approach to doing this and to synthesize the analysis is to use a technique known as force-field analysis, developed in the field of organizational psychology (Lewin, 1975). Originally conceived to help plan and understand organizational change, the technique is used to identify factors that may drive or restrain a planned change to an organization, and the likely net result of the interaction between them. To do this a force-field diagram, which symbolizes the tug of war between different factors, is produced. In the diagram those factors that represent weaker forces for or against change are placed towards the top of the diagram, those strongest toward the bottom. Once generated, the analysis can help one to understand the dynamics of a particular organization in relation to the planned change, to identify how different people are likely to influence the change, and who might need to be targeted to minimize resistance.

As noted in the opening paragraph of this chapter, new crime prevention projects can be considered a form of organisational change, and hence this force-field approach can be tailored for use in the planning of future interventions. For the current purpose we suggest a modification of this simple technique. Factors that are considered likely to impede implementation are listed on the left hand side of the diagram, and those that might counteract them on the other. Where there are many factors on the left side of the diagram for which counteracting forces cannot be reasonably identified, the intervention may be considered too risky to implement and other strategies should perhaps be explored. Alternatively, this exercise may help to identify factors that need to be addressed before implementation begins to guard against failure. Thus, the purpose of conducting the exercise is to perform a risk assessment and to determine whether any risk factors identified are so serious that successful implementation is unlikely, or whether solutions to them can reasonably be found.

To do this, using the classification generated in Table 3, elements that are likely to impede implementation of a particular intervention can be identified, and counteracting forces where they exist highlighted. To illustrate, Figure 1 shows an example of force-field analysis for the alley-gating intervention. Referring to the first row of Table 4, we see that this intervention was somewhat innovative in nature. Looking at Table 3, one risk associated with this type of scheme is that of theory failure. The reasons for this are two-fold. First, because it was an innovative scheme, the theory would not previously have been tested. This links into the second reason. As it is an area-based scheme the logic of the intervention is susceptible to the ecological fallacy that all houses treated will be at an equal risk. In reality, it is likely that relative to the risk of burglary more generally, within the area targeted some houses will be at an elevated risk, whilst others will not and might be at significantly lower risk. Thus, many houses at an elevated risk of burglary not located within the areas selected for intervention may not receive treatment. Hence, this is added to the force-field diagram and we have placed this around the middle of the diagram to indicate that it is a medium-strength force. In this case, there

Figure 1:   Force-field Analysis for Alley-gating

Against	For
	Experienced project champion, well resourced project, appropriate infrastructure in place
Exit strategy (area based, gates may require routine maintenance to have a long-term impact)	
	Crime-specific (analysis of the problem robust), bid authors involved in implementation, targeted victims
Potential for staff turnover (consultation is highly staff intensive)	
Potential theory failure (innovative, area-based)	
	Secure funding to an appropriate level, experienced manager, appropriate infrastructure
Under-resourcing (design and manufacture of the gates, installation of gates, maintenance of gates and thus sustainability of the intervention)	
	Experienced project champion, appropriate infrastructure
Red tape (multiple agency involvement, community consent required)	

Weak

Medium

Strong

are counteracting forces which protect against theory failure, which include the fact that the scheme was to be overseen by those who originally conceived the scheme, meaning that there would be no loss in the translation of how the intervention was to work. Second, the intervention was crime-specific, meaning that the definition of the problem was likely to be more focused and, in this case the analysis of the crime problem was well articulated. Hopefully, each of the remaining elements is self-explanatory. One notable element not initially addressed was that of an exit strategy. While this might not affect the initially delivery of the intervention it would impact upon its continued effect and where this is intended to be long-term (as in this case) this could be a problem that requires attention. Note that Figure 1 has been designed so that protective factors are only identified or listed where they counteract a possible implementation weakness. Hence the factors listed under "for" are expressed in terms of whether they can counteract the particular level of implementation risk posed by the "against" factor. Therefore, their true or absolute ratings may in fact be stronger than the level at which they are shown to be protective in the figure.

The aim of discussing the above case studies was to illustrate some of the problems faced by crime prevention implementation staff in real life. Here, we attempt to link the problems experienced with the type of scheme that was implemented. One reason why the selected schemes were used as case studies was that they were all innovative in some way. The anti-theft chair scheme was a pilot; a dual landlord and tenant approach had not been implemented in this way before; Liverpool was one of the first areas to develop an alley-gating scheme; and, Business Crime Direct attempted to use a new call –centre-based approach to the administration of crime prevention assistance. As mentioned earlier, innovation is a high-risk strategy and hence it is not surprising there were some hurdles to jump.

We suggest further that there are common problems associated with multi-agency approaches (although this will not, of course, necessarily be the case with established partnerships that work well together). To explain why, consider that crime reduction partnerships can be seen as a set of agents or actors from different organisations that together form a system. The more partners involved, the more complex the system in terms of the interactions between different agents, and hence the harder it will be to anticipate the outcome of a scheme. Schemes that rely on businesses or require a very heavy community involvement or public co-operation are also likely share this feature. So too are schemes where the original team have moved on and others become responsible for the actual implementation of scheme. BCD is a classic example of this; the person who originally conceived the intervention and acquired funding for it was involved in the recruitment of staff to work on the scheme, but was not directly involved with implementation on the ground. This can cause problems, particularly when it is not absolutely clear what is being proposed. Here, a clear map of how the intervention is expected to work and what is required can be of much help.

It is perhaps also worth making some observations in terms of distinctions between people-centred and equipment-centred schemes and victim- and offender-orientated ones. The scheme that focused on reducing the available local pool of offenders suffered a number of implementation issues that the others had less of a problem with. This scheme did not have a water-tight theoretical approach to begin with, and also suffered from low participation, with only a small proportion of tenants and landlords actually signing up to the scheme. Where implementation relies on the actions of individuals, rather than physical measures, it is important to factor in the inertia of the population at large: those actors not part of the implementation team.

Finally, we turn to the issue of intensity. In general, highly intensive schemes may be less resilient to implementation failure. The more that needs to be co-ordinated in terms of the organisation of equipment and human resources, the more difficult the task can become. Hence, it was less time consuming to install the anti-theft chair measures than to alley-gate a large proportion of the terraced alleyways in Liverpool. The latter was only made possible by the establishment of an organisation whose sole purpose was to deliver the implementation of the gates. The lesson here is that an appropriate infrastructure for the delivery of an intervention is of critical importance. Even a huge amount of investment might not lead to effective crime reduction if an appropriate infrastructure for delivery is not established. This becomes particularly problematic as the scale of the implementation project and complexity increases.

In summary, practitioners are advised to be aware of the balance that needs to be struck between the overall benefits of a scheme and the risks of implementation failure. It is important to be aware that certain types of scheme, whilst they might look beneficial on paper, and whilst they may yield positive returns if realised, may be at an increased risk of implementation failure. The tables presented in this chapter could be used as a rough guide to implementers when they are still considering different options at the planning stage of an intervention, and to guide the implementation process. There is nothing wrong with taking a high-risk strategy, but the practitioner (and other interested parties) should walk into this with their eyes firmly open.

Address correspondence to: Dr. Kate Bowers, UCL Jill Dando Institute of Crime Science, University College London, Brook House, 2-16 Torrington Place, London WC1E 7HN; e-mail: k.bowers@ucl.ac.uk

NOTES

1. In a recent study, Bangs and Weir (2005) found that in a sample of police crime analysts, around 50% could produce kernel density maps, and only 20% could identify repeat victims of crime.
2. However, the mechanisms by which they operate are the same regardless of whom they target: i.e., they attempt to alter an offender's decision to commit crime by changing the difficulties, risks, rewards, provocations and possible excuses inherent in a situation. See Clarke (2005) for further explanation.
3. Although, the precise targeting of those at most risk combined with the potential for a diffusion of benefit from treated to non-treated households can mean that schemes with a smaller dosage of intervention can have a similar impact to those that target a wider area, particularly where publicity is used to generate uncertainty about the coverage of intervention (e.g., see Johnson and Bowers, 2003).

REFERENCES

Bangs, M., & Weir, R. (2005). Taking forward crime mapping and analysis in police forces and CDRPs. Workshop given at the *3rd UK National Crime Mapping Conference*, April 2005, University College London.

Bowers, K. J. (2001). Small business crime: The evaluation of a crime prevention initiative. *Crime Prevention & Community Safety: An International Journal*, 3(1), 23–42.

Bowers, K. J., Johnson, S. D., & Hirschfield, A. F. G. (2004). The measurement of crime prevention intensity and its impact on levels of crime. *The British Journal of Criminology, 44*, 419–440.

Clarke, R. V. (2005). Seven misconceptions of situational crime prevention. In N. Tilley (Ed.), *Handbook of crime prevention and community safety*. Devon: Willan Publishing.

Clarke, R. V. (Ed.). (1997). *Situational crime prevention: Successful case studies* (2nd ed.). Monsey, NY: Criminal Justice Press.

Ekblom, P. (1997). Gearing up against crime: A dynamic framework to help designers keep up with the adaptive criminal in a changing world. *International Journal of Risk, Security and Crime Prevention, 214*, 249–265.

Ekblom, P. (2002). The five I's: Experimental framework for a knowledge base for crime prevention projects. In *European Crime Prevention Conference 2002*, 1, 62–97. Copenhagen: Danish Crime Prevention Council.

Ekblom, P., Law, P. H., & Sutton, M. (1996). *Safer cities and domestic burglary.* Home Office Study, 164. London: Home Office.

Felson, M. (2002). *Crime and everyday life* (3rd ed.). Thousand Oaks, CA: Sage.

Gill, M., & Spriggs, A. (2005). *Assessing the impact of CCTV*. Home Office Research Study 292. London: Home Office.

Johnson, S. D., & Bowers, K. J. (2003). Opportunity is in the eye of the beholder: The role of publicity in crime prevention. *Criminology and Public Policy, 2*(3), 497–524.

Laycock, G. (2001). Scientists or politicians – Who has the answer to crime? *Inaugural lecture*, University College London, March 26, 2001 (www.jdi.ucl.ac.uk).

Lewin, K. (1975). *Field theory in social science: Selected theoretical papers*. Westport, CT: Greenwood Press.

Pawson, R., & Tilley, N. (1997). *Realistic evaluation*. London: Sage.

Pease, K. (1998). *Repeat victimisation: Taking stock*. Crime Detection and Prevention Series, Paper 90. London: Home Office.

Mindsets, Set Minds and Implementation

by

Ken Pease

Jill Dando Institute of Crime Science
University College London

"All modern aircraft have four dimensions: span, length, height and politics." Sir Sidney Camm[1]

"Hypocrisy is a tribute which vice pays to virtue." Duc de la Rochefoucauld[2]

Abstract: *The most frequent reason for implementation failure is asserted to be that crime reduction is typically peripheral to the purposes of those tasked with it, a state of affairs which they cannot acknowledge overtly. Three examples are given of marginalisation of the crime reductive purpose in practice. The neglected role of cognitive social psychology in understanding the implementation process alongside the political mindset of implementers is highlighted and asserted to be a necessary element in translating sound crime reduction theory into practice.*

Implementation in engineering is the practical application of a method or algorithm to fulfill a desired purpose. This chapter argues that crime reduction cannot be assumed to be an important desired purpose among those tasked with the realisation of initiatives labelled as crime reductive.

Insofar as the argument holds, attempts simply to systematise the process of implementation will prove fruitless.

Implementation generally refers to the translation of intent into action. It thus has a cast of at least two, the intender and the implementer, although the two may coincide, making implementation easier. (I intend to have breakfast. I prepare and eat breakfast.) The interface between intender and implementer may be direct (as between manager and worker) or indirect (as between lawmaker and police officer). The intent is more conventionally seen as residing in the heads of powerful people such as legislators, business leaders or senior public servants. The tools of the intender include motivating implementers (including setting targets), rule-making, rule-administration and rule-adjudication. From a less elitist view of the process, the world looks different. Those who are designated implementers, being human, have intentions of their own. The intention of the designated implementer may be (and often is) to thwart the plans of the designated intender. This will occur when the aims of the intender are in tension with the aims of the implementer. Successful implementation does not require common aims, but it does require congruent purposes. Specifically, if money or promotion for the implementer becomes more likely with the achievement of the intender's aims, implementation is likely. Where the wellbeing of the implementer is independent of the achievement of the intender's aims, or negatively linked to it, implementation is unlikely. Where aims are in tension, the short-term competitive advantage typically lies with the designated implementer, since the latter is in control of what happens. The more complex a plan, the more designated implementers there are, and hence the greater the likelihood of subversion. Historically, the subversion of manufacturing is linked with the disruption caused by Ned Lud, who led opposition to the introduction of new machinery in the textile industry, at the cost of the livelihoods of many workers. The tradition is revered as a mode of opposition to change at the cost of human welfare (see Weir, 1993). Neo-Luddism is the revival of Luddite ideas in the context of the information economy, and flirts with the anti-technological ideas of the Unabomber.[3] The emergence of cyber crime can be seen as a form of neo-Luddism. Game theory may be seen as the formal working out of relationships between the plans and actions of people, and is perhaps a fruitful source of heuristics about implementation problems, albeit one beyond the scope of this chapter. This brief expedition into a wider discussion is intended merely to show that there is no shortage of history and theory with which to come to terms with implementation issues.

This chapter takes the view that implementation failure is widespread in many contexts, even where the consequences of non-implementation are fatal and/or extremely costly. The most typical reason for that is taken to be that the aims of the intender diverge from those of the implementer, often in contexts where the implementer cannot be candid about his or her real aims. Implementation failure is represented in folk wisdom by proverbs such as "There's many a slip twixt cup and lip" and "Don't count your chickens until they're hatched." This suggests recognition of the ubiquity (but not inevitability) of such failure. An important source for this view came to my attention late in the preparation of this chapter (Ormerod, 2005). This is excusable because it had not been published when the chapter was drafted! To précis the argument, Ormerod noted that most firms fail and most species become extinct, and the primary reason is not external shock but endogenous characteristics of the system of which they form part. Longevity of firm or species is no protection against failure. To quote Ormerod:

> ...a key phrase which needs to be hard-wired into the brain of every decision-maker, whether in the public or private sector, intent is not the same as outcome. Humans, whether acting as individuals or in a collective fashion in a firm or government, face massive inherent uncertainty about the effect of their actions.... Species, people, firms, governments are all complex entities that must survive in dynamic environments which evolve over time. Their ability to understand such environments is inherently limited. These limits are a fundamental feature of... systems... in which the individual agents are connected through networks which evolve over time. (p. 221)

Implementation failure will later in the chapter be illustrated by chilling examples from military and engineering contexts. The most common cause of implementation failure in these contexts, as in the writer's experience in crime reduction, is taken to be contrasting world views (and associated motives) of designated intenders and designated implementers, sometimes manifest in self-interested subversion of intent and sometimes in neglect of the work to be implemented in favour of activity deemed more central to the designated implementer's conception of core tasks (or in favour of acceding to pressures from elsewhere), the whole constituting the ineffable evolving network of Ormerod's passage reproduced above. The implications of this analysis for crime reduction will be discussed. As noted earlier, they contrast with the prescription for systematising the implementation process suggested in some other chapters. Perhaps the first step should be illustrating the points in my life when the scales fell from my eyes and I realised that crime reduction was not the primary agenda of those charged with the task. Three examples will be given from the writer's experience.

Self-Proclaimed Achievement among Community Safety Officers

Many former students of the writer have gone on to careers in U.K. local authority departments as community safety officers. These officers, as co-equals with police officers, are supposed to lead local crime reduction efforts. In time, my former students apply for more senior jobs and ask me for references in connection with their applications. I always ask them to send me a recent curriculum vitae. Reading these is instructive. A literal understanding of the role of the community safety officer would suggest that the successes they identify should be couched in terms of crime reduction, public perceptions of security, and the like. In fact, they almost invariably do not (I add "almost" only to insure against possible memory failure, not because I recall any exceptions). Their claimed successes are in terms of amounts of central government and European Commission money attracted to their locality. Bear in mind these are applications to local authority employers for *senior* positions. The core purpose implicit in them is area enrichment, not crime reduction. Of course spending the money attracted may have crime reductive effect, but that seems not to be central in their characterizations of success. This perception is strengthened by meetings with local authority representatives at conferences, and with the emergence of a cottage industry of personnel in local authorities whose primary work is to write grant applications.

Police Promotion – What Matters

While community safety officers labour to attract money, their police colleagues seek to process individual events efficiently, since failure to do that leads to discipline hearings and other professionally destructive outcomes. My epiphany about crime reduction's real and subsidiary role among police purposes came when seeking to help a close friend, a police officer seeking promotion after 20 years. His skills lay precisely in understanding crime patterns and trends, more by talking to citizens than by formal analysis. He was (and remains) in my view exactly the sort of person who should enjoy seniority within the police service because he can tell the crime problem wood from the crime event trees. At the time of writing, he has failed both the examination (which he later went on to pass) and the role-play exercise where examiners simulate members of the public complaining about *individual* events. These experiences persuaded me that, while the aggregation of events into problems is the absolute starting point for situational prevention and problem-oriented policing (Scott, 2000; Clarke and Eck, 2003), with few exceptions (notably the investigation of serial murderers and rapists) the disaggregation of events is the way in which the police and criminal justice typically make their work manageable. The "Part 1 Promotion Crammer for Sergeants and Inspectors 2004" (Barron and Mitchell, 2004)[4] is an important book for ambitious police officers. It portrays itself as follows:

> This book is designed to help you pass the Sergeants' and Inspectors' exams at the first attempt. It is a "no nonsense – no frills" book aimed at people who want to get as much as possible from their time spent studying, with all the verbiage thrown overboard together with everything else that seems to cloud the issues with facts, leaving only the bare bones of what you need to know to pass the exam. . . . There are no semantic somersaults or linguistic limbo dancing in this book – just what you need to know. (p. ii)

The things to bear in mind in looking at the content of the crammer are:

1. It has near universal readership among those preparing for the examination;

2. It is for people who, if successful, will be involved in supervising the work of many of their colleagues, will have to shape local strategy, and sit on Crime and Disorder Partnership committees;

3. Part 2 of the examination does not remedy the deficiencies of Part 1, being a role-play examination of individual contacts with members of the public.

The book is interesting in identifying relatively unexplored byways of the law. For example, how many people know that the offence of "intimidation by violence or otherwise in relation to labour relations" covering offences like hiding colleagues' tools, does not apply to seamen (p. 131)? Clearly this is important information for Police Inspectors even in the landlocked counties of England and Wales, far more important than the liaison arrangements for which they will be responsible upon promotion.[5] Among the facts not mentioned among the legal arcana are the following, all from the same Act:[6]

1. The responsibility for reducing crime and disorder is shared between police and local authority, acting jointly as a local Crime and Disorder Reduction Partnership (s5, CDA, 1998);

2. Local authorities must consider the crime consequences of all their decisions (s17, CDA, 1998);

3. The police are required to share information of crime-reductive relevance with local authorities (s115, CDA, 1998).

Most important, the entire book is concerned with police powers in respect of individual events, with no suggestion that there is any part of the police task which goes beyond this. The only times when the law specifies an offence in terms of repeated occurrences, appears for example in the offence of putting people in fear of violence where:

> ... a person whose course of conduct causes another to fear, on at least two occasions, that violence will be used against him is guilty of an offence if he knows or ought to know that his course of conduct will cause the other to fear on each occasion. (p. 73)

In short, the implicit agenda is that the prepared police manager will exhibit knowledge of:

1. Police powers

2. Evidentiary tests

3. Possible defences

4. Social skills in one-to-one role-play encounters (tested in Part 2 of the examination).

There is no suggestion of the responsibility to aggregate data to yield putative problems. This is in many ways typical of criminal justice, which fails to reflect cumulative harm. What is the evidence that the criminal justice system takes a situation involving cumulative harm and treats it as a one-off event? These include:

1. The use of sample charges in circumstances where a relationship involves numerous offending events (such as incest);

2. The practice of taking crimes into consideration which, while pragmatically defensible, converts a lifestyle into an isolated crime;

3. The circumscription of use of similar fact evidence, which treats similarity of behaviour across putative crime events as often problematic;

4. Home Office counting rules, which designate a principal event under which a set of related events is categorised (for example a hook and cane burglary of car keys and subsequent theft of a vehicle from the drive being subsumed under a single offence of domestic burglary).

To summarise, the absolutely basic step of crime-reductive policing, the aggregation of events into problems, is conspicuously absent from police promotion procedures, its absence chiming with the priorities of criminal justice generally. I believe that this reflects the subordinate position of crime reduction relative to the trouble-free processing of individual complaints or cases. Certainly the thing that an ambitious police officer should avoid at all costs is a bungled investigation, not the failure to reduce local crime levels.

Despised Successes

The third example of the relegation of crime reduction to other world-views comes from direct personal experience. The successful Kirkholt burglary reduction programme (see Pease, 1991) had two phases. In the first, action centred on the reduction of risk to those burgled and their immediate neighbours, and yielded large burglary reductions. One of the elements in this was "cocoon watch," the pared-down mutual help and vigilance version of Neighbourhood Watch incorporating six homes contiguous with one recently burgled. In the second phase of the project, more "partners" became involved, prominently the probation service. It became clear that the essentially simple precautions of cocoon watch were being progressively abandoned. The writer's protest about this was met by the lead probation officer's contemptuous response, "We've moved far beyond that!" This and the whole attempted thrust of the project thereafter bespoke an attitude of mind which privileged offender support over crime reduction. Offender support was deemed fundamental; situational measures, however successful, as mere tinkering.

While the Kirkholt experience was particularly painful (because I did not then understand the subordinate position of crime reduction in professional ideologies), more recent examples are probably more important. These come in meetings to discuss local crime reduction strategies (of which I have now attended many). These typically exhibit "balance"

between location, victim and perpetrator perspectives. However, the perpetrator perspective typically features some form of diversion from custody
(or other sanction, for example by "restorative justice"). The interesting
point is what happens when the meeting is invited to justify the inclusion
of such elements in a crime reduction strategy. I have never encountered
in such meetings any reference to a research base justifying the local
scheme in its particulars (although bluster by proponents in terms of self-
evident truth or an unspecified large literature is occasionally heard). It
becomes clear that a perpetrator-based element is justified on some semi-
articulated humanitarian grounds. At such meetings, some police officers,
apparently liberated from a potential charge of callousness, eagerly explore
the situational prevention opportunities forgone by the inclusion of offender diversion, but the notion of perpetrator diversion from sanctions
seems deeply rooted as a politically necessary demonstration of "balance,"
however uneasily it sits in a crime reduction strategy.

Implementation, Sustainability, Publicity and Ambition

Consider the career of the ambitious police officer or (to a lesser extent)
community safety professional. In a career totalling (in the U.K.) 30 years,
the ambitious officer cannot afford to spend more than a few years at a
given rank or in a given role. This means that any career advancement
yielded by an initiative must come at or near its inception. An initiative
which takes five years will if successful yield credit to a successor and
competitor. If it fails, blame can be shuffled off. At its most Machiavellian,
this would mean that the ambitious officer should launch a mix of short-
term initiatives which are likely to be successful and longer-term initiatives
which are likely to fail. This would allow him or her to say something
along the lines of "The things I completed on my watch were successful.
It's obvious that the things I left and which failed are the result of my
successor's incompetence." While it is not suggested that such cynicism
is common, it is the case, as Bowers and Johnson (2003) showed for a raft
of burglary reduction projects, that the peak in publicity intensity preceded
that for implementation, suggesting that the schemes tended to promote
their interventions *before* they were implemented.

This volume is about implementation. The last paragraph suggests
that the interplay between presentation and substance in crime reduction
is subtle enough to make the insertion of the time dimension necessary.
Implementation (conventionally considered) is perhaps a special case of

sustainability. This can be clarified by thinking about the relationship between time and initiative penetration into the available universe of interest. An initiative that is *sustained* for zero time in no places is not *implemented*. One that is sustained indefinitely over all available places is fully implemented. One that is sustained indefinitely over *some* available places is partially implemented, as is one that is sustained for *short periods* in all available places. Some of the possible relationships are illustrated in Figure 1, where the ordinate represents (for example) the proportion of the maximum possible penetration in terms of number of police officers acting in accordance with the initiative, and the abscissa time from introduction. Nearly all trajectories are possible. Three are illustrated. The fader persists in trial areas for a while before being abandoned. The stumbler enjoys modest success and is not abandoned by any of those who adopt it. The winner swiftly moves to universal use.

The point of Figure 1 is simply to assert the need to consider time as a dimension in implementation/sustainability. The never implemented would be a line along the abscissa. Faders cease to be implemented. Stumblers are implemented in only a few areas where they were not trialled. Winners seem to propagate. Notions of implementation failure which consider only the first line (zero implementation ever), and contrast it with swift implementation everywhere, would be impoverished indeed. In

Figure 1: Sustainability as Implementation

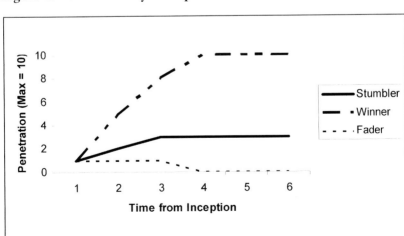

what follows the word implementation should be taken as implementation/
sustainability in the sense outlined above. The issues in engineering (and
specifically disaster prevention) contexts are set out by Perrow (1999).
His Normal Accident Theory concentrates on unforeseen interactions in
complex systems, and is of limited relevance to crime reduction. However,
the process of practical drift, which he discusses in the context of a "friendly
fire" tragedy, has resonance for crime reduction (see for example Tilley,
1993). In crime contexts, one can think of it less in terms of drift, more
as assimilation to a view of the work. This makes collaboration between
those with different working scripts particularly difficult.

> Organisations and large systems probably could not function without
> the lubricant of minor deviations to handle situations no designer
> could anticipate. Individually they were inconsequential deviations,
> and the system had over three years of daily safe operations. But
> they resulted in the slow, steady uncoupling of local practice . . . from
> the written procedures. . . . " (Perrow, 1999, p. 378)

The types of implementation trajectory distinguished above are obviously only a subset of the possible. Some winners lose as times change
(the police rattle)[7] and some stumblers start to gallop when their time
comes. This chapter does not aspire to a complete typology. However it
does argue that the integration of implementation and sustainability
changes the landscape somewhat. One of the ways in which it does so is
through the insight that in the long run nothing is implemented beyond
the currently available means to satisfy an underlying purpose. Who now
wishes to argue for the implementation of the police rattle? What survives
is the motive to summon help, realised by whatever imperfect means
current technology allows. This realisation may serve to frustrate those
whose genuinely good idea is not taken up, or to consider variants of tactic
which chime more closely with designated implementers' world-view.
Consistent with the emphasis on congruence of purpose is the assimilation-
contrast theory of attitude change (see Insko, 1967; Olson and Zanna,
1993), which (to oversimplify somewhat) suggests that attitudes will move
towards a persuasive communication relatively close to currently held
views, but away from a persuasive communications more distant from such
views. This suggests that, to be implemented, initiatives should be relatively
close to current purposes and couched in terms consistent with the perceptions of the implementer. The time dimension is relevant in that some
ideas will take off when the *zeitgeist* moves towards them, and others will
stumble when the *zeitgeist* moves away.

The obstacles to implementation in crime reduction can be seen in better relief when one considers the fate of innovations when the purposes and priorities of intender and implementer are in tension and when the stakes are high in human life and money, as the following examples illustrate. A much wider range of examples in the military context are available in Dixon (1976) and David (1977).

The Tank, the Tug and the Jet Engine: Why They Stumbled

The notion of an armour-clad vehicle had been anticipated by such luminaries as Leonardo da Vinci[8] and H.G. Wells (1903). In 1912 the inventor E.L. de Mole presented the U.K. War Office with a design for a tracked vehicle to facilitate troop movement across barbed wire and trenches, which the War Office put to one side. Nonetheless some (particularly naval officers) championed the tank, and some were built. After premature deployment in small numbers on the Somme and at Ypres during World War I, their worth was demonstrated at Cambrai, although tactical naiveté and inflexibility about their use (they advanced faster than anticipated but the supporting infantry's timetable did not change) limited eventual success. After the war, the case for mechanisation, and in particular for the tank, was made by one Major General J.F.C. Fuller, who wrote an award-winning essay and subsequent books on tank warfare, and was rewarded by unemployment in his rank for three years and subsequent forcible dismissal. The Chief of the Imperial General Staff Field-Marshal Montgomery-Massingberd, attacked Fuller's books "while admitting that he had never read them because it would make him so angry if he did" (Dixon, 1976, p. 113). It is of particular interest that it was *naval* officers who championed the tank. The naval use of armour had long been established (it will be recalled that Wells's "The *Land* Ironclads" (1968 [1903]) reflects the earlier use of the term for ships). Armoured machines were by then part of the *navy's* construct system but not the *army's*.

Liddell Hart (1965), another advocate of mechanisation and the revision of tactics necessary to make best use of machines opined:

> If a soldier advocates any new idea of real importance he builds up such a wall of obstruction – compounded of resentment, suspicion and inertia – that the idea only succeeds at the sacrifice of himself: as the wall finally yields to the pressure on the new idea it falls and crushes him. (p. 50)

We are reminded of George Kelly's (1950) characterisation of aggression as the response to the threat to core constructs. This is no doubt accompanied by allegiance to the horse. Dixon (1976) noted that in 1935–6, with the threat of war on the horizon, army spending on forage for horses was £400,000. The spend on motor fuel was £121,000. Dixon continues:

> Presumably to justify the forage, while at the same time making amends for having mentioned petrol, this same field-marshal laid down that in future all cavalry officers should be provided with two horses, and that horses should also be provided for officers of the Royal Tank Corps, presumably in a prophylactic role. (p. 117)[9]

Dixon describes the bloody events signalling the end of cavalry warfare. His book provides a series of historical examples of similar implementation failures as a result of resistant and conflicting construct systems. Some would be desperately funny (such as the faked naval demonstration that battleships could easily shoot aircraft out of the sky) had they not been so costly in human life. Dixon (1976) quotes Winston Churchill's bitter rebuke about military failure to innovate:

> . . . if only the generals had not been content to fight machine-gun bullets with the breasts of gallant men, and think that that was waging war. (p. 86)

David Divine (1964, p. 19) reflects the generality of implementation failure in the Royal Navy thus:

> Of the twenty major technological developments which lie between the first marine engine and the Polaris submarine, the Admiralty machine has discouraged, delayed, obstructed or positively rejected seventeen.

The father of I.K. Brunel, the saintly and brilliant Marc,[10] reflecting upon the improvements to marine steam engines

> . . . suggested to the Admiralty that his machinery could be fitted in a steam-tug which could haul their sail-driven warships in and out of port. Their lordships were appalled at the thought of all that soot falling n the clean white sails of British men o' war and replied sternly, considering it their "bounden duty to discourage the employment of steam vessels as they consider the introduction of steam is calculated to strike a fatal blow at the naval supremacy of the Empire. (Vaughan, 1991, p. 10)

Lest the Air Force feel excluded from this litany of non-implementation, we should pause to recall Sir Frank Whittle's failure to gain support for the development of the jet engine as perhaps the most potentially catastrophic. As his obituary in the Daily Telegraph on August 10th 1996 notes:

> Although (the 1941 first test flight of a jet powered aircraft) was a moment of triumph for Whittle, it was tinged with some bitterness, for he had had to overcome years of obstruction from the authorities, lack of funding for and faith in his brilliant ideas. He felt, with justification, that if he had been taken seriously earlier, Britain would have been able to develop jets before the Second World War broke out.

Self-Deception and Disingenuousness

Some readers may wonder about the mismatch between the rhetoric of crime reduction and the reality of very imperfect implementation. Can people really deceive themselves or be so disingenuous? There are many examples of what looks like one or the other among those dealing with crime. The rhetoric of the indeterminate Borstal training provision was that young people were kept until their individual training needs were met. Remarkably, the average length of time for that to happen fell as admissions rose, so that the total Borstal population did not exceed capacity (Bottomley and Pease, 1986). Judges invoked the guideline rape judgement as a kind of crucifix-waving (to ward off adverse appellate judgements) before imposing sentences inconsistent with it (Ranyard et al., 1994). Home Secretary decisions to keep serious offenders in prison against the advice of the Parole Board miraculously increased as general elections loomed (Wasik and Pease, 1994). In recent years, the proportion of cases discontinued in England and Wales by the Crown Prosecution Service offset pressures on the court so that delays did not get out of hand, and the periods available for tagged early release expanded to offset pressure on prison places. In a culture in which self-deception and/or disingenuousness is endemic, the notion of crime reduction as a primary purpose, with implementation non-negotiable, is probably naïve. Yet traditional social psychology suggests that cognitive dissonance, where two or more inconsistent cognitions are held simultaneously, are held to be motivating. Dissonance must be reduced (see Insko, 1967; Olson and Zanna, 1993). One overlooked way of reducing dissonance is the introduction of an extra cognition which renders the others consonant. ("It will not rain" and "I carry an umbrella" is made consonant by the cognition "All smartly dressed people carry umbrellas.") I think this is probably the preferred mode of dissonance reduction in implementation failure. The judge knows that his preferred rape sentence is inconsistent with the guideline judgement, but knows too that only reference to the guideline will save him or her from the embarrassment of having his decision overturned on appeal. Home Office Prison Department introduced the third cognition that they need to put on a defensible Borstal programme, only achievable by pretending that adequate training periods became shorter so that they were not swamped by new admissions. Community safety officers persuade themselves that leavening their situational programme with offender diversion is the only way to get the latter past local politicians.

With a Single Bound they Were Free

Many years ago, Saturday morning cinema programmes featured 15-minute segments of movies starring Flash Gordon and other heroes of his ilk. At the end of each episode, the hero found himself (always him) in a position from which it was impossible to escape. At the beginning of the next episode, some means of escape presented itself, and with a single bound he was free. The chapter to this point probably seems unremittingly gloomy. Implementation failure is common and results from purposes which are not shared between intenders and implementers. The whole is played out in a shadowland where self-deception or disingenuousness is rife. If this is even partly true, what can be done? The first task is probably to be realistic and undismayed about levels of non-implementation. The second, following Ormerod (2005), is to continue to innovate, as the guiding principle which successful companies and species use to overcome inherent and pervasive uncertainty. The third is to pay more attention to the implementer purposes onto which a new approach is to be grafted, and to see whether the new approach can be located within the assimilation range of the implementer (see above). Ormerod (2005) points out the enormous advantages conferred by even the tiny improvements which are possible in understanding the consequences of actions. People vary in the way in which they represent their world, and how their behaviour is structured by that representation. Seeking to understand that mental structuring is an enduring preoccupation of many sub-disciplines within psychology. Arguably the most enduring of frameworks is George Kelly's (1950) psychology of personal constructs. Its fundamental postulate can be paraphrased as "a person's mindset is channelled by the ways in which (s)he anticipates events." The structure of grouped anticipations are termed constructs, which are the fundamentals of one's personal psychology. Kelly draws out many implications from his fundamental postulate, two of the most important being that people can only communicate insofar as they share constructs, and that aggression is the response to threats to core constructs.

While personal construct theory never gained the pre-eminence in psychological theorising that some of us think it merited, its echoes are everywhere. One is in the theory of mental models of Phil Johnson-Laird (1993; 2001a, b), another is in the concept of frames espoused by Daniel Kahneman and Amos Tversky (2000). The Kellian assertion that the framing of a problem can yield different outcomes seems banal but is profound in its implications. The Johnson-Laird (2001b, p. 434) notion that "mental models represent what is true in the premises but by default not what is false" is likewise rich in its predictions.

Frames can include value attributions. One Swedish police officer, when invited to post notifications of a recent burglary to neighbours, objected "I'm not a postman," thus framing a sensible form of crime reductive communication as outside his frame, and of lower status. In the wake of World War II, research on anti-semitism yielded the identification of the "authoritarian personality" and its measurement by the F (for fascism) scale (see Adorno et al., 1951). The irony is that the attributes regarded as abhorrent because associated with ethnocentrism (intolerance of ambiguity, rigidity, simplicity of cognitive structure) were recognisable as those celebrated in a 1938 book by the Nazi psychologist Jaensch (see Brown, 1965). Jaensch seems to have been the first to offer a systematic theory wherein variables from the psychology of perception could be used to explain variations in personality. Jaensch felt that the ideal Nazi type (the "J" type) was a person who had strong, clear and unambiguous perceptions. In the language of this chapter, the frames were similar, the value attributions different.

The core assertion is that the politics and cognitive psychology of the implementation process need to achieve prominence. One way of expressing this is to say that the SARA (Scan, Analyse, Respond, Assess) formula of problem-oriented policing should be applied to the psychology of implementers alongside the presenting problem. Repertory grid analysis and revealed preference protocols would be the means for doing this. Stupidity inheres in continuing to do the same thing and expecting different results, and we have now failed to implement often enough for us to be condemned as stupid if we fail to seek to understand the psychology of implementation better. The greatest gain from this will be the retrieval of many activities whose failure has been condemned as theory failure which were actually implementation failure – the mistake which we should be most reluctant to make and most ashamed of ever making.

Address correspondence to author at: k.pease@lboro.ac.uk

Acknowledgments: The author is grateful to Dr. Nick Pease for discussion of the process of implementation of engineering innovations in manufacturing contexts.

NOTES

1. Camm was, inter alia, designer of the Hawker Hurricane. Cited in obituary for Sir Frederick Page, *Daily Telegraph*, June 7th 2005, p. 21.
2. *Maximes*, 1678, No 218.
3. http://en.wikipedia.org/wiki/Neo-luddism
4. http://www.policereform.gov.uk/ptdb/promotionreview/ describes proposed changes to promotion procedures. These will not affect Part 1.
5. In case of doubt, I'm being ironic.
6. All references are to sections (s) of the Crime and Disorder Act 1998, the primary legislation structuring crime reduction in England and Wales.
7. The rattle predated the whistle as the communication device issued to police officers, in England and Wales at least.
8. http://www.museoscienza.org/english/leonardo/carro.html
9. At the strategy meetings described earlier, one could regard offender diversion projects as likewise a means of "making amends" for situational prevention.
10. His reward for his major contributions to success in the Napoleonic Wars by the mass-production of waterproof boots for soldiers and blocks for the rigging of sailing ships was tardy payment by the Government and consequent imprisonment for bankruptcy (see Vaughan, 1991).

REFERENCES

Adorno, T. W., Frenkel-Brunswik, E., Levinson, D. J., & Sanford, R. N. (1951). *The authoritarian personality*. New York: Harper.

Barron, T., & Mitchell, J. (2004). *Part 1 Promotion Crammer for Sergeants and Inspectors 2004*, 6th ed. Coulsdon: Janes Information Group.

Bottomley, A. K., & Pease, K. (1986). *Crime and punishment: Interpreting the data*. Milton Keynes: Open University Press.

Bowers, K. J., & Johnson, S. (2003). *Reducing Burglary Initiative: The role of publicity in crime prevention*. Home Office Research Study 272. London: Home Office.

Brown, R. (1965). *Social psychology*. New York: Free Press.

Clarke, R. V., & Eck, J. (2003). *Become a problem-solving crime analyst*. London: Jill Dando Institute.

David, S. (1997). *Military blunders: The how and why of military failure*. London: Robinson.

Divine, D. (1964). *The blunted sword*. London: Hutchinson.

Dixon, N. R. F. (1976). *On the psychology of military incompetence*. London: Jonathan Cape.

Insko, C. A. (1967). *Theories of attitude change*. New York: Meredith.

Jaensch, E. R. (1938). *Der Gegentypus*. Leipzig: Barth.

Johnson-Laird, P. N. (1993). Inference and mental models. In S. E. Newstead & J. St. B. T. Evans (Eds.), *Perspectives on thinking and reasoning*. Hove: Lawrence Erlbaum Associates.

Johnson-Laird, P. N. (2001a). Mental models and human reasoning. In E. Dupoux (Ed.), *Language, brain, and cognitive development: Essays in honor of J. Mehler*. Cambridge, MA: MIT Press.

Johnson-Laird, P. N. (2001b). Mental models and deduction. *Trends in Cognitive Science, 5*, 434–442.

Kahneman D., & Tversky, A. (2002). *Choices, values and frames*. Cambridge: Cambridge University Press.

Kelly, G. (1950). *The Psychology of personal constructs* (2 vols.). New York: Norton.

Liddell Hart, B. H. (1965). *Memoirs*. London: Cassell.

Olson, J. M., & Zanna, M. P. (1993). Attitudes and attitude change. *Annual Review of Psychology, 44*, 117–154.

Ormerod, P. (2005). *Why most things fail*. London: Faber and Faber.

Pease, K. (1991). The Kirkholt Project: Preventing burglary on a British public housing estate. *Security Journal, 2*, 73–77.

Perrow, C. (1999). *Normal accidents*. Princeton: Princeton University Press.

Ranyard, R., Hebenton B., & Pease, K. (1994). An analysis of a guideline case as applied to the offence of rape. *Howard Journal, 33*, 203–217.

Scott, M. S. (2000). *Problem-Oriented Policing: Reflections on the first 20 Years*. Washington, DC: Department of Justice.

Tilley, N. (1993) *After Kirkholt: Theory, method and results of replication evaluations*. Crime Reduction Unit Paper 47. London: Home Office.

Vaughan, A. (1991). *Isambard Kingdom Brunel: Engineering knight errant*. London: John Murray.

Wasik, M., & Pease, K. (1994). Parole and party politics. *Criminal Law Review*, 379–382.

Weir, S. (1993). *Progress without people: In defence of Luddism*. New York: C. H. Kerr.

Wells, H. G. (1968, originally published 1903). The Land Ironclads. In P. Curtis (Ed.), *Future tense*. New York: Dell.

Knowing and Doing:
Guidance and Good Practice
in Crime Prevention

by

Nick Tilley
Jill Dando Institute of Crime Science,
University College London

Abstract: *Good practice involves knowing what to do and being able to do it. There are a number of generally accepted attributes of good practice: it must be ethical, effective, without significant negative side-effects, and economical. There have been, and continue to be a number of efforts to provide catalogues of good practice or good practice guides. What is to be reproduced as good practice can, however, be construed in differing ways: for example as a specific set of preventive activities or interventions; as a methodology for selecting preventive interventions to be adopted, or the informed activation of tested principles or mechanisms by whatever means are available; or as the exercise of well-honed tacit craft skills. Likewise, good practice can be identified in a number of ways: for example from rigorous experimental studies associating specific practices and intended outcomes, from first principles, from informed opinion, or from coherent and tested theory. For the policy-maker attempting to disseminate good practice, for the practitioner committed to implementing it, and for the researcher or educator concerned to inform practice these are important issues. This paper identifies and compares two major approaches to good practice guidance: "What works?" and, "What's to be done?" It reviews their relative strengths, weaknesses and potential uses. It* *also discusses common shortcomings, in particular neglect of the tacit, and what might be done about it.*

INTRODUCTION:
TARGETS AND TYPES OF GOOD PRACTICE

There is no shortage of guidance on what to do to prevent crime. Giving it to the public has been a major part of government policy. For example in 1988–90, of the £11.5 million spent by the British Home Office on crime prevention, £5.3 million went on publicity (Barclay, 1991), and for 1993/4, the corresponding amounts were respectively £13.1 million and £5 million (Barclay, 1995). Almost all the publicity involved guidance to citizens about what they could do to reduce their own risks.[1] There still continues to be extensive advice to the public through advertising, leaflets, and web sites. Private companies with security products to sell also provide crime prevention advice, as do police officers in general and specialist Crime Prevention Officers in particular. As well as central government, the police and the private sector, some local authorities also disseminate advice to the public on ways to avoid risk.

This paper will take a step back from guidance to private citizens on what they should do to reduce their own risks and focus instead on that directed at organisations, in particular public bodies, on what they can do to prevent crime to themselves and to third parties. Again, there has been no shortage of good practice guidance. Some of this has been written by members of the research community, and some informed by research though actually written by others. The basis of other guidance is less certain and appears to be driven as much by anecdote, politics, ideology, commercial interests and wishful thinking as by research findings. The specific concern of the discussion here will be on research or evidence based guidance on good practice, since it is taken for granted that good practice in good practice guidance includes use of research findings. The aim of the paper is, thus, to work through what needs to be included by way of good practice and good practice guidance in crime prevention when aimed at policy-makers and practitioners at local and national levels.

A long list of questions faced by those attempting to produce evidence-based crime prevention guidance is shown in Box 1. This indicates that many decisions have to be made in identifying and communicating it. Often the decisions will be made without much thought. Moreover, different items of evidence-based guidance on good practice will assume different

Box 1: Some Questions Relating to Evidence-based Good Practice Guidance

1. *How is good practice to be construed?*
   - Is it to be defined by method?
   - Is it to be defined by theory?
   - Is it to be defined by specific measures or tactics?
   - Is it to be consistent with specific values?

2. *What count as research findings?*
   - Must they be "experimental"?
   - Must they have internal and/or external validity?
   - Must the research be independent?
   - Must there have been peer review?

3. *What should be done where research findings appear to contradict one another?*
   - Should only the best or most plausible findings be drawn on?
   - Should the findings be aggregated in a meta-analysis to find net effects?
   - Should the conclusion be that patterns really vary by place, time and sub-group?
   - Should the conclusion be that the intervention differed in more or less subtle ways?

4. *What should be done where there is a shortage of research findings to draw on?*
   - Should guidance remain silent?
   - Should lack of evidence just be noted?
   - Should evidence for the underlying theory behind the practice be described?

5. *At what threshold of quality, consistency or volume of relevant research findings can policies or practices be described as good practice?*
   - Must research consistently indicate no unintended harm?
   - Must research show consistent benefits, at least for a sub-set of intended subjects?
   - How many studies or how many subjects are needed as a basis for establishing good practice?

(continued)

Box 1: *(continued)*

6. *How are research findings to be applied in good practice?*

   - How is successful work replicated?

   - How is successful work rolled out?

   - What of what was done in a successful project is to be represented as good practice?

7. *What should be included in good practice?*

   - Should it include evidence used to identify the problem?

   - Should it include methods used to analyse the problem?

   - Should it include means by which the decisions to put the measure in place were taken?

   - Should it include methods by which the measures were applied?

   - Should it include results?

8. *How are research-based good practice guidance messages to be communicated?*

   - Should there be clear and specific injunctions about what to do?

   - Should there by clear injunctions about what not to do?

   - Should advice be given about what is promising?

   - Should there be discursive advice on methods of approaching crime prevention, evidence about their track record to date, and factors to be taken into account in choosing among them?

   - Should advice be pitched at specific problems or general issues?

9. *Are there aspects of good practice which lie beyond research findings?*

   - Are there ideological issues that need to be mentioned?

   - Are there tacit features of successful measures that need to be acknowledged?

positions in relation to the questions. The reader may be relieved that the remainder of this paper does *not* constitute a painful and painstaking discussion of each main question and sub-question in turn. Instead, two broad approaches to good practice guidance are identified. These lie behind most of the evidence-based guidance issued and produce distinctive patterns of answers to the questions listed. Each approach will be described, and examples given. Their respective strengths and limitations will be discussed. The circumstances in which each may have a part to play are considered, and common limitations and uncertainties, relevant to both approaches, will be described.

MODELS OF EVIDENCE-BASED GOOD PRACTICE

Both the approaches that follow are avowedly aspiring to bring the standards and methods of science to the identification of good practice. They also share a large degree of pragmatism – they are focused primarily on informing practice so that it can become more effective in reducing crime. They are to that extent united in departing from accounts of good practice rooted in conventional wisdom, ideology or wishful thinking. They also share scepticism over much that is ordinarily undertaken in the name of crime prevention, be this the requirement of standard agency practice or the result of the exercise of untutored discretion by policy-makers, practitioners, or partnerships.

The first approach described below is labelled "What works?"(WW), and the second "What's to be done?"(WTBD). WW guidance catalogues for policy-makers and practitioners what has or has not been found to work, generally on the basis of "experimental" studies. WTBD guidance aims to help policy-makers and practitioners decide what to do in particular practice or policy circumstances and how to do it. It may draw in part on studies feeding into WW guidance, but is much more catholic in its evidence base. What follows next describes the suite of attributes of each of these models in more detail, together with some examples. The examples illustrate what are intended as instructive, idealised, but highly recognisable ideal-types of the guidance issued. Though rather clearly falling into one category or the other, the examples do not necessarily entirely follow all elements.

1. "What Works" Good Practice Guidance

Most evidence-based WW guidance is derived from findings of experiments, where what is understood by "experiment" is a trial in which an intervention is applied to one (experimental) group or place but not another (the control), and changes in the two are then compared. Most experiments are targeted at finding out what works. There is some non-experimental WW guidance, and there are some experiments which address WTBD, but they are the exceptions.

Experimentally-based WW guidance concerns what works and does not work. It is rooted in rigorous evaluations that aim to find out whether given measures do or do not have their intended crime prevention effects, or do or do not produce damaging or beneficial side-effects. The studies that best gauge this are conventionally believed to be randomised control trials (RCTs) or their nearest practicable equivalent. The first purpose of the guidance is to prevent policy makers or practitioners from inadvertently doing harm. The second is to enable decisions to be made about which interventions produce the largest positive effect size at lowest cost, in order to inform resource allocation decisions.

Guidance may be based on single studies, but ideally draws on several. Program "fidelity" or "integrity" is important to test the effectiveness of the measures put in place, and the measures must be put in place in a consistent way as required by the intended program. The logic of individual studies is to ensure that only the programme measures could produce the effects, by excluding all other factors. This is deemed to be achieved best by RCTs, where there is random assignment to treatment and non-treatment, ideally without the subjects, practitioners or those making measurements knowing which is which; and then comparing changes amongst the treated or untreated or those subject to different treatments. Both the presence of an effect and the effect size can be gauged. Each study is considered high on internal validity (change in the experimental group really was different from that in control groups). A series of studies increases confidence in external validity (that findings can properly be generalised).

Guidance on what to do and what effects can be expected is thus built up over time as more and more interventions in stronger and stronger studies are tested and confidence about effectiveness can increase.

WW guidance informed by RCTs is more readily produced and provided in relation to treatments for individuals than for schemes targeting neighbourhoods or cities, especially where the individual is a relatively passive object of the treatment. The most important reason for this is probably that RCTs providing the grounds for the guidance are more straightforward where the individual is the target of the intervention. It is easier and cheaper randomly to allocate individuals to different treatment modalities than it is to assign localities or cities to differing treatments.

Moreover, there are greater prospects of some "blindness" amongst subjects and practitioners about the experiment being conducted. It is almost certainly easier when individuals are being provided a special program, to make sure that the service that controls receive is not somehow "infected" by the treatment.

This is not to say that there has been no evidence-based WW guidance relating to interventions at city or neighbourhood level. It has, however, generally been based on studies using what advocates of experimentalism consider weaker designs than those used in RCTs. Most often this involves finding one or more area that can be deemed similar to the area receiving the intervention being tested to act as a "control," and comparing changes in crime rates in the experimental and control areas.

Let us look briefly at three examples of experimentally based WW guidance.

a) Meta-analyses and British Youth Justice Board Guidance on Youth Crime and Early Intervention

The Youth Justice Board based its guidance relating to youth crime and early intervention on an overview of the available evidence, in particular research reviews and meta-analysis over the previous 20 years. It noted that, "Meta-analyses . . . have played a particularly important part in confounding the once widely-held view amongst policy makers that, 'nothing works' " (Youth Justice Board:103).

Meta-analyses combine findings from numbers of studies using experimental and comparable control groups to look at aggregate effects. The varieties of studies and combined sample sizes allow small statistically significant effect sizes to be estimated. Meta-analytic studies by Mark Lipsey (1992; 1995) are drawn on in particular in the Youth Justice Board guidance (Youth Justice Board, 2001). Lipsey is cited as showing that across 440 evaluations of treatment programmes for young offenders, 45% of participants had a further police contact or arrest within an average of six months compared to 50% with no intervention or "treatment as usual."

Broken down into subsets, effects varied somewhat by background and by broad programme type. For example, programmes designed to improve personal and social skills, those focussed on changing behaviour, and multiple service programmes, all produced net average recidivism rates of 20% or more below the control group average, whilst vocational counselling and deterrent or "scared straight" programmes produced net negative effects. Cognitive behavioural programmes emerged as a particularly effective sub-set of all programmes evaluated. More generally, programmes with higher dosage, in terms of length and intensity of treatment, tended to be more effective.

Meta-analytic studies sometimes tease out moderators and mediators in working out guidance to policy-makers and practitioners about conditions needed for measures that have been found sometimes to be effective, to produce their effects more reliably. Thus, Lipsey's work found that substantially greater effectiveness is observed where researchers were actively involved in the design and implementation of programmes, which he accounts for by the greater "fidelity" or "integrity" of such programmes (Lipsey, 1995):

1. With a researcher involvement moderator, mediators included relatively high program fidelity, leading to relatively greater programme impact.

2. With a researcher non-involvement moderator, mediators included relatively low program fidelity, leading to relatively lower programme impact.

On the basis of these findings, the Youth Justice Board advises that,

> ...to be confident of the effectiveness of prevention strategies, a relatively prescriptive approach on the part of policy-makers is desirable ... Indeed, the promotion of new initiatives that are faithful replications of existing successful and evaluated programmes is the most likely means of ensuring success. (Youth Justice Board, 2001:122)

The Youth Justice Board report rues the lack of rigorous U.K. evaluation studies, the small numbers involved, the limited duration of many projects and the lack of an evaluation culture (Youth Justice Board, 2000:112). Whilst the guidance is evidence-based it is avowedly rooted in what the authors acknowledge to be very limited evidence. And what is advised is that very specific recipes be followed. This guidance is rooted in the notion that what at least partly explains the success of the higher impact projects is involvement of researchers who help ensure fidelity, i.e., detailed adherence to the programme rules, procedures and practices.

b) Campbell Collaboration Reviews and Scared Straight

The Campbell Collaboration aims to do for guidance on social policy and practice what the Cochrane Collaboration does for health policy and practice. Both attempt to summarise the findings of rigorous evaluations of the outcome effectiveness of specific types of intervention. What is defined as rigorous is made explicit in each review. Systematic efforts are made to track down all studies that meet the minimum standards for inclusion in the review. This is important given a publication bias towards studies that show a positive effect. All study findings that are included are then summarised, and reasons given for excluding studies that might at first sight look as if they fit. The strong preference is for RCTs, though it is acknowledged that these are not always practicable. What is minimally required as a rule is some equivalent comparative counterpart to the recipients of the intervention to act as a benchmark against which to determine whether the intervention is having an effect and, if so, the size and direction of that effect. There is provision for regular updates of reviews to take account of findings from new studies eligible for inclusion.

One completed example of a Campbell Review relates to "Scared Straight" and similar programmes. The idea behind Scared Straight is to "deter juvenile delinquents or children at risk of becoming delinquent from further involvement with crime" (Petrosino and Turpin-Petrosino, 2002) by taking them on a prison visit and exposing them to a more or less confrontational presentation by inmates serving a life sentence. The literature was scanned for studies that used random or quasi-random procedures (alternate assignment) to assign delinquents or "pre-delinquents," including at least some aged 17 or less, to treatment or no-treatment groups, with or without blinding. Prison visits had to be included. Most evidently included a presentation by inmates, but this could be more, or less, "graphic" or "educational." A measure of subsequent offending was needed, be this by arrest, conviction, police contact or self-report. Of 487 items of literature, 30 evaluation studies were identified of which 11 were potential randomised trials. Of the 11, 2 had to be eliminated either because data could not be obtained or because there was not random assignment. The nine remaining were all from the United States, and one was excluded from some of the analysis due to violations in random assignment protocols.

The findings of the studies included in the review were fairly consistent: a small but negative effect. In studies going back over some 35 years, more participants tended, relative to controls, to be involved in crime following the prison visit. "The (randomised trials) provide empirical evidence – under experimental conditions – that these programmes likely increase the odds that children exposed to them will commit offences in future" (Petrosino et al., 2003).

On the basis of these findings, the authors of the review concluded that:

> Despite the gloomy findings reported here and elsewhere, "Scared Straight" and its derivatives continue in use, although a randomised trial has not been reported since 1992. . . . We believe that our review places the onus on every jurisdiction to show how their current or proposed program is different than the ones studied here. Given that, they should then put in place rigorous evaluation to ensure that no harm is caused by the intervention." (Petrosino et al., 2003)

c) The Maryland "What Works, What Doesn't, What's Promising" Review, and Property Marking (Sherman et al., 1997)

The University of Maryland Department of Criminology and Criminal Justice was commissioned by the U.S. Congress in 1996 to review the scientific literature on what was known about effective methods of preventing local crime problems. The influential report that followed assigns studies to a scale of scientific methods, running from one to five (Sherman, 1997a, 2:18–19):

1. Correlation between a crime prevention program and a measure of crime or crime risk factors.

2. Temporal sequence between the program and the crime or crime risk outcome clearly observed, or a comparison group present without demonstrated comparability to the treatment group

3. A comparison between two or more units of analysis, one with and one without the program

4. Comparison between multiple units with and without the program, controlling for other factors, or only minor differences are evident in a non-equivalent comparison group.

5. Random assignment and analysis of comparable units to program and comparison groups.

This review then divides programs into four categories (Sherman and Gottfredson, 1997:4–5):

1. Works: if two or more studies with methodological rigor equal to three or more report significance tests for the program condition and found positive effects, and where the effect size, where given, is at least 0.1 (of a standard deviation) better than that of the control

condition, and the preponderance of evidence supports the same conclusion.

2. Doesn't work: if two or more studies with methodological rigor equal to three or more report significance tests and found no positive effect of the program, and the preponderance of evidence supports the same conclusion.

3. Promising: if one or more studies with methodological rigor equal to three report significance tests for the program condition and found positive effects, and where the effect size, where given, is at least 0.1 (of a standard deviation) better than that of he control condition, or the preponderance of evidence supports the same conclusion.

4. Don't know: categories with empirical evidence which do not fit under 1–3.

Higher scores go to studies which are judged to use methods yielding higher levels of internal validity. Seven chapters of the review divide programs up into the following categories: communities and crime prevention, family-based crime prevention, school-based crime prevention, labour markets and crime risk factors, preventing crime at places, policing and crime prevention, and criminal justice and crime prevention. Each chapter is then subdivided. Chapter 8 on policing, for example, covers: "numbers of police," "rapid response to emergency calls," "random patrols," "directed patrols," "reactive arrests," "proactive arrests," "community policing," and "problem-oriented policing" (Sherman, 1997b). Chapter 7 on places covers "apartments and residences," "retail stores, banks and money-handling places," "bars, taverns and drinking places," "public transportation," "parking lots and garages," "airports," "open public spaces," and "public coin machines" (Eck, 1997). Within each area different tactics are then considered by chapter subdivision. Under apartments and residences, in Chapter 8 these tactics include: "restricting pedestrian access and movement," "target hardening," "property marking," "closed-circuit television," "multitactic interventions and repeat victimisation," and "reducing drug dealing and crime in private rental places." There is then some discussion of the evidence in relation to each tactic. Two studies of property marking are mentioned. That by Thomas Gabor (1981) is given a scientific methods score of three and is reported as showing a 75% increase in burglary, based on seasonally adjusted burglaries per dwelling unit, comparing 24 months before the program to 18 months after it. That by Gloria Laycock

(1985, 1991) is also given a scientific methods score of three and is reported as showing a 40% reduction in burglary based on a comparison on participating and non-participating residences. The conclusion is that, "with two contradictory studies we cannot be confident that property marking is an effective measure for reducing burglaries of residences" (Eck, 1997:9). It is, therefore, defined as a "don't know" (category 4).

2. "What's To Be Done" Good Practice Guidance

Evidence-based WTBD guidance has more to do with ways of defining and prioritising problems, analysing their source and tailoring one or more responses most effectively and ethically to tackle them, than with cataloguing what specific measures are effective and ineffective in the manner of WW, though it can and often does draw – among others – on the kinds of studies that inform WW guidance. WTBD informs the use of discretion in making informed judgements about strategies to adopt, be it at the level of the neighbourhood, city, region or nation. WTBD guidance attempts to help answer the question, "What is to be done in these circumstances?," whilst WW guidance attempts to answer the question, "Will this (specific intervention or approach) work?" WTBD guidance also often gives guidance on how to implement measures or to have them implemented.

Principle and tested theory play a large part in WTBD guidance. Much WTBD guidance extols the virtues of adopting a scientific approach, mimicking that taken in medicine or engineering. Hypotheses about problem patterns are formulated and tested, using whatever data are available or suitable. Tested general theories about underling causes are explained. Methods of applying these theories are described, often through illustrative case studies.

It is not assumed that specific measures will often, if ever, be unconditionally effective. It will be quite rare that specific measures could be unequivocally advocated. The appropriateness of responses will generally be a function of context. Guidance is designed to help line up specific presenting problems and their contexts with measures or suites of measures that promise, but can rarely guarantee, effectiveness. The counterpart in medicine is problem diagnosis and treatment that fits the specific, properly understood underlying condition and the circumstances of the individual patient.

Much of the research feeding into WTBD guidance springs from demonstration, or action projects, where the researcher has worked alongside the practitioner and policy-maker to deal with some specific problem or area, though RCTs may also be drawn on.

WTBD tends to refer to context and mechanism. Mechanisms describe the underlying ways in which measures produce their impacts. Contexts describe the conditions in which measures activate specific underlying mechanisms. The same measure is liable to activate different mechanisms depending on context. The same mechanism may be activated by different measures, in part depending on context. The same overall outcome may be produced through the activation of different measure/mechanism/context mixes. Theoretically informed judgement is needed to decide on which measure or set of measures offers most promise for activating preventive mechanisms with an optimal pattern of expected outcomes. WTBD guidance aims to equip policy-makers and practitioners with the required understanding.

WTBD guidance may also refer to ethical issues relating to wider social values, utilities other than numbers of crime events, and crime distributional consequences of different crime reduction strategies.

Explicitly or otherwise, problem solving lies at the heart of most WTBD guidance. In comparison with WW guidance it tends to focus on problems that manifest themselves at the area, community or national level, and at responses that also operate in relation to troublesome situations rather than troublesome individuals. It does so in part because problems are mostly understood and addressed in relation to their social and physical settings. This is not to say that interventions following the guidance will be complex – indeed, they may be very simple. It is to say only that the starting point is connectedness or interaction with other conditions which need to be understood.

Three examples illustrate WTBD guidance.

a) COPS Problem-oriented Guides and Theft of and from Cars in Parking Facilities

The Office of Community Oriented Policing Services at the U.S. Department of Justice publishes a series of guides on methods that can be used to address specific local problems (COPS guides). These have covered a range of issues, for example loud car stereos, false burglar alarms, speeding in residential areas, bullying in schools, rave parties, and acquaintance rape of college students. Each guide has a similar structure. A description of the problem is followed by an account of factors contributing to it, guidance on how readers can understand their local problem, and then an account of responses and evidence concerning their potential effectiveness. The evidence drawn on in these guides is wide-ranging. It is the best available. It is certainly not confined to RCTs or to studies that otherwise still score highly in the scale used in the University of Maryland review to Congress. Gaps in research are noted.

Each COPS guide also includes an appendix that sets out, in a table, possible responses to the problem under a series of standard headings, including:

- Response number

- Page number (reference back to more detailed discussion in the text)

- Response (brief summary of response)

- How it works (the mechanisms through which the response might address the problem)

- Works best if . . . (contextual conditions favouring the response's effectiveness)

- Considerations (other factors that might inform decisions as to whether to include the response).

The number of potential responses, unsurprisingly, varies widely by problem covered in the guide.

The idea behind the COPS guides is that problems are specific and need to be understood in their local contexts if good decisions are to be made about the responses to make to them. These decisions are improved if guide users are made aware of the weight of evidence about the ways in which the responses work, the conditions needed for them to work and their apparent effects when they have been put in place.

The guides solicit responses from users and reports of further relevant work, and on the basis of these it is said that updates will be produced. The guides are published both in hard copy and through the Internet. Updates to the guides based on emerging research and reviews of unpublished police project reports are planned.

Problem-Oriented Guides for Police No. 10 relates to thefts of and from cars in parking facilities (Clarke, 2002). In the introduction it lists related problems, including cars parked on streets, and at housing complexes, vandalism to cars, theft of and from commercial vehicles, thefts of motorcycles, insurance frauds relating to car thefts etc., though it is noted that each of these requires its own analysis and response. Factors contributing to the problems relate to car security, regional location, car make and model, size and location of car park, principal car park users, multi-storey vs. flat car parks, and car park design and management. Guide users are advised that these general factors need to be combined with detailed analysis of their local car park theft problem. Specific questions to be asked in local analysis are under a number of headings: "for all thefts," "for theft of cars," "for theft from cars," "for thefts at all parking facilities," "for deck (multi-storey) and underground car parks," and for "lots" (flat car parks). For lots, for example, the questions include the following:

- Are entrances and exits staffed?
- What proportion of the perimeter is fenced?
- Do the fences prevent people from wandering through the lot?
- Do the fences present an effective barrier to determined thieves?
- Do the fences or foliage screen the lot from view of passersby?
- Do passing motorists and pedestrians provide natural surveillance of the lot?
- Can the lot be viewed from nearly buildings?
- Are parts of the lot screened from any natural surveillance?

Altogether 43 specific questions are listed, though in no case of course would all have to be asked in relation to a specific car park.

Fourteen specific responses are listed that relate to what can be done to lots, alongside evidence in relation to their effectiveness. These comprise:

1. Hiring parking attendants
2. Improving surveillance at deck and lot entrances and exits
3. Hiring dedicated security patrols
4. Installing and monitoring CCTV
5. Improving lighting
6. Securing the perimeter
7. Installing entrance barriers and electronic access
8. Adopting rating systems for security features

9. Arresting and prosecuting persistent offenders

10. Conducting lock-your-car campaigns

11. Warning offenders

12. Promoting car alarms and other "bolt-on" security

13. Using decoy vehicles

14. Redirecting joyriders' interest in cars.

Of these it is suggested the first nine are worth considering but not the last five, whose effectiveness is "limited." It is said to be "critical that you tailor responses to local circumstances, and that you can justify each response based on reliable analysis" (Clarke, 2002:15).

The recommended responses clearly do not exhaust what might be done in relation to theft of and from motor vehicles, insofar as rates will also be a function of some factors such as car design that lie beyond the scope of local agents.

Some guidance is also given on local implementation, including advice to calculate the respective costs of differing measures, to convince car park operators they can recover increased costs with higher charges, and to mobilise local businesses, local authorities and the media respectively to put pressure on and to provide incentives for operators to introduce preventive measures.

All 14 responses are included in the summary annex. The key fields of the first two are shown in Table 1.

b. Preventing Repeat Victimisation: The Police Officers' Guide

A succession of studies, stimulated initially by the Kirkholt Burglary Reduction Project (Forrester et al., 1988, 1990), has found repeat victimisation patterns across a wide range of places and offence types. A variety of demonstration projects, building again on Kirkholt's apparent success in preventing domestic burglary, have attempted to implement preventive strategies that try to reduce repeat incidents. On the basis of the observed patterns and some apparent successes in reducing crime, the Home Office established a Repeat Victimisation Task Force to try to stimulate, inform and build capacity for repeat victimisation crime prevention within police services. One product of this was *Preventing Repeat Victimisation: The Police Officers' Guide* (Bridgeman and Hobbs, 1997).

Table 1: Sample Summary Responses for Dealing with Theft of and from Cars in Parking Facilities (from Clarke, 2002)

Response	How it works	Works best if . . .	Considerations
Hiring parking attendants	Improves surveillance of facilities, especially at entrances and exits	. . . the facility's perimeter is secure, so those who enter and exit must pass the attendant, and the attendant booth is designed to facilitate surveillance	Expensive; usually justified only in large facilities; effective in reducing theft of cars – less so theft from cars
Improving surveillance at deck and lot entrances/exits	Increases thieves' risk of detection entering and leaving	. . . the facility's perimeter is secure	Methods include improving the lighting, removing signs and other obstructions, and encouraging vendors to set up shop near entrances and exits

After first noting the consistent research findings about patterns of repeat victimisation, Bridgeman and Hobbs provide a simple practical guide to methods of defining, identifying, measuring and analysing repeats. There is also a related appendix with a worked example showing in detail simple methods of calculating rates of repeat victimisation and the potential preventive benefits from reducing them. Bridgeman and Hobbs then provide advice on the establishment of an overarching force strategy, with targets, to address repeats, and another at a divisional level to reflect local priorities. They emphasise that implementing an effective strategy will call for partnership with third party agencies. A critical examination of existing services to victims is likely to throw up gaps that need to be filled in an effort to deal with repeats. Where the police are not the critical organisations to make good the gap, partner agencies may need to be persuaded to develop new or alter existing practices and this, in turn, may require the application of levers of various kinds (such as highlighting any potential savings that may follow, or in extreme cases threatening to withdraw services) to persuade them to do so. So far as the police are concerned, Bridgeman and Hobbs suggest that they need to:

- Demonstrate a high-level commitment
- Develop a planned and managed response to victims, taking into account the resources available and victim needs
- Ensure the plan can work in practice
- Develop a training programme for staff, and
- Develop a strategy for keeping the public involved.

Bridgeman and Hobbs go on to describe in some detail what can be delivered in practice to reduce repeat incidents. After initial guidance on some general principles of tactic design (for example that measures should be as simple as possible, that they need to be implemented quickly and that they should be proportionate to the size of the problem), they describe a graded response model, drawn from the Killingbeck domestic violence project (see Hanmer et al., 1999), that includes three levels, with suites of specific actions that can be taken at each in relation to the victim and perpetrator. This model normally involves (prompt) stepped activities as repeat incidents occur, but flexibility is built in to decide in specific cases what would be most appropriate. For the most part the activities are conventional, including for instance dispatch of information letters, mobilisation of watch arrangements, and the application of warnings to offenders. What is distinctive is only the ways in which they are applied systematically to address a specific problem pattern.

Bridgeman and Hobbs also briefly explain Routine Activities Theory to help users of their guide to think through intervention opportunities in any repeat victimisation problem and to work through what the elements of a graded response might include.

In the next stage of their guidance, Bridgeman and Hobbs discuss the management of work focused on reducing repeats. This includes:

- The collection and communication of timely and accurate information to decide what to do;
- A planned and managed response with clearly specified roles, responsibilities and lines of accountability, clear processes, the necessary equipment, routine administrative support and regular reviews; and,
- Partnership arrangements that involve the right people who understand what they are to do and communicate effectively with one another.

The final main part of this Guide relates to the assessment of what has been done. This includes advice on methods of measuring impact by focusing on changes in incidence, prevalence and concentration, by making comparisons with changes in neighbouring areas or wider areas, and by looking out for displacement and diffusion of benefits effects. Bridgeman and Hobbs also suggest that quality of service be assessed by looking at such issues as patterns of service delivery, victim satisfaction levels, victim action on the advice given to them, and worker reactions to the processes introduced. This can all feed into program improvements.

It can be seen basically that Bridgeman and Hobbs spell out in some detail what is involved in applying a problem-solving approach to a generic problem pattern turned up through empirical research.

c. Working Out What to Do: Strategies and Tactics

A guide produced with joint support from the British Home Office and U.S. National Institute of Justice gives general advice on the development and conduct of evidence-based crime reduction through problem-solving (Tilley and Laycock, 2002).

Tilley and Laycock offer guidance on the development of a strategic approach to crime reduction. Their main focus is on situational crime prevention given their view that the strongest research base exists for that approach, though they say that the general advice would hold also for other methods of prevention. The guidance takes the form of a series of concepts that the authors deem to be useful in developing a local crime reduction strategy. These include:

- Aims – the overall crime reduction or problem-solving aspirations of the strategy

- Problem-specification – detailed evidence-based statements of the aims

- Tactics – the interventions put in place to achieve the aims by addressing the specified problems

- Mechanisms – the underlying means by which the tactics applied are expected to solve the specified problem and achieve the aims

- Context – the conditions present that should allow the tactics to activate the mechanisms that will solve the specified problem and achieve the stated aim

- Replication – the translation of past achievements to present conditions by understanding how aims were achieved through solving specified problems by applying tactics in contexts that successfully activated preventive mechanisms.

The guide stresses the need to tailor tactics to varying conditions on the grounds that specified problems and contexts differ. Tactics that will successfully activate preventive mechanisms will vary by place and time. Past research can only successfully guide future prevention if the ways in which the measures worked when and where they were put in place are appreciated. Those deciding if they should adopt them can then make an informed (evidence-based) judgement on their relevance to the specific presenting problem and the circumstances surrounding it.

Tilley and Laycock draw on research showing varying ways in which crime has been found to be concentrated: by place, by victim, by offender, by presence of low-level disorder, and by availability of "facilitators." They suggest that those developing local strategies need to understand how problems that they are addressing are concentrated in these ways. They explain a range of mechanisms through which preventive tactics may produce their crime reduction consequences (and side-effects), given relevant attributes of the context for the measures. They describe circumstances in which attempted replications have failed because the same measures have activated different mechanisms in different contexts. They describe in some detail the underling mechanisms through which a range of specific situational measures may produce their preventive outcomes. They highlight potential negative and positive side-effects and the need to consider them in deciding on tactics. They stress the need to consider both the short- and long-term effects of suites of measures introduced with the aim of producing quick, but also sustainable falls in crime.

Tilley and Laycock discuss burglary as an extended case study for the general guidance they give. They note finally that following their advice depends on local capacity for strategic thinking, good local data, and the (voluntary or levered) co-operation of a range of agencies for delivery of the measures identified through the analytic processes described in the guidance.

DISCUSSION

The following discussion of WW and WTBD guidance considers the relationship between them, their respective distinctive strengths and weaknesses, the circumstances in which each might be most appropriate, and their common failings.

The Relationship between WW and WTBD Guidance

Whilst WW and WTBD guidance comprise recognisable contrasting types, with a constellations of attributes summarised in Table 2, there are cross-overs and hybrids. For example, guidance from Communities that Care (1999) has expressed quite a strong preference for RCT studies to inform crime prevention activity, but also advocates local analysis analogous to that suggested in problem-solving to determine where local efforts, informed by experimental studies, should be targeted. The CTC guidance, however, construes local analysis in terms of the identification of local "risk factors" for criminal involvement, rather than an understanding of the mechanisms through which presenting crime problems are generated in their specific contexts. There has been at least one experimental WW study to inform preventive orientation that has taken problem solving as the intervention variable (i.e., following WTBD type guidance). It found in favour of problem solving (Braga et al., 1999).

Strengths and Weaknesses of WW and WTBD Guidance

The main strengths claimed by WW guidance include the following:

- It identifies practices that have been shown to be capable of working, with evidence that has high internal validity.

- By focussing on what has been shown to be capable of working, it identifies practices that are promising.

- It provides specific effect size estimates, based on empirical research, that are useful for economic modelling and which can inform resource allocation decisions.

- It can inform harm-avoidance by identifying interventions that have been counterproductive.

- It promises clear, relatively simple, practical advice on what specifically to do.

- It offers evidence on the expected net effects of planned universal services.

The main strengths offered by WTBD guidance include the following:

- It is rooted in tested theories and principles that can be widely applied because of their external validity.

Table 2: Constellation of Typical Attributes of WW and WTBD Guidance

	What works	What's to be done
Model of practitioner	Operative, following recipes and rules	Professional decision-maker
Treatments/ interventions	Same for all/consistent	Variable, by need
Type of advice	What to do/not to do	How to decide what to do/not to do
Focus of advice	The specific intervention	The presenting problem
Fidelity/integrity	To action/intervention	To application of theory (albeit that this is sometimes left unstated)
Basis of advice	Tested action	Tested theory
Ideal evidence	The RCT	Broad range, including case study/demonstration project/action project/experiments
Admissible evidence	Experimental/control comparisons	Any relevant persuasive evidence
Question addressed	Will "x" work?	What will work for "x"?
Causal factors	Variables	Causal mechanisms
Qualifications	Moderators and mediators	Contexts and mechanisms
Primary validity criterion	Internal	External
Characteristic intervention target	The individual	The situation
Core value	Error/harm avoidance	Problem-solving
Sample underlying approach	Risk factors	Situational crime prevention
Conceptions of the individual	As object of intervention	As intentional agent
Cited examples	Campbell Collaboration YJB guidance Review for Congress	COPS Guides Repeat victimization guidance Working out what to do

- By focussing on tested general theories, it provides the basis for understanding and preventing unfamiliar and new crime problems, and problems in unfamiliar settings.

- It provides reasons to act differently in differing situations avoiding waste from the application of measures that are irrelevant to the specific problem situation.

- It informs harm-avoidance by identifying interventions that are likely to be counterproductive in a specific situation.

- It provides informed and thoughtful guidance to those who are disposed to be informed and have the capacity to be thoughtful about local crime problems.

- It offers a means of thinking through the expected specific effects of measures applied in specific situations.

- It acknowledges the complexity of context.

Table 3 summarises the respective potential strengths of WW and WTBD guidance.

WW guidance promises improvements on untutored discretion or untested rule-bound practices by providing guidance on new rule-bound (do and don't) behaviour and programs that will provide for better outcomes. WTBD guidance also promises improvements on untutored discretion and untested rule-bound behaviour, but does so by providing for the informed use of discretion that will provide for better outcomes.

Each form of guidance also has some specific weaknesses. For WW guidance the main weakness relates to the extent to which it can be validly applied.

WW research characteristically comes to mixed findings, as with the studies of property marking referred to in the Maryland review mentioned earlier. Moreover, the meaning of the WW findings for replication, are unclear. The absence of attention to mechanisms and context means that what accounts for the alleged effectiveness of the measure, and the conditions for its efficacy, are generally neglected. For example, in the property marking example referred to earlier, according to Laycock (1992) it was not the property marking per se in her study which brought about the observed falls in her case study. Rather it was the publicity. The conclusion that her study comprised a corroboration of the efficacy of property marking is misleading.

Table 3:   The Potential Strengths of WW and WTBD Guidance

	What works	What's to be done
Question answered	What has worked/can work?	Why and how preventive measures work, and under what conditions?
Harm-avoidance	Avoids harm, by avoiding interventions that are on balance counterproductive	Avoids harm, by avoiding interventions that are counterproductive in specific cases
Waste-avoidance	Avoids waste by avoiding interventions that don't generally work	Avoids waste by avoiding interventions that will not work in specific conditions
For whom	Provides clear guidance for low/mixed-ability practitioners and policy-makers	Provides relatively complex guidance to reflexive practitioners and policy-makers
Economy and efficiency	Provides best buys	Provides way of selecting best buys, fit for purpose
Improvement	Improves rule-bound standard intervention	Improves discretionary intervention
Validity	Stronger on internal – what has worked in the past so . . .	Stronger on external – what tested theory tells us here so . . .

The fact that WW studies are always spatio-temporally specific means that findings are always strictly confined by the context from which assignment to treatment and non-treatment occurs. The application of positive findings as if they had external validity is always in this sense an act of faith, and one that may be little warranted in heterogeneous and changing environments (see Ekblom, 2002).

It might seem that WW could be useful in providing guidance about what does not work. Sadly, this is not the case either, since many innovations require much development work before they can become effective. Moreover, even where findings are fairly consistently negative, in the absence of understanding why failures occur, conclusions beyond the individual study or series of individual studies cannot, again, strictly be drawn.

If Scared Straight failed, was it because the children were not scared? Or that they liked being scared so were unintentionally encouraged to be criminal? Or, were they risk-hungry and therefore inclined to undertake activities that had a revealed significant risk? Or, did different subsets of children react differently, some being put off and but others encouraged by the prison visits? Or, was the dosage too low to have an effect? Or for those already inclined to commit crime, was prison demystified and hence less frightening? Scared Straight may not seem a very sensible programme from the point of view of the theoretically much more sophisticated situational crime prevention. The painstaking summary of atheoretical experimental evaluations is rather unhelpful, however, in learning whether the underlying ideas (whatever these are) are fundamentally flawed or whether their manner of implementation, or the contexts for their application, has been such that they have so far tended to generate negative net effects, if any. Indeed, rather than simply counselling against further such programmes the best advice that the Campbell Review can come to is that future analogous programs be evaluated to see if they work. The RCT experimental findings, that they have failed often and produced some counter-productive outcomes, show strongly that these programmes – at least somehow and amongst some – can fail, and suggest that they may be capable of generating real negative effects. A similar positive outcome would show only that – at least somehow and amongst some – positive effects can be generated. They can do this, but no more.

Meta-analysis bundles programmes together to look at net effects, in an effort to increase external validity. There is some arbitrariness in this. What makes for similarity, difference and common family membership for guidance about what to do and when to do it in most crime prevention lacks theoretical foundation or clear operational definition. And, where specific actions are the subject of evaluation studies and on that basis are advocated, then further problems have emerged in practice.

Peter Raynor (2004) discusses the adoption of WW guidance in accredited probation programmes within the U.K. Crime Reduction Programme. He cites a meta-analysis by Lipsey (1999), which compared evaluated results of 196 "practical" (routine, real world) with 205 "demonstration" (pilot, experimental) programmes, and found that the former were only about half as effective on average as the latter. Achieving "demonstration" programme impacts levels in "practical" programmes was clearly a substantial challenge. The solution to weak implementation of WW interventions, as advocated in the YJB guidance referred to earlier, was slavish adherence to programme protocols, which was assumed to be the means to programme fidelity and integrity. Raynor notes a series of implementation problems that were encountered, many to do with resistance from members of the probation service. He also comments on the dire consequences:

> ... the reduction of officers' discretion, although producing a more consistent approach, also helped to increase the number who failed to complete programmes. (Raynor, 2004:318)

> (There was) a tendency to be preoccupied with implementing programmes or "interventions" rather than with providing an experience of supervision which would be effective as a whole. Although this had been pointed out by early British Research (Raynor and Vanstone, 1997), by the Chief Inspector of Probation when he warned against "programme fetishism" (Her Majesty's Inspectorate of Constabulary, 2002) and by the Correctional Services Accreditation Panel which insisted on continuity as one of its accreditation criteria (Correctional Services Accreditation Panel, 2003), little attention was paid to the need for effective case management until attrition rates started to cause concern. (Raynor, 2004:318-9)

Moreover in relation to these prescribed programmes Raynor notes also, that:

> Unless we know how outcomes are produced we are unlikely to be able to replicate them. Just as the drive for "programmes" overshadowed significant contributions to effectiveness such as case management, practitioner skills and indeed sentencing patterns, so a one-dimensional approach (RCTs) to outcome measurement is in danger of concentrating on the dependent variable without sufficiently exploring what all the independent variables might be. . . . (Raynor, 2004:319)

Though Raynor is far from hostile to WW guidance per se, he notes the negative consequence of an eclipse of discretion and stresses the importance of supervision within which the exercise of discretion is presumably guided and accountable. He also highlights a need for a range of research to underpin treatment decisions. What he seems to favour slides into WTBD.

The specific weaknesses in WTBD guidance are rather different from those for WW guidance. The main one relates to the heavy demands on those charged with using the guidance. Whether or not the guidance is valid, its use requires strong data, extensive thought, analytic capacity and some imagination by those trying to follow it properly. Many policy-makers and practitioners want simple, practical answers, and WTBD guidance fails to deliver it. Moreover WTBD guidance fails to yield effect size estimates: Those charged with decisions among competing demands for resources need estimates of the expected respective returns from different actions, and WTBD guidance is generally thin on this.

The Respective Relevance of WW and WTBD

One basis for determining the relevance of WW and WTBD guidance relates to the nature of the presenting problems and states of understanding them. Another relates to the nature of the agencies and organisations deciding and delivering the response to the problem.

Where there is a high level of homogeneity in the presenting problem, or where the problem is so well understood that homogenous subsets can be identified, and where there are also well-tested specific responses, WW guidance would seem to make sense. However in other circumstances, where presenting problems are heterogeneous, varying by place and time, or where specific response-relevant problem-subtypes have not or cannot be identified, and where there is a shortage of well-tested and well-specified responses, WTBD guidance would seem to make more sense.

Moreover, in organisational settings where there is a high degree of accountability, surveillance and control and/or a highly compliant practitioner group, WW guidance would seem to have a fighting chance of being followed. In organisational settings where practitioner groups are not compliant, and where their actions cannot easily be observed, or where there are not lines of authority and accountability, it may be difficult to implement WW guidance however appropriate it may be. WTBD guidance may have its best prospects of delivering improved outcomes in organisational settings where decisions are in the hands of those who are informed, interested, research-literate, imaginative and highly intelligent, with the time and resources to attend to the guidance and to go through the problem-solving processes that are advocated.

Some crime problems in relatively stable closed settings, such as shop theft, customer credit card fraud, and pilfering, may comprise examples where WW guidance is fitting. The problems may be sufficiently homogeneous and the organisational structures such that compliance can be well-enough monitored and adjusted that WW guidance is relevant and open to implementation. Recent efforts to build the capacity of local crime analysts in police services and local neighbourhoods represent an effort to

Table 4: Circumstances Appropriate for WW and WTBD Guidance

	What works	What's to be done
Presenting problem	Standard across space, time, subgroup and individual	Varying by place time, subgroup and individual
Policy option	Standard service to all in relevant eligibility/target group	Discretionary/varying service by area or sub-group
Practitioner	Uninformed, biased and liable otherwise to do harm	Well-educated, open, expert and committed to solving problems
Organisation	Disciplined, accountable, command structure	Informed, educated, reflective, organic, flexible, participatory

create a cadre of informed, interested, research-literate, imaginative and intelligent workers capable of delivering routinely on WTBD guidance in relation to that welter of crime problems in community settings that have so far defied categorisation into relatively homogeneous categories with promising set responses.

The respective circumstances in which WW and WTBD guidance may be most useful are summarised in Table 4.

A Common Dilemma for WW and WTBD Guidance

Both WW and WTBD guidance face a problem in selecting levels of specificity. Level of specificity here refers in the case of WW guidance to the detail or particularity of the intervention, its targets and the conditions in which it is applied. Insofar as WW guidance tells practitioners and policy makers what to do, how precise is the prescription about what is to be done, to whom and by whom? Greater detail provides less scope for error, less ambiguity, and increased fidelity, but the price paid is that meta-analysis becomes impossible unless replicas are close to exact copies of the original, and precise duplication can never strictly be achieved (Tilley, 1996). Moreover, generalisation of findings about the potential of programmes which differ in any detail, is not possible in the absence of theory. The Youth Offending Team guidance refers to fidelity, but fidelity can never be perfect and criteria for selecting what counts as faithful are arbitrary in the absence of theory providing grounds for selecting what does and does not matter. Rough, family resemblance is achieved in meta-evaluations and in study reviews as in the case of the "Scared Straight" Campbell Review, but generalisation from this in terms of WW guidance is not strictly possible. WW overviews of broad classes of programmes may provide rough guidance on whether to invest in this approach, based on the assumption that the future will resemble the past sufficiently. They can, however, offer no more than this. The Maryland review provides findings at several levels, but mixed findings and confusion at the most detailed level, as shown in the case of property marking, reveal the problems of bundling cases and railroading details.

Level of specificity in WTBD guidance relates to problem-definition and form of response. Greater detail allows for more precise diagnosis of any concrete problem faced by a policy-maker and practitioner, but limits the range to which the guidance is relevant. Rougher categories broaden the scope of the guidance, but at the price of less precise advice on how to analyse the particular problem. The working out what to do guidance referred to earlier is pitched at a relatively high level of generality (but with a worked example), the repeat victimisation guidance at a relatively detailed level of specificity, and the COPS car park car crime guide at a level somewhere in between.

Evidence-based guidance has to assume that families of some type or at some level can be created in order that past findings can be stretched to the future. In the absence of explicit theory the grounds for family creation and generalisation, however, are unclear, even if rough and ready common sense categories may be adequate for some practical purposes and be easily recognised by practitioners and policy-makers. The bases for taxonomies and the level at which they are pitched are issues for both WW and WTBD guidance.

WTBD guidance tends towards theoretically defined categories (for example repeat victimisation rather than a specific crime type) or prac-titioner-recognisable problem types (for example car crime in car parks). WW guidance tends towards specific interventions or surface-similar types of intervention, as in the Youth Justice Board guidance, and Maryland and Campbell reviews.

Common Failings in WW and WTBD Guidance

Two major weaknesses are faced both by WW and WTBD guidance. The first is that it is widely ignored. The second is that even when it is not ignored, it is poorly followed.

With regard to the first of these weaknesses, it is apparent that poor ideas, supported by neither WW nor WTBD guidance, travel as well as good ones. There is no natural selection mechanism favouring the effective. For example, Scared Straight type programmes have not withered in spite of consistently negative research findings. Reports on the implementation of problem-oriented policing, which essentially attempts to follow WTBD guidance, show limited and episodic implementation (Her Majesty's Inspector of Constabulary, 1998, 2000; Read and Tilley, 2000; Scott, 2000). There is a plethora of advice from a host of sources with scant knowledge of or interest in evidence. For much crime prevention work there is little WW evidence-based guidance to give. Salient influences at a local level are likely to be others who are known personally, as much or more than paper or Internet-based guidance written by members of the research community. The voices of evidence-based WW and WTBD guidance compete with many others in a veritable Babel of advice, and decision-makers and practitioners are likely to find it difficult to discriminate among them. Moreover, locally known, trusted, powerful and persuasive advice from familiar sources is liable to trump the impersonal writings of more distant members of the research community. Finally, the politics and practices of partnerships, staff turnover, political imperatives, externally imposed performance indicators, power-brokering and so on all militate against the analytic approaches advocated in both WW and WTBD guidance.

With regard to the second weakness, the WW guidance probably tends to fail in part because few organisational settings provide for the detailed oversight of its implementation (see Hanmer, 2003), in part because of the limited number of problems that are sufficiently homogeneous or with sufficiently powerful known responses to make WW guidance appropriate, and in part because precisely what is required of replication is often unclear (Tilley, 1996). The WTBD guidance probably fails in part because of the sophistication it demands of its followers – who lack the education, time, or skill to follow it – and in part because the organisational structures in place enabling discretion provide ample opportunities for influences that are not informed by WTBD guidance. Moreover, much in local settings provides for the continuation of routine practices for which there is support from neither WW nor WTBD guidance, perhaps because these practices contribute to social, personal or organisational goals.

There may, finally, also be one further and more profound reason why guidance is neglected and its implementation is poor, be it WW or WTBD. This is the neglect of "tacit" elements of implementation – those that cannot be expressed in formulaic or recipe terms.

Michael Polanyi (1958), who was professor of both physical chemistry and social studies at Manchester and who also wrote on the philosophy of science, emphasised the importance of tacit, personal knowledge in everyday life and in the conduct of science. He noted that the deployment of a tacit understanding of physics was common in day-to-day conduct, as when we successfully ride a bicycle. The sociologist of scientific knowledge, Harry Collins (1985), picked up on this in empirical work related to the construction of lasers, and found that it was a long time before a replica functioning laser was produced without the personal involvement of someone who had previously been involved in constructing one. There was an ineffable, personal element to the construction of the laser that required personal contact for its transmission. As Collins put it,

> The flow of knowledge was such that, first, it travelled only where there was personal contact with an accomplished practitioner; second, its passage was invisible so that scientists did not know whether they had the relevant expertise to build a laser until they tried it; and third, it was so capricious that similar relationships between teacher and learner might or might not result in the transfer of knowledge. (Collins, 1985:56.)

The importance of the tacit is largely taken for granted in the training of professional practitioners. Doctors, dentists, accountants and, for that matter, researchers learn their craft not just by reading books, attending lectures and understanding theory, but also by undergoing a form of apprenticeship where they have personal contact with those from whom they learn to practice. Indeed, there is a good deal of show-and-tell learning and supervision as discretion is gradually passed from master to apprentice. There appears to be an art and craft to successful practice as well as the science in which it is rooted. Written guidance, be it paper or Internet-based, is not able to transmit this personal understanding. Perhaps we expect too much of it in crime prevention. The reason researcher-involved pilot projects seem to work better than their copies may have much to do with the coaching/transmission of the tacit that is involved in the implementation of these programs, but that is not present in recipe-book copies, however assiduously efforts are made accurately follow the instructions.

Over time, as successful practice develops common, easily reproducible essential elements for effectiveness may emerge, with the removal of identified common errors and the discovery of critical features for achievement. At this point it might be possible to produce practice recipes provided that what is crucial to conditions is clear. This seems largely to be the case with developments in engineering (Petroski, 1982, 1994). In human flight many attempts failed before there was success. One success showed it was possible. Much more was needed to make it predictable. And many further developments were needed before foolproof manuals were available. Moreover, aeronautical engineers still go through apprenticeships. There appears to be science, art, craft and the tacit in engineering and the transmission of engineering skills. Even the humble motor mechanic learns by apprenticeship and comes to develop an intuitive understanding of the engines he or she works on. Indeed, the intuitive, tacit, unspoken, personal art and craft of applying science is catered for in many spheres of professional and technical practice.

Both WW and WTBD guidance neglect the tacit, in the first case in the delivery of specific practices and in the latter in the conduct of analysis, problem solving and application of theory to novel situations. Both tend wrongly to assume that written guidance and/or classroom guidance are enough for policy-makers and practitioners. The tacit may also need to be transmitted.

CONCLUSION: WW AND WTBD ABOUT WW AND WTBD?

It has been argued that WW and WTBD comprise two major forms which good practice guidance has taken. There may be conditions in which WW guidance is appropriate and possible, but for much crime reduction it is either premature or may never be possible. WW guidance will be most appropriate with well-understood, well-specified recurrent problems in relatively closed and stable settings where standard responses can be made with constant net effects. These conditions are currently rather rare, but may for example be found in some supermarket chains and in some forms of credit card fraud. WTBD guidance is in principle of much wider relevance, involving the deployment of well-tested theories across both familiar and relatively unfamiliar conditions. Its application is, however, intellectually challenging and requires organisational conditions in which time, information technology, strong data, good will and influential, able research-literate personnel are all present. This is rarely, if ever the case at present. Both forms of guidance thus face huge challenges. Neither can be seen much to be succeeding. Both forms of guidance compete with many other influences over practice and policy, and both neglect the tacit. So, WW and WTBD about it?

The foregoing discussion suggests that WTBD guidance currently has more to offer crime reduction than pure WW guidance, though clearly WW studies can and do feed into WTBD guidance. If we look at ways in which guidance is taken up, it has generally involved direct personal contact. It has not been confined to the written word or to the spoken word in the classroom, or to just to a mix of these. Direct contact has been needed. If we want WTBD guidance to be taken seriously, forms of delivery may need to take the form of apprenticeships, personal involvement in its implementation, directly supervised practice, and dissemination through face-to-face, direct-contact methods. This is how guidance in other areas of activity seems to be delivered. Even within the police, where it is crucial that new practices are followed, there is direct contact personal training with supervision. It is the practice too in the private sector.

One possible model would involve the simplest possible text guidance backed by personal training and supervised practice, offering limited but growing discretion as the apprentice practitioners come to show that they have sufficient skill and understanding to make their own decisions and depart from strict rules without discussion and approval. At a certain point those who have developed the understanding and skill to a sufficient degree might themselves be charged with supervising further apprentice practitioners in like manner. Alongside this, action research involving researchers and competent practitioners should be developing improvements in understanding and tested practice that can be drawn on to enrich and further extend, effective, theory-based evidence-based practice. In some cases this may suggest that there are set procedures that should be mandatory for specific conditions. In some cases intelligent application of newly tested theory and principles will be needed. This is the basic model of medicine and engineering. Perhaps we should take our lead from them.

Address correspondence to: Nick Tilley, Jill Dando Institute of Crime Science, University College London, Brook House, 2-16 Torrington Place, London WC1E 7HN, UK; e-mail: NickJTilley@aol.com

NOTE

1. Publicity does, of course, have other functions, and some is directed at offenders. For an overview see Bowers and Johnson (2005).

REFERENCES

Barclay, G. (1991). *A digest of information on the criminal justice system*. London: Home Office.

Barclay, G. (1995). *Digest 3: Information on the criminal justice system*. London: Home Office.

Bowers, K., & Johnson, S. (2005). Using publicity for preventive purposes. In N. Tilley (Ed.), *Handbook of crime prevention and community safety*. Cullompton, Devon: Willan.

Braga, A., Weisburd, D., Waring, L., Green Mazerole, L., Spelman, W., & Gajewski, F. (1999). Problem-oriented policing in violent places: A randomised controlled experiment. *Criminology, 37*, 541–580.

Bridgeman, C., & Hobbs, L. (1997). *Preventing repeat victimisation: The police officers' guide*. London: Home Office.

Clarke, R. (2002). *Thefts of and from cars in parking facilities*. Problem-Oriented Guides for Police Series No. 10. Washington: U.S. Department of Justice.

Collins, H. (1985). *Changing order: Replication and induction in scientific practice*. London: Sage.

Communities that Care (1999). *A Guide to promising approaches*. London: Communities that Care.

Eck, J. (1997). Preventing crime at places. In L. Sherman et al. (Eds.), *Preventing crime: What works, what doesn't, what's promising*. Office of Justice Programs Research Report. Washington, DC: U.S. Department of Justice.

Ekblom, P. (2002). From the source to the mainstream is uphill: The challenge of transferring knowledge of crime prevention through replication, innovation and anticipation. In N. Tilley (Ed.), *Analysis for crime prevention*. Crime Prevention Studies, vol. 13. Monsey, NY: Criminal Justice Press.

Forrester, D., Chatterton, M., & Pease, K. with the assistance of Brown, R. (1988). *The Kirkholt Burglary Prevention Project*. Crime Prevention Unit Paper 13. London: Home Office.

Forrester, D., Frenz, S., O'Connell, M., & Pease, K. (1990). *The Kirkholt Burglary Prevention Project: Phase II*. Crime Prevention Unit Paper 23. London: Home Office.

Gabor, T. (1981). The Crime Displacement Hypothesis: An empirical examination. *Crime & Delinquency, 26*, 390–404.

Hanmer, J. (2003). Mainstreaming solutions to major problems: Reducing repeat domestic violence. In K. Bullock & N. Tilley (Eds.), *Crime reduction and problem-oriented policing*. Cullompton Devon: Willan.

Hanmer, J., Griffiths, S., & Jerwood, D. (1999). *Arresting evidence: Domestic violence and repeat victimisation*. Police Research Series Paper 104. London: Home Office.

Her Majesty's Inspectorate of Constabulary (1998). *Beating crime*. London: Home Office.

Her Majesty's Inspectorate of Constabulary (2000). *Calling time on crime*. London: Home Office.

Laycock, G. (1985). *Property marking: A deterrent to domestic burglary*. Crime Prevention Unit Paper 3. London: Home Office.

Laycock, G. (1991). Operation identification, or the power of publicity? *Security Journal, 2*, 67–72.

Lipsey, M. (1992). Juvenile delinquency treatment: A meta-analytic enquiry into the variability of effects. In T. Cook, H. Cooper, D. Cordray, H. Hartmann, L. Hedges, R. Light, T. Louis, & F. Mosteller (Eds.), *Meta-analysis for explanation: A casebook*. New York: Russell Sage Foundation.

Lipsey, M. (1995). What do we learn from 400 research studies on the effectiveness of treatment for juvenile delinquents? In J. Maguire (Ed.), *What works: Reducing reoffending*. Chichester, UK: John Wiley.

Lipsey, M. (1999). Can rehabilitative programs reduce the recidivism of juvenile offenders? An enquiry into the effectiveness of practical programs. *Virginia Journal of Social Policy and the Law, 6*, 611–641.

Petrosino, A., & Turpin-Petrosino, C. (no date). "Scared Straight" and other prison tour programs for preventing juvenile delinquency: Protocol. Philadelphia: Campbell Collaboration.

Petrosino, A., Turpin-Petrosino, C., & Buehler, J. (2003). "Scared Straight" and other juvenile awareness programs for preventing juvenile delinquency. In *The Campbell Collaboration Reviews of Intervention and Policy Evaluations (C2-RIPE)*. Philadelphia: Campbell Collaboration.

Petroski, H. (1982). *To engineer is human*. New York: Vintage Books.

Petroski, H. (1994). *The evolution of useful things*. New York: Vintage Books.

Polanyi, M. (1958). *Personal knowledge*. London: Routledge.

Raynor, P. (2004). The probation service "pathfinders": Finding the path and losing it. *Criminal Justice, 4*, 309–325.

Read, T., & Tilley, N. (2000). *Not rocket science? Problem-solving and crime reduction*. Crime Reduction Research Series Paper 6. London: Home Office.

Scott, M. (2000). *Problem-oriented policing: Reflection on the first 20 years*. Washington, DC: U.S. Department of Justice, Office of Community Oriented Policing Services.

Sherman, L. (1997a). Thinking about crime prevention. In L. Sherman, D. Gottfredson, D. MacKenzie, J. Eck, P. Reuter, & S. Bushway (Eds.), *Preventing crime: What works, what doesn't, what's promising*. Office of Justice Programs Research Report. Washington, DC: U.S. Department of Justice.

Sherman, L. (1997b). Policing for crime prevention. In L. Sherman, D. Gottfredson, D. MacKenzie, J. Eck, P. Reuter, & S. Bushway (Eds.), *Preventing crime: What works, what doesn't, what's promising*. Office of Justice Programs Research Report. Washington, DC: U.S. Department of Justice.

Sherman, L., & Gottfredson, D. (1997b). Appendix: Research methods. In L. Sherman, D. Gottfredson, D. MacKenzie, J. Eck, P. Reuter, & S. Bushway (Eds.), *Preventing crime: What works, what doesn't, what's promising*. Office of Justice Programs Research Report. Washington, DC: U.S. Department of Justice.

Sherman, L., Gottfredson, D., MacKenzie, D., Eck, J., Reuter, P., & Bushway, S. (1997). *Preventing crime: What works, what doesn't, what's promising*. Office of Justice Programs Research Report. Washington, DC: U.S. Department of Justice.

Tilley, N. (1996). Demonstration, exemplification, duplication and replication in evaluation research. *Evaluation, 2,* 35–50.

Tilley, N., & Laycock, G. (2002). *Working out what to do: Evidence-based crime prevention*. Crime Reduction Research Series Paper 11. London: Home Office.

Youth Justice Board (2001). *Risk and protective factors associated with youth crime and effective interventions to prevent it*. London: Youth Justice Board for England and Wales.